DEBATING BRAIN DRAIN

DEBATING ETHICS

General Editor
Christopher Heath Wellman
Washington University of St. Louis

Debating Ethics is a series of volumes in which leading scholars defend opposing views on timely ethical questions and core theoretical issues in contemporary moral, political, and legal philosophy.

Debating the Ethics of Immigration
Is There a Right to Exclude?
Christopher Heath Wellman and Philip Cole

Debating Brain Drain
May Governments Restrict Emigration?
Gillian Brock and Michael Blake

Debating Brain Drain

May Governments Restrict Emigration?

GILLIAN BROCK

MICHAEL BLAKE

OXFORD
UNIVERSITY PRESS

Oxford University Press is a department of the University of Oxford.
It furthers the University's objective of excellence in research,
scholarship, and education by publishing worldwide.

Oxford   New York
Auckland   Cape Town   Dar es Salaam   Hong Kong   Karachi
Kuala Lumpur   Madrid   Melbourne   Mexico City   Nairobi
New Delhi   Shanghai   Taipei   Toronto

With offices in
Argentina   Austria   Brazil   Chile   Czech Republic   France   Greece
Guatemala   Hungary   Italy   Japan   Poland   Portugal   Singapore
South Korea   Switzerland   Thailand   Turkey   Ukraine   Vietnam

Oxford is a registered trademark of Oxford University Press
in the UK and certain other countries.

Published in the United States of America by
Oxford University Press
198 Madison Avenue, New York, NY 10016

© Oxford University Press 2015

Library of Congress Cataloging-in-Publication Data
Brock, Gillian.
Debating brain drain: may governments restrict emigration? / Gillian Brock
and Michael Blake.
pages cm.—(Debating ethics)
Includes index.
ISBN 978-0-19-931562-8 (pbk.: alk. paper)
ISBN 978-0-19-931561-1 (hardcover: alk. paper)
1. Emigration and immigration—Economic aspects.   2. Emigration and
immigration—Government policy.   3. Brain drain—Government policy—Developing
countries.   4. Manpower policy—Developing countries.   5. Skilled labor—Developing
countries.   I. Title.
JV6098.B76 2015
331.12'791—dc23
2014014465

1 3 5 7 9 8 6 4 2
Printed in the United States of America
on acid-free paper

CONTENTS

PART II BY MICHAEL BLAKE

PART III RESPONSES

DEBATING BRAIN DRAIN

Introduction

The Brain Drain and Global Justice

THE WORLD AS WE KNOW it is a terribly unequal place. It is unequal in terms of simple dollars and cents: the average citizen of Malawi has an annual income of US$320, while the average citizen of Japan has an annual income of almost US$48,000.[1] This sort of inequality has been much discussed in recent political philosophy; philosophers have spent a great deal of time trying to understand precisely what sorts of inequality might be regarded as unjust, and why.[2]

The world is terribly unequal in other ways as well, and philosophers have spent comparatively little time dealing with some of these. Consider again Malawi and Japan: Japan has around twenty-one physicians per ten thousand people, while Malawi has only one physician for every *fifty thousand* people.[3] This radical inequality in medical skills and talents has bad consequences for health; people born in Malawi will live, on average, thirty-two years fewer than their counterparts born in Japan.[4] These facts are troubling in themselves. They become even more troubling when we start asking *why* nations like Malawi have so few physicians. The answer, it seems, is not that the citizens of developing countries have no interest in becoming physicians or a lack of opportunity for medical training. In fact, many developing societies spend a great deal of money training new physicians, and spots in medical school are avidly sought in these countries. The reason for the low numbers of physicians has much to do with what medical training provides: namely, the opportunity to *leave* the developing society and enter into a more developed one. Developed societies such as the United States and the United Kingdom have made immigration comparatively easy for those with desirable medical skills. Those who are trained abroad will often choose to take their newly minted skills to the developed world, leaving their impoverished compatriots behind. The result is a continued shortage of medical personnel in sub-Saharan Africa. No matter how much a developing country invests in medical education, it is unlikely to obtain an adequate stock of medical personnel. In 2000, for example, Ghana trained 250 new nurses—and lost 500 nurses to emigration.[5] In 2001, Zimbabwe graduated 40 pharmacists—and lost 60.[6] In 2002 alone, Malawi lost 75 nurses to the United Kingdom—a cohort that represented 12 percent of all the nurses resident in Malawi.[7]

This phenomenon is often referred to as the *brain drain*. This term has a multiplicity of uses, but it is often used—as we use it here—to refer to the movement of talented (and often expensively trained) people from developing nations to developed ones.[8] The phenomenon is found most acutely in the medical context, but it is more general than that; it emerges wherever there is a net movement of talented and educated persons away from an impoverished society to a wealthier one. It is found, in the words of Thabo Mbeki, in the stock of "physicists, engineers, doctors, business managers and economists" who grew up in a developing society but live and work in a developed one.[9] The brain drain is, or should be, troubling to those of us who care about global justice. The brain drain seems to result from a shared history of colonialism and violence; the countries from which it occurs are, most frequently, those that have been most brutalized by Western powers. The phenomenon, moreover, seems poised to perpetuate the inequality in life-chances between developing and developed societies. The absent talent of the emigrant undermines both the life-chances of present citizens of the developing society—a society with fewer doctors, after all, is a society in which more people will die avoidable deaths—and the chances for that society to develop flourishing institutions for future citizens. The phenomenon, finally, seems almost ludicrously unfair: the wealthy citizens of the United States, already well-equipped with medical services, are increasing their stock of medical personnel by depriving the most needy global citizens of medical practitioners. It is tempting to conclude, as a recent headline in the *New York Times* had it, that America is stealing the world's doctors.[10]

This book is about what is wrong with the brain drain—and about how we might, consistent with our values, respond to these wrongs. It is perhaps important, before we go any further, to say a few words about what the authors of this book cannot claim. We are not specialists in development economics, but philosophers; as such, what we offer is ethical reasoning about which pathways to development are legitimate—not which of those pathways are most likely to be effective. We emphasize this to note that, while we discuss some empirical results about what effects different interventions might have, we do this with a due sense of modesty about our empirical skills—and with a hope that others, more skilled in empirical research than ourselves, will take this book as an opportunity for further cross-disciplinary conversation. Neither are we global activists; we are specialists, again, in what might be morally rightful for us to do in response to the brain drain but not in how we might begin to marshal the global forces necessary to make an effective response. True global change, we accept, requires not just good reasoning but skilled agents, adept at the tasks of coalition-building and institutional design. While we hope that such agents continue the work we discuss here, we cannot hope that we ourselves shall specify how that work should be completed.

What, then, can we claim? We are both political philosophers, who have written on how justice might be understood when applied to the global context.[11] We are both interested in applying the core liberal intuition—that persons, all of them, are alike in moral dignity and must be treated as such by the institutions that shape their lives—to the world as a whole. We are capable, then, of providing some argument about how justice as a concept might deal with the apparent problem of the brain drain.

Our responses, however, will be markedly different. Despite our similar intuitions at the level of political morality, we offer distinct takes on how developing societies might legitimately respond to the emigration of skilled persons from within their borders. The most important disagreement we have—one that shapes the range of acceptable policy alternatives we defend—is whether or not a state may, consistent with the liberal morality we defend, condition or prevent exit from its borders. Gillian Brock argues that it may, and that the range of policy options available to work against the brain drain is comparatively large. Michael Blake will argue that it may not, and that the range of acceptable policy options is therefore rather small.

In Part I, therefore, Brock describes several reasons to think that the developing state may legitimately seek to make exit from that state more difficult. To begin with, she notes that there is a deep unfairness in allowing those who have been trained by an impoverished state to simply leave that state and sell their talents to the highest bidder; those who have sacrificed to train that individual deserve some reasonable return on their investment. More centrally, however, those individuals who depart from the state are often those who are most likely to be energetic and skillful builders of social and political institutions; when they leave, they deprive their compatriots not only of their particular skills but of the institutions that might emerge from the use of those skills in the broader political context. Brock therefore concludes that the developing state has a wide array of potential tools with which to respond to the brain drain. These tools include programs of mandatory service prior to departure from that state and programs of taxation after departure.

In Part II, Blake describes several reasons to think that this vision is illiberal. By his account, it is fundamentally unfair that the burden of building developing societies should be placed on those who happen to have been born within them; the world as a whole has the duty to assist with development, and it is unjust for a state to restrict the mobility of the talented simply because it might be useful to do so. More centrally, though, the liberal state simply should not take itself as having the right to prevent exit from within its territorial jurisdiction; both historical and philosophical considerations tell us that such powers are not rightly held by states. The range of policy options available to us, in Blake's account, is correspondingly short—and Blake concludes that we may not, consistent with liberal morality, be able to deal with the brain drain in any effective way at all.

These are two distinct visions of how justice should respond to the problem of the brain drain; we agree in the foundations of political morality but disagree quite strongly about what such morality might defend. We would conclude, though, with one point of agreement. We are both convinced that the phenomenon of brain drain is worthy of attention from those who are worried about international justice; we are heartened to see increased consideration given to this issue in recent political philosophy. It is our hope that this volume will spark further inquiry into this vitally important topic.

NOTES

1. Data from 2012 World Bank survey, available at http://data. worldbank.org/country.
2. See, for a survey of some recent work on this, Michael Blake, "Global Distributive Justice: Why Political Philosophy Needs Political Science," *Annual Review of Political Science* 15 (2012): 121–136.
3. The data are from studies between 2005 and 2012; they are available at http://kff.org/global-indicator/physicians/.
4. Figures are from 2012 life expectancy data, available at http://cia.gov/library/publications/the-world-factbook.
5. Magda Awases, Akpa Gbary, Jennifer Nyoni, and Rufaro Chatora, *Migration of Health Professionals in Africa: A Synthesis Report* (Brazzaville: World Health Organization, 2004).
6. David R. Katere and Lloyd Matowe, "Effect of Pharmacist Emigration on Pharmaceutical Services in Southern Africa," *American Journal of Health-System Pharmacy* 60 (2003): 1169–1170.

7. Sue J. Ross, Daniel Polsky, and Julie Sochalski, "Nursing Shortages and International Nurse Migration," *International Nursing Review* 52 (2005): 253–262, at 260.

8. The term might also be used to describe any significant decrease in skills within a given territory resulting from migration; in this wider view, the movement of entrepreneurial young people from rural America to the cities represents a form of brain drain. We do not engage with this issue in the present work and will generally use the term in a restricted sense. See, though, Patrick J. Carr and Maria J. Kefalas, *Hollowing Out the Middle: The Rural Brain Drain and What It Means for America* (Boston: Beacon Press, 2010).

9. The list is from Mbeki's "African Renaissance" speech, which urged such individuals to return to Africa. The speech is available at http://www.dfa.gov.za/docs/speeches/1998/mbek0813.htm.

10. Matt McAllester, "America Is Stealing the World's Doctors," *New York Times*, March 7, 2012.

11. See Gillian Brock, *Global Justice: A Cosmopolitan Account* (Oxford: Oxford University Press, 2009); Michael Blake, *Justice and Foreign Policy* (Oxford: Oxford University Press, 2013).

PART I

GILLIAN BROCK

1

Introduction to Part I

THE BASIC NEEDS OF DESPERATELY poor people rightly command our normative attention.[1] We are concerned not only about the fact that there is poverty and unmet need in the world today, but also the scale of this neediness—so *many* in the world lack the basic necessities for a decent life. Some of these widespread, severe deprivations include lack of food, clean water, basic healthcare, primary education, basic security, infrastructure, and an environment that can sustain and ensure secure access to these goods and services. An important part of enjoying the basic goods and services necessary for a decent life is the availability of skilled personnel able to provide these. Here there are severe shortages, especially in developing countries where needs are gravest. For instance, about 2 million more teachers and 4.25 million more health workers are needed to supply basic health and education for all.[2] These shortages are exacerbated by high numbers of skilled personnel departing developing countries and seeking better prospects for themselves in developed ones. What, if anything, may developing countries defensibly do to stem the flow? This is the central question that orients my work in this book.

Before I can explain my approach to answering this question, further background is necessary. As noted, fueling the shortage of skilled personnel is the very high rate of emigration among those with the necessary skills, a problem commonly referred to as "brain drain." Though brain drain occurs in most sectors, brain drain among health professionals is particularly widespread and damaging for developing countries. These countries typically have poor heath care resources anyhow, so the loss of trained healthcare workers is felt even more than it might be in places that are better resourced. In some cases, the departure of healthcare workers from developing countries threatens the viability of the healthcare systems in those countries, especially in sub-Saharan Africa.[3]

Skilled workers often have good reasons for wanting to leave poor countries of origin. Inadequate remuneration, bad working conditions, lack of professional development opportunities, lack of security, and lack of funding are important factors in their decision to leave. Developed countries frequently appear to offer better pay and working conditions, or career and training opportunities that are not available in developing ones. Departure seems to be an entirely rational decision under such circumstances. Skilled workers, like everyone else, should have the right to exit countries in which they no longer wish to live. But there are normative questions about citizens' responsibilities, fair terms of exit, and whether migration should be managed to ensure the burden of migration does not fall disproportionately on the world's worst off, so that those who benefit from movement across borders do not also impose impermissible severe losses on those who suffer disadvantage because of that movement. As we discuss, these losses sometimes include significant reduction in educational and health services, poor health and educational attainment, public funds wasted on expensive tertiary training which does not benefit citizens, fiscal losses, and—more generally—loss of assets required for beneficial development. As I also discuss, there are various ways to ensure that movements work well for all significant stakeholders, but one such way, for which I argue, is that developing countries may permissibly tax citizens who depart under certain conditions. I also argue that they may reasonably expect citizens with relevant skills to assist fellow citizens for a short period of compulsory service under certain important conditions. Compulsory service and taxation are two kinds of measures that developing countries may take to help reduce poverty in their countries.[4]

While there has been considerable normative theorizing on the topic of immigration,[5] most analyses have focused on the relation between the migrant or prospective migrant and the society she will join—issues of admission, accommodation, integration, and so forth.[6] By contrast, in this work I focus on the more neglected relationship between the migrant and the society she will leave, and the normative implications of her departure. The central questions for analysis are these:

(1) Are there setbacks to significant interests that result from the departure of migrants?

(2) Even if there is such damage, is this compensated for by benefits that result from their exit?

I argue that, overall, departures can result in important net losses, which raises the following further questions for analysis.

(3) What kinds of policies might best address the identified harms?

(4) When there are important losses, what may governments permissibly do to address those losses?

(5) How should burdens associated with addressing harms best be distributed?

(6) Is it fair to impose costs on emigrants?

(7) What kind of normative account can best support appropriate burden-sharing arrangements?

Together, the answers to these seven questions form the basis of an answer to the question of what justice in emigration consists in for those who wish to exit poor, developing countries. I claim that the issue of justice in emigration is a relatively neglected topic. Indeed, the neglect in the philosophical literature seems quite marked, given the substantial amount of writing that focuses on the relationship of the migrant to the host society.[7] In trying to account for the neglect, it might seem obvious that we have rights to exit countries from which we hail. Indeed, our commitments to freedom of movement and association might seem to account fully for why this is a non-issue. However, as we come to appreciate, both these freedoms have limits, and the limits correspond, in important ways, to where setbacks to others' important interests would otherwise result. A simple appeal to these freedoms cannot fully explain the neglect.

A few preliminary remarks are in order to forestall possible misunderstandings about the views I argue for here. First, my general position is that people should be free to move across state borders so long as that movement satisfies a number of important conditions to be discussed. These can be met if we actively manage migration better and take account of relevant negative externalities.

To be clear, then, I am not arguing that people should be completely prohibited from migrating. My basic argument is for more actively managed migration and more attention to undesirable and somewhat hidden effects of this movement. I am concerned with developing reasonable and robust policy that can mitigate these negative effects and take seriously the rights and important interests of migrants, along with the concerns of others who are importantly affected.

Second, the focus in this work will be on emigrants departing from *developing countries*, because this is where vulnerabilities and losses are most pressing. The analysis does have some bearing on movement from developed countries as well, though I do not extend the analysis to developed world migration explicitly here.

Third, it is important to note that though they are important, migration policies are only one component of a full account of global justice. Indeed, given that the number of people who move is likely to remain a relatively small percentage of the world's total population, it can be only a relatively small part of seeking a more just world.[8] However, there will always be people who want to move for a variety of reasons, especially when there are significant wage differentials between economies, so it is worthwhile considering what just emigration policy consists in in such cases. But we cannot expect all the wrongs of our current global situation to be addressed solely through policies concerning migration. When considering some policy remedies, I do discuss some broader issues, though a fuller treatment of these issues can be found elsewhere.[9]

Fourth, it is important to define the core case of interest here so we have that firmly in view. As I discuss, there are many salient policy options that could be explored as potential solutions to the brain drain problem. But a key orienting question in this work is what developing countries themselves may permissibly do to solve their problems. And we are concerned primarily with skilled citizens. What can reasonably be expected of *this* group of citizens and what permissible actions may governments take with respect to them? There are many ways in which people can acquire skills. And, over time, some will change their occupations as their plans alter in the course of living a life they consider valuable. But it will help to define what I consider to be the standard highly prevalent case, and I take that to be one in which skilled workers have acquired their current skill set in developing countries and lived in those countries until the point of emigration to a developed country, whereupon they continue to work in the same general line of occupation (in that country or another developed one), usually at much more attractive remuneration packages.

Finally, there are a number of ways to view my project's motivating question and multiple entry points into the debates central to this book. I mention the following three important ways to motivate my orienting question to show that the importance of the basic concerns can be arrived at from several starting places; even if one is not compelling to a reader, she may feel the force of another.

First, if we are concerned about the unmet needs of the desperately poor, this concern should extend to the people who can provide for those needs. What can we reasonably ask those who have the abilities to meet needs to do to address other's unmet needs?

Second, the responsible state also has important obligations to ensure that citizens are equipped with core goods and services. What may it permissibly do to coerce citizens into supplying these goods and services when market incentives are insufficient to attract enough workers to do the necessary jobs?

Third, the concerns also flow from a more comprehensive picture of what global justice requires and the importance of strong institutions in promoting prosperity. Good institutions matter greatly for poverty reduction, whatever other factors are also significant. For instance, those institutions that promote respect for the rule of law and accountability make for an environment conducive to innovation and investment in education, health, and infrastructure—all key ingredients for lifting people out of poverty. Creating better institutions is a significant component in helping people out of poverty and a central factor in promoting development. One of the most worrisome setbacks developing countries can suffer from emigration is damage to institutions and institution building, and therefore the loss that is sustained in opportunities for development and escape from poverty. Helping developing countries retain their most skilled citizens is often a key issue in building the better institutions crucial to prosperity. The highly skilled, it seems, are important sources of demand and supply for better institutions. If that is right, what policy options to retain such citizens are permissible, given that on the face of it, we might be unduly restricting people's important freedoms, such as freedom of movement or association?

It is important to note that even if the institutional view is rejected, because it is found to be empirically (or otherwise) defective, more simple versions of the core issue are available, as highlighted in the first two descriptions of questions motivating interest in this project. Given the extent of unmet need in the world today, it would seem that we have several compelling reasons to attend to the core issue of whether requiring skilled citizens to assist with deprivation can be justified.

An overview of Part I might be helpful and is provided next. In this book I develop an account of the responsibilities skilled citizens of poor, developing countries have to contribute to deprivation reduction, especially when they wish to leave such countries. This grounds a view about fair terms of exit from such countries. I begin, in the next chapter, by briefly outlining what global justice minimally requires. I describe the nature of our obligations to one another and how states matter in working toward global justice. As we come to appreciate, states have an integral role to play in reducing global injustice, and we have obligations to assist them in providing certain core ingredients necessary for a decent life. In addition to the general obligations I identify, I also argue that agents from affluent, developed countries have important remedial responsibilities and can be expected to take up a large share of the work in the project of moving toward a less unjust world.

Chapter 3 covers some important empirical issues. In it I also outline some of the conditions necessary to promote prosperity in developing countries and the effects departing individuals can have on those left behind. As signaled, good institutions are immensely important for sustained gains in eliminating poverty. Helping developing countries retain their most skilled citizens is often a key issue in building the better institutions crucial to prosperity. Chapter 3 discusses some of the empirical evidence for these claims, a catalog of some possible policy options that deserve further consideration, and a more detailed discussion of two policy options that will be the focus here: compulsory service and taxation programs.

Chapter 4 begins the main normative work. I offer several arguments as to why the skilled citizen has important responsibilities with respect to compatriot deprivation. My claim is that the cluster of arguments provided is sufficient to make the case that carefully designed compulsory service and taxation programs can be justified under certain kinds of conditions, such as when poor, responsible, legitimate developing states are making good-faith efforts to supply core goods and services that citizens need for a minimally decent life, under severe budgetary constraints, and where there is full information about those constraints and what is expected when students accept opportunities for tertiary-level training.

Chapter 5 continues the development of the argument by considering key objections to the view along with replies. What counts as a legitimate state? Do not compulsory service programs inappropriately limit the freedom and opportunity of emigrants? Why think it is justifiable to coerce some people to labor for the benefit of others? Why distribute so much of the responsibility for assisting the needy on relatively poor compatriots rather than affluent developed-world citizens? And why think the emigrant can assist best by staying in the country of origin rather than from outside of it? These are the sorts of reasonable questions that need further analysis, and this is undertaken throughout Part I but especially in Chapter 5. Chapter 6 offers a concise summary of the central arguments marshaled for the positions defended in Part I.

NOTES

1. For outstanding comments on previous drafts of this work I thank Helen Adams-Blackburn, Christian Barry, Timothy Berry, Michael Blake, Eamonn Callan, Joe Carens, Josh Cohen, Stephen Davies, Avigail Eisenberg, Nir Eyal, Andrew Harland-Smith, Cindy Holder, Devesh Kapur, Simon Keller, Eszter Kollar, Will Kymlicka, Patti Lenard, Alistair Macleod, Colin Macleod, John McHale, Margaret Moore, Gerhard Overland, Thomas Pogge, George Rainbolt, Hamish Russell, Hugh Springford, Lucas Stanczyk, Anna Stilz, Christine Straehle, Christine Sypnowich, Christopher Wellman, Jo Wolff, and Lea Ypi. For excellent research assistance with this project I thank Hamish Russell.

2. Oxfam International, *Paying for People* (2007), available at www.oxfam.org.nz/imgs/about/070314PayingForPeople.pdf.

3. See, for instance, Jenny Huddart and Oscar F. Picazo, *The Health Sector Human Resource Crisis in Africa* (Washington, DC: United States Agency for International Development, 2003); Peter E. Bundred and Cheryl Levitt, "Medical Migration: Who are the Real Losers?," *Lancet* 356 (2000): 245–246; and Edward Mills, William A. Schaba, Jimmy Volmink, et al., "Should Active Recruitment of Health Workers from sub-Saharan Africa Be Viewed as a Crime?," *Lancet* 371 (2008): 685–688.

4. As we see, compulsory service programs come in a variety of flavors, from quite coercive to not objectionably coercive at all. Program design is important both to the defensibility of the program and the level of coercion (or otherwise) that they involve.

5. Some notable recent publications include Joseph Carens, *The Ethics of Immigration* (Oxford: Oxford University Press, 2013); Joseph Carens, "Live-in Domestics, Seasonal Workers, and Others Hard to Locate on the Map of Democracy," *Journal of Political Philosophy* 16 (2008): 419–455; Christopher Heath Wellman and Phillip Cole, *Debating the Ethics of Immigration: Is There a Right to Exclude?* (New York: Oxford University Press, 2011); David Miller, "Immigrants, Nations, and Citizenship,"

The Journal of Political Philosophy 16 (2008): 371–390; Will Kymlicka and Keith Banting, "Immigration, Multiculturalism and the Welfare State," *Ethics and International Affairs* 20 (2006): 281–304; Mathias Risse, "On the Morality of Immigration," *Ethics and International Affairs* 22 (2008): 25–33; Christopher Heath Wellman, "Immigration and Freedom of Association," *Ethics* 119 (2008): 109–141; Joseph Carens, "The Rights of Irregular Migrants," *Ethics and International Affairs* 22 (2008): 163–186. For some other influential contributions to recent debates see Veit Bader, "Citizenship and Exclusion: Radical Democracy, Community and Justice. Or, What Is Wrong with Communitarianism?," *Political Theory* 23 (1995): 211–246; Joseph Carens, "Aliens and Citizens: The Case for Open Borders," *Review of Politics* 49 (1987): 251–273; Jonathan Seglow, "The Ethics of Immigration," *Political Studies Review* 3 (2005): 317–334; Michael Walzer, "The Distribution of Membership," in Peter G. Brown and Henry Shue (eds.), *Boundaries: National Autonomy and Its Limits* (Totowa: Rowman and Littelefield, 1981), 1–35; David Miller, "Immigration: The Case for Limits," in Andrew I. Cohen and Christopher Heath Wellman (eds.), *Contemporary Debates in Applied Ethics* (Oxford: Blackwell, 2005), 193–206; Chandran Kukathas, "The Case for Open Immigration," in Andrew I. Cohen and Christopher Heath Wellman (eds.), *Contemporary Debates in Applied Ethics* (Oxford: Blackwell, 2005), 207–220; Chandran Kukathas, "Are There Any Cultural Rights?," in Will Kymlicka (ed.), *The Rights of Minority Cultures* (Oxford: Oxford University Press, 1995), 228–256; Will Kymlicka, *Politics in the Vernacular: Nationalism, Multiculturalism, and Citizenship* (Oxford: Oxford University Press, 2001); Michael Blake, "Immigration," in R. G. Frey and Christopher Heath Wellman (eds.), *A Companion to Applied Ethics* (Malden, MA: Blackwell, 2003), 224–237; Will Kymlicka, *Multicultural Citizenship: A Liberal Theory of Minority Rights* (Oxford: Clarendon Press, 1995); Will Kymlicka, "Territorial Boundaries: A Liberal Egalitarian Perspective," in David Miller and Sohail Hashmi (eds.), *Boundaries and Justice* (Princeton, NJ: Princeton University Press, 2001), 249–275, at 266–267;

Stephen Castles and Mark J. Miller, *The Age of Migration*, 3rd edition (Basingstoke: Palgrave, 2003); Susan Moller Okin, "Feminism and Multiculturalism: Some Tensions," *Ethics* 108 (1998): 661–684; Joshua Cohen, Matthew Howard, and Martha Nussbaum (eds.), *Is Multiculturalism Bad for Women?* (Princeton, NJ: Princeton University Press, 1999); Jeremy Waldron, "Minority Cultures and the Cosmopolitan Alternative," in Will Kymlicka (ed.), *The Rights of Minority Cultures* (Oxford: Oxford University Press, 1995), 93–119; Thomas Pogge, "Migration and Poverty," in Veit Bader (ed.), *Citizenship and Exclusion* (Houndsmills: Macmillan, 1997).

6. Typical questions include these: Is it morally defensible for affluent countries to restrict the entry of would-be immigrants from poorer countries? Is it fair to impose specific terms, such as the type of work that can be performed, as a condition of entry in immigration policies? What entitlements or rights should new immigrants have? What can be required or reasonably expected of immigrants in integrating into their new societies? How should clashes between immigrant and host culture be resolved? For excellent recent coverage of all these issues see Joseph Carens, *The Ethics of Immigration* (Oxford: Oxford University Press, 2013). For one of the classic treatments of all these issues see Kymlicka, *Multicultural Citizenship*. For excellent extended treatment of the first issue see Wellman and Cole, *Debating the Ethics of Immigration*.

7. Notable exceptions include Kieren Oberman, "Can Brain Drain Justify Immigration Restrictions?," *Ethics* 123 (2013): 427–455; Anna Stilz, "Is There an Unqualified Right to Leave?," in Sarah Fine and Lea Ypi (eds.), *Migration and Morality: The Ethics of Membership and Movement* (Oxford: Oxford University Press, forthcoming); Lea Ypi, "Justice in Migration: A Closed Borders Utopia?," *The Journal of Political Philosophy* 16 (2008): 391–418; Thomas Pogge, "Migration and Poverty," in Veit Bader (ed.), *Citizenship and Exclusion* (Houndsmills: Macmillan, 1997), 12–27; Miller, "Immigration: The Case for Limits"; and Eric Cavallero, "An Immigration-Pressure Model of Global

Distributive Justice," *Politics, Philosophy, and Economics* 5 (2006): 97–127.

8. If climate change is very dramatic, resulting in "environmental refugees," the numbers of people moving might alter dramatically. In considering what justice in emigration consists in for that case, we would need to address a range of other issues not covered here, such as climate justice issues. For an interesting argument on just this issue see Mathias Risse, "The Right to Relocation: Disappearing Island Nations and Common Ownership of the Earth," *Ethics and International Affairs* 23 (2009): 281–299.

9. Gillian Brock, *Global Justice: A Cosmopolitan Account* (Oxford: Oxford University Press, 2009).

2

What Does Global Justice Require?

THE PROBLEMS OF BRAIN DRAIN arise largely because there are vast disparities in life prospects in different countries, and some are not able to provide core ingredients necessary for a decent life. If a state's inability to ensure the essentials for a decent life is a fundamental factor driving migration, we should investigate what obligations there might be to remedy that situation. So, what responsibilities do we have to one another to ensure essentials for a decent life? How, if at all, should membership in states matter to our obligations? I have developed a comprehensive account of global justice elsewhere.[1] Here, I sketch only some of the central features that bear on the core issues that are our focus, so we can extend the analysis and apply it to the debates concerning brain drain.

I start with the importance of institutions to justice. There are many different ways to see that institutions are a focal point in matters of justice. The fundamental institutions that we collectively uphold structure and importantly influence how our lives will go. The most prominent contemporary political philosopher, John Rawls, makes this a central feature of his theory. The basic structure of society—which includes all the main political, economic, legal, and social institutions—is the core focus for theorizing about justice because its effects are pervasive, profound, and present from birth. Whether or not we endorse Rawls's particular claim about the impact of institutions, we must at least recognize a version of it: the institutions that govern our lives—whether at state or international levels—have an important role to play in structuring our life prospects and so it is important that we ensure these aim to approximate just ones.[2]

My next presumptively uncontroversial point is to acknowledge the importance of what one might call the "moral equality imperative"—we all must acknowledge the moral equality of all human beings. No matter where people are located on the planet they deserve to be treated as human beings that have equal value to other human beings, ceteris paribus. All human beings' needs and interests matter and, in some important sense, deserve equal consideration, ceteris paribus. Clearly, there is much more that can be said in elaborating on the ideas entailed by these moral ideals. For our purposes we should focus on the particular institutional implications.

What should commitment to the moral equality imperative mean for how we ought to structure the institutions we collectively uphold? In my view, the commitment minimally entails that we should ensure everyone is well positioned to enjoy the prospects for a decent life, and I elaborate on this via four central components.[3] First, one should be enabled to meet one's basic needs. Second, one ought to have adequate protection for one's basic liberties. Third, fair terms of cooperation should govern one's collective endeavors. And fourth, one must have background conditions (especially social and political arrangements) that support these core ingredients for a decent life.

There are various ways to make the point that these four components are important ingredients for a decent life.[4] Like human rights approaches, we might start with the individual human person and consider what she needs to live a life of dignity, fleshing out opportunities, protections, resources, and the like that are central for such a life, taking account of a wide sweep of variation in human living arrangements. That will get us some distance, but we quickly realize that how that person stands in relation to others is also a key part of enjoying a life of dignity. Is she subject to domination, exploitation, or oppression? Must she endure highly coercive terms of cooperation? If her relationships with others are characterized by certain kinds of radical inequalities, this may interfere with the ideal of a life worthy of human dignity. And so we arrive at the necessity of including relational components in our account of what global justice requires, such as fair terms of cooperation. All the details of my account of global justice need not concern us for the purposes of this work.[5] For our purposes, we need note only a few key points. First, global justice requires that we must be concerned with everyone's prospects for a decent life in designing and upholding just institutions. Second, we all have duties to one another to ensure that we are well positioned to enjoy prospects for a decent life. Third, governments frequently can act as efficient coordinators and dischargers of these responsibilities. As this view suggests, governments then have an important role to play in discharging global justice duties. So, let us also consider next the relevance of states in my account of global justice.

On my view, rather than having little importance (as some cosmopolitan global justice theorists maintain), states are highly relevant for several reasons. First, states matter to people. People are, for the most part, attached to many of their fellow citizens and care greatly about their state's standing and achievements in the world. This identification and attachment can also have an important bearing on an individual's well-being. Of course, this attachment is socially constructed and is subject to modification, though the mechanisms for modification require careful treatment, including managing rather than suppressing identities, at least over a reasonably long time frame.[6] At any rate, there are good reasons to make space in an account of global justice for *defensible forms* of such attachments, citizens' commitments to states and, indeed, flourishing forms of civic nationalism that enhance rather than undermine support for key elements of global justice. States are likely to be a core feature of our world order for many years to come and so to ignore the role they can and should play in transitioning to a more just world is a missed opportunity to further key global justice goals. Even in an ideal world, however, there are reasons to think states might be a robust part of the global institutional architecture and that a world state would be less desirable. The obvious concerns surround the concentration of power and its possible abuse. Multiple centers of power might provide better protection from potential abuse and global institutional derailment.

Second, there are many state-level institutions, policies, and practices that should be of concern in ensuring the moral equality imperative is implemented satisfactorily in state-wide institutions. State-level institutions are still highly significant in promoting or retarding human beings' prospects for flourishing lives and constitute an important site of cooperation that ought to aspire to fairness.

Third, in the world we live in, much responsibility for ensuring core ingredients necessary for a good life are devolved to states. States are therefore an important vehicle through which many key aspects of global justice are secured and protected.

Fourth, as an empirical matter, in our current world *effective* states are undeniably important for beneficial development. One of the largest-scale global injustices we currently face is the massive extent of poverty. Two billion people currently live below the $2 (US dollars) per day poverty line.[7] Many of these poor people live in developing countries (or countries that are classified as low-income or middle-income ones), and those countries especially need effective states that can actively manage the development process and pro-poor economic activities that reduce poverty. There are many reasons why effective states are indispensable to beneficial development. States ensure the availability of key goods including healthcare, education, water, sanitation, infrastructure, security, the rule of law, and at least a minimum level of social and economic stability, all of which are necessary precursors in building a dynamic economy capable of pro-poor growth. States are also in a unique position to regulate and develop the economy in helpful ways.[8] All in all, the body of evidence that confirms the positive role effective states can play in reducing poverty is huge; by some accounts, states are altogether *essential* to the process.[9] In addition, actively engaged citizens can play a key role in helping to produce and maintain effective and accountable states.[10]

Drawing on some of the strands sketched so far in this chapter, we can marshal the following argument. We all have obligations to one another to ensure we have the necessary ingredients for a decent life (and we have especially strong obligations not to get in the way of what people need for such a decent life through our harmful activities and practices). Effective states are an essential component of enjoying a decent life in our world. So we have obligations to support states' attempts to be effective, and we have a range of other obligations to help secure for others core elements of a decent life.

So far I have presented a general account of our core obligations to one another that derive from my account of global justice. This can be supplemented with an account of remedial responsibilities that addresses the distribution of responsibilities in moving toward a world that better approximates ideals of global justice. Those in developed countries have a significantly greater share of the remedial duties associated with reducing global injustice, and we can argue for this position on several grounds. While we might all acknowledge that poor citizens and their governments are key actors in relieving poverty in poor, developing countries, they can be considerably helped or hampered in these efforts through actions, institutions, practices, and policies that are under the control of those in developed countries. Developed world actors currently are too much part of the problem in undermining states' abilities to be effective through their support for a variety of institutions that govern global practices—especially those found in the global economy—including those that govern trade, investment, international financial markets, and taxation, all of which can undermine revenue-raising capacity and job opportunities in those countries. Developed countries also undermine the empowerment of citizens by failing to support an international and domestic environment conducive to accountability, self-organization, and freedom of expression, to name but a few central ways in which they are currently contributing greatly to global injustices. I have offered various arguments for these views in several other places.[11] We need not rehearse these here, though I give some examples of the problematic mechanisms that need reform below. It may be worth noting before I do so that, in the context of this debate, *that* developed world agents have many global justice responsibilities is not a contentious issue—Michael Blake (and others who are key opponents to the position I take here) agrees with this important point. The issue over which we disagree is not that developed countries have large global responsibilities but rather whether skilled citizens from developing countries should also be expected to play a special part in discharging these responsibilities and mitigating losses. I argue that they can reasonably be called on to play a special role. Michael Blake believes that this view is not justified.

At any rate, along with the arguments I advocate elsewhere, I have also offered various mechanisms for making progress on discharging our obligations of global justice. I mention one such area that has excellent potential here as it will be relevant to some of the policy options we explore below. I have agued for many taxation innovations and reforms that, if implemented, could make significant inroads in reducing global injustice.[12] These include the permissibility of levying global taxes as a way of discharging our global obligations to ensure everyone's basic needs are met, their liberties are secured, fair terms of cooperation are maintained in collective endeavors, and that social and political arrangements are in place to ensure all of this (for instance, sustaining the global public goods on which our prosperity relies). I have also argued that reforms to our global taxation and accounting arrangements are long overdue, especially those that facilitate vast tax escape thus enabling the illegitimate diversion of enormous sums away from developing countries.[13] More generally, when we examine some of the mechanisms that would help reduce global injustice, we notice that there is much that those in developed countries can do to help fortify strong local institutions for developing ones.[14] Examples include supporting the International Criminal Court or the Extractive Industries Transparency Initiative,[15] both of which promote an environment conducive to holding the powerful to account for their actions in ways that can make a tremendous difference to protection of basic liberties and the meeting of basic needs. There are plenty of good initiatives already developed—but which could benefit from more support to fortify their effects—that are good examples of strengthening effective government and empowering citizens, and do well in meeting other desiderata for good assistance.

In this chapter I have highlighted the importance of effective states in securing global justice. Skilled workers have an important role to play in helping states to be effective. What may states permissibly do to retain skilled workers or benefit from their skills? It is to those issues that we turn shortly. Before we are in a position to discuss these normative issues, we must first survey some relevant empirical evidence that suggests skilled worker migration can cause important losses. We turn to that next.

NOTES

1. Gillian Brock, *Global Justice: A Cosmopolitan Account* (Oxford: Oxford University Press, 2009).

2. Another way to argue for the importance of institutions is through recognizing the important empirical connections between institutions and promoting prosperity or beneficial development (a way we discuss in Chapter 3).

   As Allen Buchanan defines the term, "an institution is a kind of organization, usually persisting over some considerable period of time, that contains roles, functions, procedures, and processes, as well as structures of authority" (*Justice, Legitimacy, and Self-Determination: Moral Foundations for International Law* [Oxford: Oxford University Press, 2004], 2). I use the term *institution* slightly more broadly to include also *significant* practices which set up authoritative norms for interaction between individuals and groups, even if no one formal organization oversees the practices' operations, including enforcement of the rules (which might take diffuse forms).

3. Brock, *Global Justice*.

4. We can argue that these define the minimum that we can reasonably expect of one another, and we can go on to elaborate these ideas of reasonable expectation by harnessing the power of normative thought experiments, as I do in Brock, *Global Justice*, Chapter 3, for instance.

5. Though the interested reader might see Brock, *Global Justice*, especially Chapter 12.

6. Gillian Brock and Quentin Atkinson, "What Can Examining the Psychology of Nationalism Tell Us About Our Prospects for Aiming at the Cosmopolitan Vision?," *Ethical Theory and Moral Practice* 11(2008): 165–179.

7. Andy Sumner, "Where Will the World's Poor Live? Global Poverty Projections for 2020 and 2030," *Institute of Development Studies In Focus Policy Briefing* 26 (2012), available at: http://www.ids.ac.uk/files/dmfile/InFocus26-Final2.pdf.

8. I cannot elaborate on all these vast themes here, but the interested reader might consult Duncan Green, *From Poverty to Power: How Active Citizens and Effective States Can Change the World* (Oxford: Oxfam International, 2008); Duncan Green, *From Poverty to Power: How Active Citizens and Effective States Can Change the World*, 2nd edition (Rugby, UK: Practical Action Publishing, 2012); and Gillian Brock, "Global Poverty, Decent Work, and Remedial Responsibilities: What the Developed World Owes to the Developing World and Why" in Diana Meyers (ed.), *Poverty Coercion, and Human Rights* (Oxford: Oxford University Press, 2014).

9. For a comprehensive summary of literature see Green, *From Poverty to Power*, 2nd edition.

10. Green, *From Poverty to Power*, 2nd edition.

11. For a sample of arguments see Gillian Brock, "Health Inequalities and Global Justice," in Patti Lenard and Christine Streahle (eds.), *Global Health Inequality* (Edinburgh: Edinburgh University Press, 2012), 102–118; Gillian Brock, "Global Poverty, Decent Work, and Remedial Responsibilities"; Gillian Brock, *Global Justice*.

12. See, for instance, Gillian Brock, "Taxation and Global Justice: Closing the Gap between Theory and Practice," *Journal of Social Philosophy* 39 (2008): 161–184; Gillian Brock, "Reforming our Taxation Arrangements to Promote Global Gender Justice," *Philosophical Topics* 37 (2010): 141–160; Gillian Brock and Rachel McMaster, "Global Taxation and Accounting Arrangements: Some Normatively Desirable and Feasible Policy Recommendations," in Martin O'Neill and Shepley Orr (eds.), *Political Philosophy and Taxation* (Oxford: Oxford University Press, forthcoming); and *Global Justice*, Chapter 5.

13. Some of the egregious culprits are that we permit a variety of accounting measures to count as perfectly legitimate, including tax havens and so-called transfer pricing schemes. See Brock, "Taxation and Global Justice"; and *Global Justice*, Chapter 5.

14. For a summary of these see Brock, "Global Poverty, Decent Work, and Remedial Responsibilities"; and Brock, *Global Justice*.

15. The Extractive Industries Transparency Initiative (EITI) is an excellent example of the kind of initiative worthy of support. EITI aims to address the enormous problem of lost revenue that arises from natural resource sales that are not adequately transparent or accountable. In many cases, the revenue that poor, developing countries could obtain from resource sales would be more than enough to finance reforms necessary to address poverty, that is to say, if the revenue were actually received and appropriately disbursed. Approximately 3.5 billion people live in countries rich in resources, yet all too often many poor citizens see little benefit from the extraction of their resources. On the contrary, these resources often undermine effective states and the empowerment of citizens. Citizens, governments, and multinationals (both from within and outside the country) could play a very important role in assisting countries to receive such revenue. Currently, many resource sales occur through non-transparent processes where prices and amounts sold are not disclosed, thus providing ample opportunities for private gain and corruption, not to mention extensive damage. On the EITI scheme, companies disclose their tax and royalty payments for resources to governments. Governments disclose what they receive in payments. The tax and royalty payments are then independently verified and made public in a process overseen by several key stakeholders, including representatives from governments, companies, and civil society. This initiative provides mechanisms for relevant information gathering, such that citizens and the private sector in those countries can help improve governance conducive to promoting effective and legitimate states. Citizens of countries in the developed world can assist poor citizens in resource-rich developing countries by mobilizing to make participation in the EITI mandatory when operating in key organizations under their

jurisdiction. For instance, they could require that all multinationals that list on developed world stock exchanges comply with transparency practices such as those outlined by the EITI. They could make membership of EITI mandatory for participation in desirable opportunities such as being involved in contracting agreements with government. (See the EITI website at http://eiti.org for more details.)

3

Prosperity in Developing Countries, the Effects Departing Individuals Have on Those Left Behind, and Some Policy Options

ACCORDING TO THE WORLD BANK, "if rich countries allowed their workforce to swell by a mere 3 per cent by letting in an extra 14 million workers from developing countries between 2001 and 2025, the world would be $356 billion a year better off, with the new migrants themselves gaining $162 billion a year, people who remain in poor countries $143 billion, and natives in rich countries $139 billion."[1] If this truly is a win-win situation for everyone involved, surely one ought not to obstruct the movement of migrants who want to leave their poor countries of origin?

While I do not deny that there is evidence to suggest that considerable benefits may accompany migrants' moving across borders, we should also examine some of the ways in which their departure can result in important losses as well. There is much evidence to review here. In this chapter we examine relevant empirical issues showing why there can be important losses when skilled workers exit poor, developing countries. Once we understand what these losses are, I outline important policy options that could address them. Armed with relevant empirical knowledge, the following chapter, Chapter 4, focuses on the normative analysis necessary to deciding whether particular measures are defensible.

3.1 PROSPERITY IN DEVELOPING COUNTRIES AND HOW DEPARTING INDIVIDUALS CAN UNDERMINE IT

One of the big push factors in migration is the vastly different life prospects people enjoy in different countries. Prominent among the many differences are vast income disparities among countries, especially between developing and developed ones. Furthermore, at least 1.5 billion of the world's population lives in poverty. If poverty and poor life chances are key drivers of movement away from developing countries, tackling these problems seems important. What are the causes of poverty and poor life chances and how can they be adequately addressed? A lively debate flourishes on this topic.[2] There is compelling evidence to suggest that institutions matter greatly in this process, *whatever other factors are also significant.*[3] Creating better institutions is a significant component in helping people out of poverty and a key factor in promoting development. As I go on to discuss, one of the most worrisome setbacks developing countries suffer from emigration is damage to institutions and institution building, and therefore a loss in opportunities for development and escape from poverty.

What do we know about absent human capital? Some sectors are especially hard hit; for instance, there is much awareness concerning the outflows of healthcare workers. Indeed, brain drain in the health sector is particularly widespread and damaging for citizens of developing countries, sometimes of such a scale that it undermines the effectiveness of whole healthcare systems.[4] Some countries lose a staggering percentage of the healthcare professionals they train. For example, in 2001 Ghana lost five hundred nurses, which is more than double the number of new nurses graduated in that year.[5] About a third to a half of South African medical school graduates emigrate to the developed world, and about half the physicians trained in Ghana between 1985 and 1994 have left the country.[6] These kinds of substantial losses, born by developing countries already struggling with inadequate human resources, result in major loss of healthcare delivery capacity, with important consequences for the health of those in developing countries.[7]

While negative effects in the health sector are worrying, other damage is pervasive. Here I identify four types. First, there are important fiscal consequences.[8] Skilled workers typically contribute more to a country's tax receipts than they get in government expenditures.[9] The loss of such workers can mean significant loss of revenue and opportunities for more progressive taxation regimes. Desai, Kapur, McHale, and Rogers estimate the fiscal cost of the brain drain for India as roughly 2.5 percent of Indian fiscal revenues, or 0.5 percent of the Indian GDP.[10] Gibson and McKenzie calculate that for those in the United States, this is about $4,120 per migrant aged twenty-five and older, per annum.[11] The exact fiscal loss a particular country experiences depends on the tax system in the country of origin and how progressive it is. So Micronesia and Tonga, which have low and flat income tax rates, experience losses of approximately $500–$1,000 per migrant. By contrast, Ghana has higher and more progressive income tax rates, and so suffers losses of approximately $5,500–$6,300 per migrant per annum.[12]

Second, there are knowledge spillover effects.[13] Skilled workers' knowledge spreads to others in the economy and in a context where knowledge about best technical practices, organization methods, and so forth is scarce, the loss of workers with highly specialized skills can be quite devastating.[14] Third, on at least one model of growth, high skilled worker migration "reduces income levels and long-term economic growth."[15] But, fourth, the most worrisome effects are institutional. Highly skilled people are "close to indispensable" in building domestic institutions.[16] As institutions are crucial in promoting development, when those most likely to contribute to institution building are absent, development suffers.

People build institutions, and the skilled people who leave are potentially important institution builders. Skilled and talented citizens are both important sources of demand and supply for institutional reform. Generally, for institution building to occur, you need a critical mass of people with high levels of human capital.[17] For instance, in the United States it has been argued that an "intellectual vanguard of university-trained professionals, economists, and other progressive thinkers was among its most valuable state-building resources during the early twentieth century. These individuals played key roles in developing a more professional and bureaucratic state by providing new ideas about better organization and the exercise of power."[18] The loss of those with high skill levels often promotes more emigration, thus further undermining that critical mass necessary for institution building. In addition, the World Values Survey Data suggests a strong connection between a pro-democracy stance and class and education, so when the more educated leave, there may be less local support for democracy.[19] Developing countries tend to have a limited middle class. If members of this segment leave in high numbers, maintaining robust democracies may be challenging.

It is important to point out that there are at least three distinct types of harms that have been identified in this brief survey of detrimental effects from compatriots' departures on those left behind:

(1) Purely financial loss (such as costs of training or loss of tax revenue);
(2) Loss of skills and services; and
(3) Loss of institution-building assets.

In many ways, the third set of harms is the most difficult to address, but all of these losses are not insignificant and can anyhow affect this third set. Some losses of types (2) and (3) have an important indirect effect on the quality and capacity for better institutions. For instance, loss of tax revenue can play a vital role in states' abilities to be effective, and having sufficient funds to build and sustain institutions is also obviously important. Also, providing some kinds of goods (such as basic education and healthcare) might be necessary precursors for the right kinds of institutions to take root and so may be necessary conditions for institution building.

3.2 PROSPERITY IN DEVELOPING COUNTRIES AND HOW DEPARTING INDIVIDUALS CAN PROMOTE IT

Do the positive effects that result from emigration outweigh or compensate for the losses identified? It is often suggested that there are a number of ways in which high-skill migration can have good poverty-reducing or institution-enhancing effects, and can benefit countries of origin. These include:

(1) *Increased human capital formation*: the prospect of leaving to seek a better life elsewhere incentivizes many to acquire skills they would not otherwise.

(2) *Network or diaspora effects*: emigrants residing abroad can become assets to countries of origin, for instance, enhancing trade links or facilitating additional mutually beneficial opportunities which would not arise in the absence of migrants living abroad.

(3) *Temporary migration and return*: migrants often bring many benefits back to countries of origin when they return, such as enhanced human and other forms of capital, or progressive ideas, including the importance of promoting freedom, equality, or democracy.

(4) *Remittances*: Migrants often send sizeable funds back to friends and family in countries of origin.

The volume of such cross-border transfers is huge
and standardly is much greater than official development assistance.[20]

In Part III we explore these considerations further and
examine the state of the empirical literature on these topics, especially in response to Michael Blake's claims, which
rely in part on this evidence. At this more introductory
stage, I believe an extended analysis of the empirical literature is not needed for several reasons, but importantly,
both Michael Blake and I agree that despite a huge range of
benefits that accrue to countries of origin, there are some
cases in which net losses may be occurring, so the key normative question is worthy of consideration. Thus it is pertinent to consider the key normative question, namely: when
there are important net losses for poor developing countries, what may they do to remedy these? And we share the
view that there are enough real-world cases of tragic losses
that this core normative issue has some important bearing
for the world we live in and so deserves analysis.

As we see from surveying some of the empirical evidence in Part III, the effects for countries of origin are
complex and multifaceted. There are many ways in which
high-skill migration can have important consequences
for countries of origin. The main channels of influence
that I discuss in this book include fiscal losses, human
capital formation, temporary migration and return,
network or diaspora effects (especially on trade, foreign
direct investment, technology adoption, and home country institutions), remittances, impacts on services or
outcomes involving core goods (notably health and education), knowledge spillover effects, effects on income

and growth, and of course, effects on institutions and institution-building possibilities. Given this range of considerations, it is not surprising that research confirms that the effects of brain drain vary considerably for different countries of origin, especially given population size, skill levels within those populations, and so forth. While the argument I make in this book aims to be well informed by current evidence, it is not, strictly speaking, dependent on it, in the sense that I am not relying on there *always* being important losses, as a key assumption in my argument. Obviously, if there are no relevant losses, there is nothing to offset. So it is relevant to my project that at least in some cases we can identify relevant losses. And it is also pertinent that we can identify many of the types of losses that accompany high-skill migration so we can identify appropriate policy that could mitigate these categories of losses. But we need not be committed to the view (that is surely false) that the losses identified must *always* accompany high-skill migration. Again, and for emphasis, my central question is a conditional one: when there are relevant losses that accompany high-skill migration, what may governments from poor, developing countries do about such losses?

Two key points are worth highlighting at this stage of our inquiry (with further analysis to come in Part III). First, according to many studies, brain drain (or the migration of high-skill workers) "is becoming a dominant pattern of international migration and a major aspect of globalization."[21] Second, because there is a dominant assumption in some literature that remittances are a widely neglected mechanism of positive change for developing countries, it may be testing readers' patience to ask them to wait until

Part III before I address this issue. Therefore, I make some brief comments about that next.

It is widely assumed that financial remittances can compensate for the departure of citizens, "substituting one scarce factor (financial resources) for another (human capital) that is critical for development."[22] But these factors are not substitutable. Though there are some notable successes from remittance programs, these are not necessarily of the right type or scale to provide the needed economic changes.[23] There is a vast literature on this topic and more empirical work is underway which is relevant to an assessment of the power of remittances.[24] However, as Devesh Kapur and John McHale argue, "there is as yet no evidence that remittances can catalyze broad economic transformations, the kind that is essential to alleviate structural poverty in the long term."[25] And unless remittances have good institution-building effects, I think we should be cautious about their power to be the main vehicle for transforming poor, developing countries into the kinds of places that can provide reasonably decent life prospects for all citizens, even though they can have good poverty-reducing effects for select individuals lucky enough to feel the direct or indirect effects of remittances. We should be cautious about the power of remittances because there are a number of worrisome negative effects that can accompany significant remittance flows, such as the following: the inflow of funds can create dependence for recipients encouraging further migration especially among the working-age, productive adults; both home and host countries can become dependent on continuing migration arrangements and may fail to invest in local economic arrangements that would eliminate the dependence; economic activity can become depressed in countries of origin thus encouraging more emigration; needed economic reforms can be neglected, as can be the creation of rewarding opportunities in the home country; remittances may have a positive effect on transient poverty, but do not by themselves reduce structural poverty; and remittances tend to decline over time.[26]

In this section I have noted that how the effects of high-skill migration play out varies enormously among countries. Though I do not deny that there can be considerable benefits, I also want to emphasize that, when we do the aggregation, we need to consider both benefits and costs, and we need to evaluate whether net resulting benefits are sufficiently large as to outweigh some of the pervasive harms that also flow from migration. In trying to arrive at an overall assessment, we should be especially careful in taking into account factors that might undermine the fundamental features necessary to sustain the right kinds of prosperity-promoting conditions. Prominent among such conditions are those that sustain robust institutions and effective states.

3.3 POLICY OPTIONS THAT MIGHT ADDRESS SOME OF THE LOSSES IDENTIFIED

A variety of policy options to address important losses deserve consideration. I identify three main (sometimes interrelated) strategies that could be deployed, and these have implications for a number of developed and developing world agents. I then identify the core ones that are my focus here, namely those that concentrate on what developing countries themselves may permissibly do to solve their own problems.

(i) Control outflow by trying to change behavior of those in developed countries: Developed countries could mandate that codes of practice be followed in recruitment, and prohibit certain practices such as highly aggressive targeting of scarce talent (in which, for instance, recruiters aim to lure the entire graduating class of a university or the entire staff of a hospital away from communities already experiencing critical shortages). Developed country agents could consider employing migrants for short-term assignments, such as clearing the backlog, rather than permanent positions.

(ii) Require compensation: For mandatory compensation programs to be effective, most require cooperation between developed and developing countries. We could link development aid with human capital recruitment. We could work on arrangements to share streams of taxation revenues. We could establish programs requiring emigrants to pay exit taxes in which revenue accrues to source countries (such as the Bhagwati tax[27]). We could provide conditional education grants repayable on emigration.[28] We could require compulsory service from citizens.

(iii) Create opportunities and incentives: Both developed and developing countries could explore various strategies to create more human capital. Developed countries could focus on their own policies surrounding human capital creation, such as affluent countries systematically underinvesting in sectors such as healthcare and education, which leads to permanent skill shortages, and they could consider a more appropriate level of investment in these high-need areas.[29] Developed countries could reduce barriers to temporary migration. Both could create more incentives for migrants to want to return to countries of origin, such as depositing funds in special accounts that can only be accessed when emigrants return.[30] Developing countries could try to leverage connections in the diaspora to promote mutually beneficial opportunities (such as in trade or investment).

All items listed in the first set of policy options that primarily target the actions of those from developed countries seem worthy of further consideration. Controlling the targeting of scarce talent seems important. There are a number of ways of doing this that have yielded some successes, though there is much scope for further gains in this area. Reaching more agreement on codes of best practice for international recruitment of workers from developing countries would be a significant advance. Ensuring recruitment transactions are more beneficial for source countries seems key. This often entails compensation in one form or another (so this shades into the second set of policy considerations).[31] Compensatory measures could take a number of forms, including technological, technical, or financial assistance; setting up training programs; or helping with institution building. Since governments issue work visas, they have a natural intervention point for checking that recruitments do conform to agreements. To ensure governments continue to play their parts in recruitment agreements, it would be best for an international agency to oversee activities, broker compensation, punish violators (perhaps by levying meaningful fines), and so forth.

Someone might object that while these ideas are noble theoretical aspirations, none of these policies will be able to gain traction in our current world. Even if we reach agreements on recruitment or compensation, who will enforce them? Currently we have several willing and able such bodies. A number of agencies deal with migration issues, including the United Nations (UN), the International Labor Organization, the World Health Organization, and the International Organization for Migration (IOM). The main one is the IOM, which was set up in 1951 and has 105 members. There are also calls for a World Migration Organization, which would function like the World Trade Organization and could gather data, provide information, facilitate the forging of agreements, monitor and help enforce any agreements that are made, and so forth. Whether or not that comes to pass, it is worth pointing out that there are already organizations in existence, such as the IOM or the UN, that are well positioned to assist with policy implementation.

As we have seen in this section, there are a variety of policy options that deserve our consideration in attempting to reduce damage to those left behind. The ones I am particularly interested in discussing here are the permissibility of compulsory service programs and taxation arrangements that target citizens who have departed or those who wish to do so. Is it permissible to coerce (whether directly or indirectly) highly skilled citizens to provide service for payment in their skill areas for a short period? Are programs that tax non-resident citizens justified?

3.4 COMPULSORY SERVICE PROGRAMS

First of all, what do I mean by a "compulsory service program"? The basic idea is that on completion of a course of study, a period of service is required and the state may be quite specific about where that service should take place. Typically, the state directs service toward underserved areas —those areas for which it is hard to attract staff capable of delivering the necessary services, given normal market incentives. A common reason for an area being underserved is that it is geographically remote or far from typical attractions that urbanized areas offer, such as many schooling or lifestyle opportunities often desired by potential providers—especially those with families. For this reason, compulsory service is frequently directed toward rural areas.

Programs of compulsory service may include a large variety of schemes. In a comprehensive study, Frehywot, Mullan, Payne, and Ross survey seventy compulsory service programs currently in use that attempt to deploy and retain a professional health workforce within particular countries.[32] They identify a number of programs as instances of compulsory service, some of which are more accurately characterized as incentive schemes, in my view.[33] While I reject the authors' particular typology, the study is useful in bringing to our attention the range of programs classified as compulsory service. Surveying and reflecting on these programs, we might distinguish seven common types of programs.[34] I list them next, ordered loosely from ones that may be considered more coercive, to those that could reasonably be seen as less coercive and perhaps are more accurately described as incentive schemes:

(1) Some required service must be performed as a condition of completing the education needed to be awarded a degree. For instance, a requirement

to complete a module of underserved community service (typically in rural areas, but other communities are sometimes included) is part of the degree requirements to become a medical doctor.

(2) Service in underserved communities is required on completion of the degree. (The state may be quite directive about exactly where service will be performed.)

(3) There is a delay (such as one year) between completing the education necessary to be awarded the degree and the awarding of the degree.

(4) There is a requirement to complete a module of service in an underserved community in order to gain a license to practice in that state.

(5) There is a requirement to complete a term of service in an underserved community in order to be considered for postgraduate training.

(6) Completing a term of service in an underserved community is considered an advantage in applications for postgraduate training.

(7) Incentives are offered to serve in various underserved areas. These incentives could take various forms, including offering employees subsidized or free housing, education for their children, higher salaries, or low-rate loan opportunities.

In my view, (6) and (7) are not at all coercive and are more accurately described as incentive schemes. A dominant assumption is that compulsory service involves programs such as (2), but in the literature we find quite a range of possibilities. Compulsory service programs could take the form of (3) or (4), which involve fairly low levels of coercion. In practice, (3) may have almost the same desired result as (2) because newly trained but not yet officially graduated healthcare workers may lean heavily on government-provided opportunities during that period, which might involve performing less desired work in underserved communities. At any rate, many of the newly trained (but not yet graduated) are likely to remain in the country for at least the length of time required to get the paperwork needed to receive the qualifications, and so in effect will serve in countries of origin for that period. Under (4), if one wants a license to practice in the state, one must perform a period of compulsory service. If one does not wish to practice in the state, (4) would hardly be coercive.

Another interesting fact we learn from examining the literature on compulsory service is that the most common way to enforce service requirements is through withholding certification necessary to practice legally within a particular country, in other words, programs such as (3) and (4). Freywot et al. report that 64 percent of the compulsory service programs they surveyed do this.[35]

3.5 TAXATION PROGRAMS

The basic idea with the taxation programs that are our focus here is that departing citizens would be eligible for taxation, and the taxes could be levied in various ways. These include departure taxes, ongoing taxation on income (at least for a certain period such as ten years after exit), or tax sharing arrangements between home and host countries. A high-profile proposal concerning ongoing taxation is the Bhagwati tax proposal, which has undergone several revisions since its initial formulation in 1972.[36] As originally conceived, the Bhagwati tax would enable developing countries to receive revenue streams from emigrants living in developed countries to offset some of the effects of brain drain.[37] Another reason offered for such taxes is that if those who leave countries of origin still retain the right to vote (as many do), they have "representation without taxation." Those who have a say in determining the life of a community should also be prepared to help support that community financially.[38]

In Bhagwati's preferred form, the tax would be collected and administered via the institutions of the UN. The tax would be levied for a certain period, such as the first ten years after an emigrant departs from a developing country. The UN would have the authority and the means to direct the revenue to countries of origin, and could deal with the issue of any corrupt or dictatorial countries by disbursing funds to developed countries to spend as part of their normal development spending. Early reactions to the proposal focused on anticipated legal, administrative, and practical problems. But a further wave of attention challenged the idea that these issues were insurmountable. More than three decades on, there is considerable cooperation among jurisdictions (especially about taxation matters) in such a way that many obstacles to its implementation have been cleared.[39] In practice, we see that several countries do tax their citizens who live abroad. Countries such as the United States (currently) and the Philippines (prior to 1998) use citizenship as the basis for ongoing taxation, taxing their citizens on worldwide income received, regardless of where they reside. The US experience shows that it is not only possible to tax citizens living outside of their countries of citizenship, but that it may be less complicated than previously argued and can bring in considerable sums from some of the most high-income citizens who are globally mobile.[40]

Why would it be fair to expect citizens who wish to exit a country to pay taxes to the country they leave? Are compulsory service programs a defensible instrument of social or global justice? We need to turn to the important normative issues next and explore the responsibilities emigrants and destination countries have to those left behind. We discuss some of these policy options in more detail after exploring the normative case for there being important responsibilities that need to be discharged, especially on the part of the emigrant.

NOTES

1. Philippe Legrain, *Immigrants: Your Country Needs Them* (London: Little, Brown, 2006), 19.
2. For an accessible introduction to the debate, see Gillian Brock *Global Justice: A Cosmopolitan Account* (Oxford: Oxford University Press, 2009), Chapter 5.
3. See for instance, Douglas North, *Institutions, Institutional Change, and Economic Performance* (Cambridge: Cambridge University Press, 1990); Daron Acemoglu, Simon Johnson, and James Robinson, "The Colonial Origins of Comparative Development: An Empirical Investigation," *American Economic Review* 91 (2001): 1369–1401; Dani Rodrik, Arvind Subramanian, and Francesco Trebbi, "Institutions Rule: The Primacy of Institutions over Geography and

Integration in Economic Development," *Journal of Economic Growth* 9 (2004): 131–165; Dani Rodrik, "What Do We Learn From Country Narratives?," in Dani Rodrik (ed.), *In Search of Prosperity: Analytic Narratives on Economic Growth* (Princeton, NJ: Princeton Univserity Press, 2003), 1–19, at 10–11.

4. For a synthesis of just some of this vast literature, see Peter E. Bundred and Cheryl Levitt, "Medical Migration: Who are the Real Losers?," *Lancet* 356 (2000): 245–246. See also Edward Mills, William A Schaba, Jimmy Volmink, et al., "Should Active Recruitment of Health Workers from sub-Saharan Africa Be Viewed as a Crime?," *Lancet* 371 (2008): 685–688; World Health Organization, *World Health Report: Working Together for Health* (2006), available at http://www.who.int/whr/2006/whr06_en.pdf. For an excellent recent survery of recent literature see Eszter Kollar and Alena Buyx, "Ethics and Policy of Medical Brain Drain: A Review," *Swiss Medical Weekly* 143 (2013), available at http://www.smw.ch/content/smw-2013-13845/.

5. Magda Awases, Akpa Gbary, Jennifer Nyoni, and Rufaro Chatora, *Migration of Health Professionals in Africa: A Synthesis Report* (Brazzaville: World Health Organization, 2004).

6. Tikki Pang, Mary Ann Lansang, and Andy Haines, "Brain Drain and Health Professionals: A Global Problem Needs Global Solutions," *British Medical Journal* 324 (2002): 499–500. Nearly 25 percent of America's physicians are trained outside America, and almost two-thirds of them come from low- and lower-middle-income countries. Fourteen percent of recently licensed nurses are trained abroad. See, for instance, Amy Hagopian, Matthew J. Thompson, Meredith Fordyce, Karin E. Johnson, and L. Gary Hart, "The Migration of Physicians from Sub-Saharan Africa to the United States of America: Measures of the African Brain Drain," *Human Resources for Health* 2 (2004); also Linda Aiken, James Buchan, Julie Sochaliski, Barbara Nichols, and Mary Powell, "Trends in International Nurse Migration," *Health Affairs* 23 (2004): 69–77.

7. See, for instance, Huddart and Picazo, *The Health Sector Human Resource Crisis in Africa*; Bundred and Levitt, "Medical Migration: Who are the Real Losers?"; and Mills, Schaba, Volmink, et al., "Should Active Recruitment of Health Workers from Sub-Saharan Africa be Viewed as a Crime?"

8. For some excellent surveys by economists of these types of effects, see Devesh Kapur and John McHale, *Give Us Your Best and Brightest: The Global Hunt for Talent and its Impact on the Developing World* (Washington, DC: Center for Global Development, 2005); Devesh Kapur and John McHale, "Should a Cosmopolitan Worry about the 'Brain Drain'?," *Ethics and International Affairs* 20 (2006): 305–320; Devesh Kapur and John McHale, "What is Wrong with Plan B? International Migration as an Alternative to Development Assistance?," in Susan Collins and Carol Graham (eds.), *Brookings Trade Forum 2006: Global Labor markets?* (Washington, DC: Brookings Institution Press, 2006), 137–186.

9. Kapur and McHale, *Give Us Your Best and Brightest*, Chapter 6.

10. Mihir Desai, Devesh Kapur, John McHale, and Keith Rogers, "The Fiscal Impact of High-Skilled Emigration: Flows of Indians to the U.S.," *Journal of Development Economics* 88 (2009): 32–44.

11. John Gibson and David McKenzie, "Eight Questions about Brain Drain," *Journal of Economic Perspectives* 25 (2011): 107–128, at 123–124.

12. Gibson and McKenzie, "Eight Questions about Brain Drain," 124.

13. Francis Fukuyama, *State Building, Governance and World Order in the 21st Century* (Ithaca, NY: Cornell University Press, 2004); Albert Hirschman, *Exit, Voice, and Loyalty: Responses to Decline in Firms, Organizations and States* (Cambridge, MA: Harvard University Press, 1970); Dani Rodrik, "Institutions for High-quality Growth: What They Are and How to Acquire Them," *NBER Working Paper 7540* (Cambridge, MA: National Bureau of Economic Research, 2000); Lant Pritchett and Michael Woolcock, "Solutions

When *The* Solution is the Problem: Arraying the Disarray in Development," *World Development* 32 (2004): 191–212.

14. Kapur and McHale, *Give Us Your Best and Brightest*, 95. See also Chapter 6, for more detailed treatment.

15. Kapur and McHale, *Give Us Your Best and Brightest*, 97.

16. Kapur and McHale, *Give Us Your Best and Brightest*, 96. See also Daron Acemoglu and James Robinson, *Economic Origins of Dictatorship and Democracy* (Cambridge: Cambridge University Press, 2006); Edward Glaeser et al., "Do Institutions Cause Growth? *Journal of Economic Growth* 9 (2004): 271–303; Edward Glaeser, Giacomo Ponzetto, and Andrei Shleifer, "Why Does Democracy Need Education?," *NBER Working Paper 1218* (Cambridge, MA: National Bureau of Economic Research, 2006); Albert Hirschman, *Exit, Voice and Loyalty: Responses to Decline in Firms, Organizations, and States* (Cambridge, MA: Harvard University Press, 1970); Rodrik, "Institutions for High Quality Growth," 2000; Fukuyama, *State Building*; Pritchett and Woolcock, "Solutions When *The* Solution is the Problem."

17. Kapur and McHale, *Give Us Your Best and Brightest*, 97; Hirschman, *Exit, Voice and Loyalty*; Fukuyama, *State Building*.

18. Kapur and McHale, *Give Us Your Best and Brightest*, 97.

19. Kapur and McHale, *Give Us Your Best and Brightest*, 108–109.

20. For more on these topics, see Gillian Brock, *Global Justice: A Cosmopolitan Account* (New York: Oxford University Press, 2009), Chapter 8.

21. Frederic Docquier and Hillel Rapoport "Globalization, Brain Drain, and Development," *Journal of Economic Literature* 50 (2012): 681–730, at 681. In this excellent article the authors comprehensively document four decades of research, focusing especially on more recent contributions.

22. Kapur and McHale, *Give Us Your Best and Brightest*, 145.

23. Included in the success stories would be the Mexican "three for one program" in which remittances from Hometown Associations are matched with federal, state, and local authorities contributing equal amounts. Overall, though, it is not clear that the programs have generated much in the way of income-producing jobs. Also not clear is whether

they are simply funding future migration through enhanced training. For a good explanation of the concern see Kapur and McHale, *Give Us Your Best and Brightest*, 152.

24. For excellent, detailed, very current data on remittances, see the dedicated World Bank website on migration and remittance effects at http://econ.worldbank.org/WBSITE/ EXTERNAL/EXTDEC/EXTDECPROSPECTS/0,,contentMD K:21121930~menuPK:3145470~pagePK:64165401~piPK: 64165026~theSitePK:476883,00.html. For older data, see Brock, *Global Justice*, Chapter 8.

25. Kapur and McHale, *Give Us Your Best and Brightest*, 162.

26. Fernando Lozano-Ascencio, *Bringing It Back Home: Remittances to Mexico from Migrant Workers in the United States* (San Diego: Center for U.S. Mexican Studies, 1993); also Deborah Waller Meyers, "Migrant Remittances to Latin America: Reviewing the Literature," in Rodolfo O. de la Garza and Briant Lindsay Lowell (eds.), *Sending Money Home: Hispanic Remittances and Community Development* (Lanham, MD: Rowman and Littlefield, 2002), 53–81; Richard Black, "Soaring Remittances Raise New Issues," available at http://www.migrationinformation.org/Feature/display.cfm?ID=127.

27. For more on the Bhagwati tax, see Jagdish Bhagwati and Gordon Hansen, *Skilled Migration Today: Prospects, Problems, and Policies* (Oxford: Oxford University Press, 2009). See especially John McHale's contribution, "Taxation and Skilled Indian Migration to the United States: Revisiting the Bhagwati Tax," available at http://web.business.queensu. ca/faculty/jmchale/research3/Taxation%20and%20 Skilled%20Migration%20to%20the%20Uniited%20 States%20%20Revisiting%20the%20Bhagwati%20Tax.pdf. Also Jagdish Bhagwati and Martin Partington, *Taxing the Brain Drain* (Amsterdam: North Holland Publishing Co., 1976).

28. Though John Gibson and David McKenzie caution that many developing countries lack the capacity to recover loans, sometimes recouping less than 10 percent of loans issued. The same problem plagues even developed countries; for instance, New Zealand has a high rate of default.

See Gibson and McKenzie, "Eight Questions about Brain Drain," 123.

29. Also, developed countries should not waste the talent that does arrive by not recognizing skills that often function as a screen for protection of domestic competition.

30. Such a scheme applies to migrant workers from Mozambique and Lesotho who work as miners in South Africa. A portion of their wages is sent to banks in their home countries (Kapur and McHale, *Give Us Your Best and Brightest*, 187).

31. Gillian Brock, "Health in Developing Countries and Our Global Responsibilities," in Angus Dawson (ed.), *The Philosophy of Public Health* (Farnham: Ashgate, 2009), 73–83.

32. Seble Frehywot, Fitzhugh Mullan, Perry Payne, and Heather Ross, "Compulsory Service Programmes for Recruiting Health Workers in Remote and Rural Areas: Do They Work?," *Bulletin of the World Health Organization* 88 (2010): 364–370.

33. These programs are all governed by some type of regulation, ranging from a parliamentary law to a policy within the ministry of health. Depending on the country, doctors, nurses, midwives, or all types of professional allied health workers are required to participate in the program. Some of the compliance-enforcement measures include withholding full registration until obligations are completed, withholding degree and salary, or imposing large fines.

34. In the real world, programs may combine several features. I also separate out here different features of the programs, while acknowledging that in practice programs sometimes combine more than one feature. I also broaden the scope of such programs to include not just healthcare workers but all other skilled citizens trained at the tertiary level who are involved in the provision of core goods and services necessary for citizens to flourish.

35. Frehywot et al., "Compulsory Service Programmes: Do They Work?," 366.

36. Jagdish Bhagwati, "The United States in the Nixon Era: The End of Innocence," *Daedalus* 101 (1972): 25–47; Jagdish Bhagwati and Martin Parlington (eds.), *Taxing the Brain Drain: A Proposal* (Amsterdam: North-Holland,

1976a); Jagdish Bhagwati and Martin Parlington (eds.), *The Brain Drain and Taxation: Theory and Empirical Analysis* (Amsterdam: North-Holland, 1976b).

37. Bhagwati and Parlington (eds.), *Taxing the Brain Drain.*
38. Jagdish Bhagwati and William Dellafar, "The Brain Drain and Income Taxation," *World Development* 1 (1973): 94–101.
39. Domenico Scalera, "Skilled Migration and Education Policies: Is there still scope for a Bhagwati Tax?," *The Manchester School* Vol 80 (2012): 447–467; John Douglas Wilson, "Taxing the Brain Drain: A Reassessment of the Bhagwati Proposal," available at http://hdl.handle.net/10022/AC:P:8484; Mihir Desai, Devesh Kapur, and John McHale, "Sharing the Spoils: Taxing International Human Capital Flows" *International Tax and Public Finance*, 11 (2004): 663–693.
40. Desai, Kapur, and McHale, "Sharing the Spoils."

4

Whose Responsibility Is It to Remedy Losses Caused by the Departure of Skilled Migrants?

4.1 SOME NORMATIVE CONSIDERATIONS

Consider the following case, which I call "attempting to be a responsible government, even though poor," or "responsible, but poor" for short. A legitimate government of a poor, developing country attempts to address and provide for its citizens' needs in a responsible way. It makes projections of current and future citizens' needs, and good-faith plans to meet them. It realizes it will have to invest in training in a number of areas: the country needs more nurses, doctors, and a range of other healthcare workers, but also more engineers, legal experts, teachers, skilled construction workers, architects, quantity surveyors, information technology experts, economists, social workers, experts in finance and entrepreneurial skills, workers skilled in best administrative practice, and those with skills in a host of other categories, in order to build robust, well-functioning institutions and the necessary ingredients to sustain decent lives for citizens. After thoroughly reviewing its budget, the government decides that it has sufficient funds to train only a small number of people in each skill category every year. For emphasis, let us make that number very small. Let us say only five people can be trained in each of the identified need categories. The government widely publicizes the state of its budget, which is available for all to see (on its web-based transparency portal), as is the budgetary calculation indicating why it is a sensible decision, under the circumstances, to train only a limited number of people at public expense every year. The government also widely publicizes its view that given the scarcity of resources, acceptance of the training would create some weighty expectations: on completion of the course of study, the qualified person would provide benefits to citizens in their field of training in the future. The government also suggests that under the circumstances, it believes that the following policy would be justified, namely, that those who accept places in these limited tertiary training opportunity courses acknowledge that such acceptance creates an obligation for the graduates to provide services in their chosen occupation for a period of one year. The government proposes that it be made part of a formal agreement that anyone trained in tertiary institutions in that country will be required to provide service to that country for a period of one year. It further proposes adding an additional clause stating that should the trained citizen leave the country (at any stage), she would be required to pay either an exit tax or an ongoing income tax back to that government for a period of five years.

The government realizes it needs to provide some normative argument for why these prudent decisions might also be morally justified. It enlists the help of a political philosopher, who is to compile a report of normative arguments that the government might like to consider. This is what I would advise in my report.

I would begin with a general account as a prelude to setting out several more focused arguments. I would point out that there are a number of benefits that typically flow to members of a community that is functioning minimally well. A variety of public and private goods are on offer, directly or indirectly. There will be a certain level of peace, protection for people's basic liberties and property, some level of developed infrastructure, education, and so forth. Arguably, one of the most overlooked and under-appreciated benefits of all of these is providing a level of peace and security so that people can go about their lives without fear of imminent danger at all times. Enjoying such benefits accumulates debts that are typically discharged by being a productive member of that society in adulthood. However, if one's adulthood is not spent in that community, other ways of discharging that debt might be appropriate.

Furthermore, well-governed communities make plans to enable the satisfaction of members' needs by investing in the training of those able to provide educational services, build infrastructure, deliver healthcare, and the like. Those investments in developing human resources are prudent, and are part of what good planning and governance of a community requires. Those people who have received the necessary training are, in *a way* and *in part*, community investments.

When a highly skilled citizen of such a community leaves to take up employment elsewhere, there are a number of costs she now imposes on the community she leaves. Notably, there are the training costs, which are frequently heavily subsidized by the community, but there are other costs that are likely to have just as important an effect on development, such as the stream of services she would have provided (in this case, disrupting significant plans and projections for responsible provision of services), the loss of income from taxed wages, the loss of progressivity in fiscal arrangements, the fact that worse-off citizens must now bear more of the cost of public goods, the contribution that person would have made to a well-governed community (including participating in civic and political affairs), and, in general, the loss of people likely to be important sources of both demand and supply for better institutions. The departing individual therefore imposes burdens on those left behind and as a beneficiary of the community's public resources, hospitality, nurturance, and protection, she has a duty to address the loss she has created for the community that helped her become the person she now is, notably, one who has been educated to a sufficiently high level that she is able to take up well-paying opportunities in a global employment market. She has typically received a range of benefits and therefore has incurred some relevant duties.

There are several ways to substantiate this last point, but a version that simplifies many elements is this. Basically, states provide important benefits unlikely to arise in their absence, and they standardly do this without asking citizens to make unreasonable sacrifices. For instance, each of us gains from general compliance with state laws that guarantee peace and security. A certain amount of state coercion of its residents is justified when this is necessary to ensure the peace and security from which we benefit. We also have to be willing to do our fair share in providing key public goods.[1]

However, my report would continue, we need to consider an anticipated challenge likely to be offered especially from emigrants, which we might call "the bad luck objection." Why expect the skilled citizens to absorb all the costs? The fact is that whatever luck came her way, she still was not lucky enough to be born into a better community, namely the one to which she would like to move. It is no fault of hers that she was born where she was. What of all those in developed countries who, through no achievement of theirs, found themselves lucky enough to be born into those countries? Why should they not be made to compensate the source communities? The short response is that developed countries' citizens do have a duty to contribute to these less well-off communities as well. After all, they will gain from adding to the stock of well-educated, highly skilled citizens, who will be able to contribute to political, civic, economic, and social affairs in that country. Indeed, even if no benefits were to accrue directly, they have obligations to the global poor that derive from a number of sources, as Chapter 2 highlighted. But conceding this point does not settle the issue of whether the skilled citizen still has *some* responsibility here as well. As we see in the following, there are a number of arguments that can be collected that point in the direction of there being some important obligations for her, in addition to the responsibilities that others will also have to contribute to addressing the problem.

There are various ways to locate the source of the duties. Some of these source considerations are outlined next with some further thoughts.[2]

(1) *Fairness, the requirements of reciprocity, and the prohibition against free-riding:*[3] Fairness, or the fair provision of benefits, demands a fitting response. Others have made sacrifices to support a mutually beneficial scheme by, for instance, paying their taxes or complying with laws that secure peace. Skilled citizens must assume a fair share of burdens or make some fitting response in virtue of the requirements of reciprocity, fair play, or general considerations of fairness. Failure to reciprocate for the benefits provided by others' cooperation, support, and sacrifice involves taking advantage of others or free-riding unfairly.[4]

(2) *Exploitation and the creation of disadvantage:* By leaving without compensation, emigrants create disadvantages for others. Emigrants' actions would now create a burden that must be recognized. Several burdens are potentially relevant: there is the fact that those left behind must provide services to more people and must typically work harder or leave citizens' important needs unattended. There is the loss of revenue that can entail insufficient funds for core services. More generally, there are losses associated with institution building and its precursors. Whereas the focus in (1) was the receipt of past benefits, here attention passes to the burdens emigrants now create for others by leaving. Those left behind

are made more vulnerable by the emigrants' decisions, as the viability of a decent society could be under threat. Those left behind deserve protection from the disadvantages the emigrants have now created for them. And it is worth drawing attention to the fact that those who have left acquired their advantage-generating skills while making use of citizens' contributions (to civil accord, taxes, mutual cooperative schemes, and the like), so they can be accused (not inappropriately) of exploiting the contributions of their fellow citizens. That there is disadvantage created is clear when we consider that citizens left behind are worse off than if someone had taken up one of the limited training opportunities and had remained in the country for the rest of her life, thereby providing a much-needed stream of services to citizens.

(3) *Thwarting governments' attempts to discharge their duties*: Governments have extensive duties to their citizens. By leaving without compensating for losses, emigrants create burdens for governments who have responsibly been making plans based on these citizens' staying and being part of a productive workforce. Emigrants thwart governments' efforts at planning to meet their citizens' needs if they leave without compensating for losses imposed on fellow citizens through their departure.

(4) *Undermining citizens' abilities to support their governments*: Uncompensated departures that result in governments being unable to discharge their

duties undermine citizens' abilities to support their governments. Fair-minded citizens will support legitimate governments that responsibly plan to help them meet their needs, ceteris paribus. If governments are unable to do this, this can undermine citizens' abilities to support governments, which could manifest in destructive behavior or even lead to state failure. And fair-minded citizens will not undermine fellow citizens' abilities to support legitimate governments that attempt to discharge their duties in good faith.

(5) *Duties of loyalty*: As fellow participants in shared institutional schemes, we have duties of loyalty to compatriots to enable them to support their institutional schemes. Emigrants' uncompensated departures undermine governments being able to discharge their duties and therefore threaten to undermine citizens' support for governments in these efforts. To play a central part in this process is to show disregard for our compatriots and to fail to help them support their institutional schemes.

(6) *Responsibilities in virtue of unintended harmful side effects*: We have duties to show due concern for *certain kinds* of unintended harmful side effects of our actions—actions which may in themselves be perfectly morally acceptable. Certain kinds of dire distributional consequences of our perfectly permissible actions should attract *appropriate concern*.[5]

(7) *Fair returns on investment*: When governments invest scarce resources in creating human capital

to provide for the needs of their citizens, they are entitled to fair returns on their investment. Indeed, for governments not to claim a fair return on their investment would be to use public resources unwisely. Governments are entitled to claim compensation from those who will benefit from their investment, especially when the beneficiaries are non-citizens. After all, non-citizen beneficiaries are gaining services for which their governments did not pay. But emigrants can be called on to play some part too, since they are major beneficiaries as well.

The report would then summarize two key lines of argument that run through several of the more specific arguments outlined in the preceding list. First, by leaving without compensation, skilled citizens create disadvantages for others. Their actions create a burden that must be recognized. Those left behind are made more vulnerable by the emigrants' decisions, as the viability of their enjoying a decent society could be under threat; so they deserve protection from the disadvantages the emigrants have now created for them. Second, when governments invest scarce resources in creating human capital to provide for the needs of their citizens, they are entitled to fair returns on their investment and so are entitled to claim compensation from those who will benefit from their investment; indeed, not to do so would be to squander public resources.

A big issue that is yet to be resolved is how to distribute responsibilities for the losses identified. Who should do what? We cover this next (in section 4.2), before considering (in section 4.3) whether the argument holds more generally for cases not characterized by the assumptions of the "responsible, but poor" case.

4.2 SHARING RESPONSIBILITIES FOR LOSSES: WOULD TAXATION AND COMPULSORY SERVICE PROGRAMS BE JUSTIFIED?

As we have cataloged, there can be considerable costs generated when skilled citizens leave. How should these be distributed? In assigning remedial responsibility, we can usefully draw on dominant patterns of connection which can link particular agents (A) to people suffering deprivation (D).[6] Three connective grounds are especially salient, which I make use of here.

Causal or contributory connection: If one causes or significantly contributes to deprivation, this can be one sufficiently connective ground on which to allocate remedial responsibility.

Benefit: A might have had no role in a process leading to D's deprivation, but might nonetheless have benefited from it. Benefiting from such a process might be sufficient to make A remedially responsible for helping D.

Capacity: Here the focus is on who is capable of assisting. There are actually two issues related to capacity: first, the effectiveness with which one can render aid, and second, the costs to the rectifier of remedying the situation. For instance, the strongest swimmer might be expected to effect the rescue, but only if this is also going to involve low cost to him.

How should we allocate responsibility for sharing the costs that result when skilled citizens depart? Who should do what? We could assign all the responsibilities to those who are beneficiaries of the departure on the grounds that those who benefit from certain actions should bear their costs.[7] Alternatively, we could assign all the remedial costs to those who have greater capacity to absorb them. Or those who cause or substantially contribute to a problem could be expected to fix it, ceteris paribus. And combinations are possibilities too. Sometimes these three considerations pull in different directions and we need to evaluate their contrasting strengths. However, in the domain under review, they relevantly converge in appropriate ways to suggest how costs may fairly be distributed, at least for our core cases. I show how by considering the policy options previously introduced that are my focus here: the permissibility of taxation and compulsory service programs, respectively.

4.2.1 Policy Options Concerning Taxation

Would it be fair to require skilled citizens who emigrate from developing countries to pay exit or ongoing income taxes? Might it also be fair to expect citizens of host countries to share tax revenues with developing countries?

While considering the permissibility of policy options here, it will be useful to consider the matter from the perspective of the main groups affected. Let us simplify and take it to be the case that three groups are the primary stakeholders: the emigrants, the citizens of the source country, and the citizens of the host country. The emigrant is a major beneficiary of the move, she has greater capacity to pay than her typical compatriots, and by leaving, she causes or contributes to relevant losses. However, similar reasoning also applies to those in the host country: they will typically be greatly benefited by the skilled migrant's arrival, compatriots in host countries have superior capacity to pay than either the group of emigrants or source country citizens, and considerations of causal responsibility may seem to point strongly in their direction. I have suggested that by taking in the emigrant (without relevant compensation), host countries facilitate harm to developing countries. Furthermore, they arguably play a significant role in undermining good institutions in developing countries.[8] The arguments can be pressed in a number of forms. For one, developed countries dominate all the major international decision-making fora in which the rules of international interaction are decided (such as the WTO, IMF, or UN) and have in the past often used their superior power to impose terms of agreements that vastly favor the interests of developed countries at the expense of developing ones, such as in their trading arrangements, practices surrounding taking loans, or conventions about the permissible use of military force. Developed countries also currently uphold various other unjust institutions (such as unjust taxation practices and accounting regimes, or the international resource and borrowing privileges often discussed by Thomas Pogge[9]) that point to a global basic structure that is far from fair.[10] Developed countries have great responsibilities to change the underlying globally unjust situation (given the three principles outlined above, along with the arguments canvassed in Chapter 2), and so it is not unfair if we put a *large share* of the responsibilities on their shoulders.

Given the arguments surveyed above, such as the seventh one concerning fair return on investment, it does not seem in principle unreasonable to tax host country citizens to help compensate for losses when those host country citizens receive the benefits of the training an emigrant received in a developing country. However, given all of the considerations raised in the seven arguments above, it is likewise also not in principle unreasonable for emigrants to be asked to assist. Taxes can be shared among relevant beneficiaries, notably the emigrant and those in the host country, with shares to be adjusted perhaps in light of relevant factors such as occupation, income, benefits received, and losses sustained.[11] Recall again that the central questions I tackle here concern what developing countries may do to solve their problems. Whether or not they are successful in convincing developed countries to play a part in discharging their duties, the case is made that skilled citizens can be expected to do so.

So I believe there is a case for reasonable taxation programs that can justly be levied on emigrating citizens, even if we concede that distributing some cost to developed-world citizens is appropriate as well. Reasonable taxation programs include ones that respect core concerns and interests of at least three relevant stakeholders (those left behind in countries of origin, the migrants, and fellow residents in the host country) and, importantly, do not impose unreasonable costs on those who will be expected to pay the tax. Reasonable taxation programs include other features as well, such as that they are compassionate and do not undermine activities communities should encourage (though a broader treatment of the large issue of a theory of reasonable taxation is beyond the scope of this particular project).[12] If the tax is small enough it should not have anticompetitive effects or provide perverse incentives. I believe something like the Bhagwati tax can be sufficiently carefully crafted to take account of such factors, or at any rate, we could devise a tax that could.

4.2.2 Compulsory Service

Some might object that taxing emigrants lets them off too lightly. According to some of the evidence surveyed in Chapter 3, what developing countries most need is for skilled or talented citizens to remain in the country, so what policies are permissible in trying to encourage people to stay, return, or delay departure? I have been working with an indicative proposal in constructing the case that a period of compulsory service be attached to accepting a position in a particular course of study at public tertiary institutions. (That is the proposal more explicitly stated as (P3) below.) However, there are several other possibilities. Let us consider four variants of a compulsory service proposal:

> (P1) A short period of compulsory service is required on completion of the course of study when one accepts government funding of tertiary education, such as in the case of accepting a scholarship (with the clear contractual terms of service written into the agreement).

> (P2) A short period of compulsory service is required on completion of the course of study when one takes out a government loan to fund tertiary education (and service terms are written into the loan agreement).

(P3) A short period of compulsory service is required on completion of the course of study when one accepts a position in a public tertiary institution (again, this expectation can be written into agreements).

(P4) A short period of compulsory service is required on completion of the course of study when one accepts a position in a private tertiary institution, even though one self-funds (and, again, this can be made part of a formal agreement).

We leave for more detailed later consideration what qualifies as a short period of compulsory service. For now, let us consider that the period is ridiculously short—as short as one week, or one day, or even one hour. If the arguments can be made for this case, I will argue that they also work for a more extended (but still short) period of compulsory service, such as one or two years.

Given the seven normative arguments described, I have suggested that it can be permissible for countries to endorse proposals for compulsory service such as (P1)–(P3). Would one week of service not be a completely reasonable exchange given the benefits those trained at public expense have received? In my view, this would be a reasonable exchange. Proposals described as (P1) and (P2), which have the terms written into *funding* agreements, are reasonably uncontroversial in the context of this debate. Michael Blake and I agree that such contracts could be reasonable, though we differ importantly on our reasons for the position. Those who accept the funding do so on the terms explicitly mentioned, and these include compulsory service. These kinds of contracts can be morally permissible, given the conjunction of normative arguments supplied.[13]

(P3) might be thought more controversial, as we are attaching the compulsory service terms to the acceptance of an opportunity to be included in a course of study, even when one pays tuition fees oneself. Again, we can appeal to the conjunction of the normative arguments (1)–(7) to justify why this can be reasonable. Compare two students: the first student takes up the opportunity to become a physician's assistant and on completion of her training remains and performs such service. The second student takes up the position and leaves after graduating, never to look back. Clearly, the first student is a better selection from the perspective of the country's scarce resources than the second. In order to ensure that the government is investing public resources wisely (and so discharging its duties responsibly) it would seem the government can permissibly require that some benefit explicitly accrue to citizens, given its budgetary constraints.

I have been building a case as to why it might be fair and reasonable to specify compulsory service conditions as a condition of accepting places in tertiary institutions, and certainly in tertiary funding agreements. Those who accept the positions (and especially the funding) under the stated terms thereby incur contractual obligations to perform service as specified. My primary case involves the generation of duties on accepting a place in a tertiary institution subsidized (whether wholly or in part) by the state. Can the case extend to those who enroll in private colleges and who pay tuition costs themselves? Let us consider the fourth proposal, (P4), in more detail next.

Should those who pay tertiary tuition costs themselves and train in private institutions be exempt from any compulsory service terms that apply to those who accept places in public tertiary institutions? First, in the developing world, the number of people who pay the *full* cost of their own tuition is quite small compared with the number whose training is subsidized.[14] But even in the case of those who do self-fund, their training is still *heavily subsidized* by the state in both direct and indirect ways. Tuition fees rarely cover the full cost of training, so there are often quite direct subsidies involved—and these can be calculated. More importantly, there are numerous indirect subsidies that allow people to engage in training in a focused and productive way. Keeping the peace is an obvious example of this. The fact that citizens are not actively engaged in civil war allows them to get on with productive activities. The existence of reliable infrastructure, usable roads, efficient and affordable transportation, and the like are all background conditions that enable us to focus on acquiring skills. We tend to take these for granted, but without them our ability to learn is considerably hampered. Furthermore, many private institutions will also invariably lean heavily on public resources or state-funded provision of necessary goods integral to that training. So a private healthcare college might rely on the availability of adequate teachers, many of whom might have been publicly educated, as well as public research grants, professional boards, or government regulators that are publicly provided and empowered to certify, monitor, sanction appropriately, and the like.[15] Therefore, I believe a case can also be marshaled for the permissibility of *some* kinds of compulsory service programs (for instance, *perhaps* of shorter duration) even for those citizens who fund their own tertiary training at private institutions in developing countries.

At any rate, I believe the argument goes through easily enough when we have the ridiculously short period of compulsory service we have been entertaining in mind (such as one week). But what about a more lengthy term of service? Indeed, we should clarify more details about all the terms that can defensibly be part of a reasonable compulsory service program. Getting clearer on the shape of defensible programs involves tackling questions such as these: What terms of service are reasonable to impose (e.g., one year, three years, five years)? Can emigrants buy out of the compulsory service requirement for a suitably high fee? If so, can this cost be passed on to others? And can we require skilled citizens to be more active in institution building during their years of service?

Let me state my answers to this cluster of questions briefly. Balancing considerations, it would be reasonable for particular developing countries to require, say, one or two years of compulsory service as a condition of accepting funding at the tertiary level. This is certainly true in the case described as "responsible, but poor," which involved a one-year term.[16] However, it also seems reasonable that skilled citizens should be allowed to substitute a service requirement for other arrangements, if adequate terms of compensation can be organized. For instance, a Canadian doctor might go to work in South Africa for two years while a South African one goes to Canada for a comparable period. Also, for a suitably high but reasonable fee, skilled citizens should be allowed to buy out of the service requirement or transfer the costs of replacing them on to the actual beneficiaries of their services. Any agreement on an appropriate fee for such buyout should take account of as many of the real costs of the transaction as feasible—such as training, loss of service, costs of training replacements, perhaps opportunity cost to institution building, and so forth—while balancing that sum with the effects the fee would have on those who must pay it (so the cost can be moderate but must still be reasonable). The fee can be paid at flexible intervals, and need not be paid off in full on initial departure. Placing further conditions on would-be emigrants, such as to be more active in institution building during their discretionary time when they reside in the source country, would not be reasonable.

I have already indicated that people may be permitted to buy out of compulsory service requirements and they may be permitted to pass the cost on to beneficiaries of their services. Perhaps there should also be flexibility as to when compulsory service is performed. It may be that if citizens of developing countries acquire skills in host countries they will be of more benefit to developing countries not before departure but at some future point, so allowance should be made for compliance with compulsory service requirements at a point later than initial departure. This seems reasonable, though we should anticipate the objection that what is gained in flexibility may be lost in lack of enforcement. It might seem that states will have maximum power of enforcement if they require service to be completed before permanent departure is permitted, but with cooperation from host countries (as is currently the situation with a number of US visa categories) this need not be the case. If evidence comes to light that cooperation is not forthcoming, policies can be adjusted in light of current constraints.

Some might object that if the normative arguments presented above are so compelling, the terms of compulsory service should be longer. Why limit the service terms to only one or two years? Why not a longer term, or a policy of at least one year of service for every year of training subsidized? There is bound to be some tension here: the stronger the force of the arguments the more they point in the direction of longer terms. Yet longer terms might not be considered reasonable sacrifices for skilled citizens to have to make. So we have to compromise in our real-world policy proposals. I take seriously the idea that any sacrifices we can be expected to make must be reasonable ones. People make plans for their lives and their reasonable plans deserve significant consideration. Compelling them to stay in one country might significantly disrupt such plans, and the period of compulsory service must be mindful of this.

4.3 EXAMINING HOW FAR WE MAY EXTEND THE ANALYSIS OF "RESPONSIBLE, BUT POOR"

A patient reader might agree with everything argued so far, but challenge just how far we can extend the arguments from cases of responsible but poor governments when, she might object, in our actual world this hypothetical case does not map on to many real-world cases. I examine this issue next.

First of all, for my purposes, it is sufficient that I have described a quite plausible scenario in which, if a government were to conform to the assumptions of "responsible, but poor," it would be justified in setting the required terms for which I have argued as a condition of accepting places in courses of study at tertiary institutions. That is all I need to show for my argument to work.

In addition, it seems that governments might be able to conform to key features of my core case easily enough. Some already do fully disclose their budgets. And it would not be difficult for governments to indicate what skill sets are in short supply. It certainly would not be difficult for them to publicize their expectation that acceptance of training positions creates the obligations of service specified (indeed, some already do so informally or in more formal ways), and it would be easy enough for them to get students, on enrollment, to sign contracts that make them vividly aware of what they are undertaking.

To be clear, though, the position I am taking on the permissibility of taxation and compulsory service programs only applies in cases where the governments are sufficiently responsible (and poor), and being sufficiently responsible includes being reliable in resource expenditure, sufficiently free of corruption, and so forth. Also, compulsory service can only be reasonably required when the costs of staying and performing service are not unreasonable, which they would be were the state unable to provide an environment sufficiently protective of human rights. We explore more such issues in the next section. And we consider some objections to the views argued for in this section, and in response to these objections, further develop the position that developing countries may permissibly introduce programs, such as ones concerning compulsory service and taxation, thus regulating terms of exit in efforts to solve the severe problems they often face.

NOTES

1. For an excellent defense of this view, see Christopher Wellman's arguments in Christopher Heath Wellman and A. John Simmons, *Is There a Duty to Obey the Law?* (Cambridge: Cambridge University Press, 2005), 3–89.

2. While most of the relevant normative issues have been raised in political philosophy debates, prominently in marshalling a case for why we have duties to obey the law, these kinds of considerations are not usually deployed to build a case that duties may track citizens moving away from their home societies.

    What is the status of the seven arguments presented below? I believe that some of these considerations are jointly sufficient to build a case that duties may track citizens' moving away from their home societies. Perhaps (7) is sufficient by itself, but at any rate, my claim is that a cluster of such arguments could be, and that this cluster is.

3. H. L. A. Hart, "Are There Any Natural Rights?" *Philosophical Review* 64 (1955): 175–191; George Klosko, *Political Obligations* (Oxford: Oxford University Press, 2005); John Rawls, "Legal Obligation and the Duty of Fair Play," in Sidney Hook (ed.), *Law and Philosophy* (New York: New York University Press, 1964); Lawrence Becker, *Reciprocity* (New York: Routledge, 1986); Christopher Heath Wellman and A. John Simmons, *Is There a Duty to Obey the Law?* (Cambridge: Cambridge University Press, 2005).

4. While there are well-known libertarian objections to such general lines of argument, I do not find them particularly plausible in the case at issue. Robert Nozick is well known for these skeptical concerns, such as in *Anarchy, State, and Utopia* (New York: Basic Books, 1974). The kinds of cases he raises, such as the provision of entertainment benefits, are not germane to the kinds of benefits under discussion here which are central to secure fundamental interests such as in security, health, and other necessary conditions of agency.

    In recognition of others' prior beneficial actions (such as those discussed in (1) and the general narrative above), emigrants have also incurred duties to show gratitude, but I will not make much of this argument here (see, for instance, A. D. M. Walker, "Political Obligation and the Argument from Gratitude," *Philosophy and Public Affairs* 17 (1988): 191–211).

5. The standard purported counter-example to such arguments is one drawn from what appears to be perfectly legitimate business competition. Say you set up a better coffee shop than mine nearby, and I go out of business. This is perfectly permissible in a context in which there are adequate provisions to help me get back on my feet—for instance, there is unemployment assistance and other welfare benefits are available. Here appropriate concern extends to ensuring such assistance is provided. Note that in the kinds of cases under discussion the point is exactly that such institutional safeguards are not available, so appropriate concern extends to ensuring that they are. This means that invoking such examples simply begs the question.

6. Here I draw on dominant accounts in the literature, notably that of David Miller in *National Responsibility and Global Justice* (Oxford: Oxford University Press, 2007), Chapter 4.

7. This consideration seems especially strong when receiving benefits simultaneously exacerbates injustice, for instance, benefiting from unjust practices also helps sustain them.

8. See, for instance, Gillian Brock, *Global Justice: A Cosmopolitan Account* (Oxford: Oxford University Press, 2009), or Thomas Pogge, *World Poverty and Human Rights* (Polity: Cambridge, 2008).

9. Pogge, *World Poverty and Human Rights*

10. Brock, *Global Justice*, Chapters 4–9.

11. For more on such possibilities see, for instance, Jagdish Bhagwati and Gordon Hansen (eds.), *Skilled Migration Today: Prospects, Problems, and Policies* (Oxford: Oxford University Press, 2009). Also Jagdish Bhagwati and Martin Partington (eds.), *Taxing the Brain Drain* (Amsterdam: North Holland Publishing Co., 1976).

12. Other desirable features of a reasonable tax include the following partially overlapping considerations: (N1) the tax

complements or promotes important social, political, economic (and the like) objectives; (N2) it is compassionate in that it takes account of the capacity to pay and does not disproportionately burden those whose position makes it particularly difficult for them to bear more of the cost than others far better positioned (i.e., it is not regressive); (N3) it is competitive, that is to say it does not importantly undermine appropriate, fair, and non-destructive competition or prevent activities communities should otherwise encourage; and (N4) it is one that is competently collected, administered, and disbursed. I develop some of these ideas elsewhere. See, for instance, Gillian Brock and Rachel McMaster, "Global Taxation and Moving Towards Global Justice: Some Normatively Desirable and Feasible Policy Recommendations," in Martin O'Neill and Shepley Orr (eds.), *Taxation and Political Philosophy* (Oxford: Oxford University Press, forthcoming).

13. I should note that some libertarians might still challenge the validity of such contracts as, in their view, they might involve undue coercion. Taking on this strand of libertarian interlocutor is not an important focus in this work and anyhow the arguments that I would need to supply to do justice to the libertarian view would take us too far afield and would encompass discussions about the kinds of freedoms we ought to want, what the state might permissibly do to assist in promoting desirable forms of freedom, and what we can reasonably expect from one another in pursuing freedom as an important guiding ideal. In Part III, we do cover some issues concerning whether the circumstances in which such contracts are signed involve undue coercion, and there I argue why any coercion that there might be can be adequately justified.

14. Consider, for instance, that with rare exceptions, tertiary students in Africa finance only a minor proportion of their education. African governments generally fund over 90 percent of the total operating budgets of higher education institutions. See Damtew Teferra and Philip G. Altbachl, "African Higher Education: Challenges for the 21st Century," *Higher Education* 47 (2004): 21–50, at 27–28.

15. Jim Dwyer makes some of these points in "What's Wrong with the Global Migration of Health Care Professionals?" *Hastings Center Report* 37 (2007): 36–43, especially 38.
16. The rough rule of thumb that one should provide a year of service for each year of training subsidized also strikes me as prima facie reasonable. However, if we consider that training in a particular field might require a decade or so of tertiary level training, this cumulative debt might well prove too much and indeed provide perverse incentives for people to undertake less training in efforts to reduce their compulsory service debt.

5

Consideration of Central Anticipated Objections

NEEDLESS TO SAY, ANY TALK of regulating emigration is likely to be seen by some as repressive, invoking visions of Soviet-era controls, even though those are clearly not what I have been arguing for. In this chapter we consider many key concerns that are likely to be raised about the arguments so far and, in addressing them, further develop the view.

Objection 1: The communities people typically want to leave are not well-functioning, legitimate states—they do not reach the threshold for triggering the duties. What counts as a legitimate state and when do the duties get triggered?

On my view, only *legitimate* states have the permissions that I argue are sometimes justified. It is common in the literature to use as a criterion of a legitimate state that it must sufficiently respect human rights, especially core civil and political ones.[1] This concise account will be fine for the sake of the arguments here, and it will do as a rough proxy, though legitimacy probably requires more than respecting human rights. There are at least two dimensions that are relevant in judging whether a state is legitimate, and both can be important in assessments of overall state legitimacy. The first dimension concerns how those who currently hold positions of power came to power. There must have been a legitimate process governing the assumption of power, and typically this will be infused by democratic norms or at least involve political participation from citizens. The second dimension in judging legitimacy (arguably more important) involves examining how power is exercised. Power must be exercised in ways that show concern for the needs of citizens, such as by providing core public goods essential for a decent life (and doing what is necessary to provide secure access to these, such as planning for citizens' well-being). Key tests of legitimacy are that a state must be able to manage an impartial system of justice, it must be able to raise revenue fairly, and it should be able to spend revenue wisely.[2]

Clearly excluded as legitimate states are ones that are failing or failed, or ones that persecute citizens. So consider the case of Uganda, where a homosexual may face the death sentence if found out to be homosexual. In my view, this violates basic human rights. Whether or not one agrees that human rights are violated by this Ugandan practice, the costs of staying in such an environment are high and asking someone who is homosexual to absorb such costs would be unreasonable. With this practice the state is persecuting its citizens and since a legitimate state cannot do so, it would have no grounds on which to insist that citizens stay and assist others.

Objection 2: By specifying or regulating terms of departure—such as advocating for the permissibility of developing countries implementing taxation or compulsory service programs or suggesting that developed countries may be required to pay compensation for skilled citizens they admit—we are unfairly undermining the freedom of emigrants or unfairly limiting their opportunities.

This kind of objection focuses on the freedom of those who choose to leave, rather than the freedom of those left behind. Should those who remain not also be able to enjoy the freedom to live and work in their home country? Without compensatory or interventive measures, members of the developing country face important losses that we should not reasonably ask people to accept. If we are trying to secure freedom, we must be concerned with a greater range of those whose relevant freedoms are affected. We should try to secure for all a genuine opportunity to live and work in their home country. Failing to take action or "doing nothing" is not in fact doing nothing but rather ignoring the disadvantages the most vulnerable must face and favoring the interests of those who are better off. Equal consideration of the interests of the less well-off requires that their needs and interests be given at least equal weight as the interests of the emigrants. We need to give equal recognition to the freedom, rights, needs, opportunities, and interests of those left behind. I discuss some further problems concerning freedom below.

Objection 3: Would imposing costs on those who wish to leave not be a way of unjustly limiting the freedom of movement of these people?

Though freedom of movement is an important liberty that we should be allowed to enjoy, this liberty always has various limits attached to it, even within the most well-functioning communities. I may not freely move about in ways that conflict with people's property rights. For instance, I may not freely move into your house without your permission. Other cases where limiting freedom of movement can be justified include quarantining people for public health reasons or limiting people's abilities to use particular threatened habitats in efforts to protect them. The limits of my freedom of movement often coincide with harms or setbacks to others' important interests, and so it is precisely an open question if we have identified setbacks to others' important interests that should have some appropriate weight. The arguments I have been offering explore this question (rather than presupposing the answer as the objection seems to imply) and I have been arguing that third-party interests should have significant weight that may permissibly affect freedom of movement.

Objection 4: Just as people should be free to leave golf clubs or marriages that no longer work for them, so similar considerations concerning freedom of association and dissociation mean that emigrants should be able to leave their countries of origin with no conditions attached.

Different kinds of associations might generate different fair terms of exit. Consider the freedom to leave a golf club. An individual member's leaving a golf club might well impose costs on others. His leaving may mean that the cost of maintaining the course for each person will rise, and perhaps if enough people leave the club, the viability of maintaining that golf club may be called into question. However, if someone chooses to leave a golf club, as there are no significant fundamental interests that are involved in the playing of golf, maintaining clubs, and so on, no exit costs should ordinarily apply.

While we generally think freedom to dissociate should have considerable force, notice that we do sometimes think exit costs are appropriate. Our practices governing fair dissolution of marriages recognize the permissibility of specifying terms under which dissolution may proceed, especially the permissibility of requiring financial transfers to be made to parties whose important interests would otherwise be compromised and requirements concerning ongoing care for vulnerable parties, notably children. Other kinds of associations may also generate concerns about the timing of departure. While members of an orchestra should generally be free to leave the group when they no longer wish to play with the orchestra's musicians, to do so in the middle of a concert or a season might significantly harm others and thus it can be permissible to specify terms of exit, such as giving the orchestra due warning or waiting until suitable replacements can be found.

Objection 5: Why require presence when there may be other ways to discharge the duty to assist more effectively?

I believe my arguments are sensitive to the ways in which presence should, and should not, matter to our obligations, for instance, being flexible about alternative arrangements that are likely to have positive effects for all concerned. But actually "being there" is sometimes indispensable. For instance, when there is a severe shortage of skilled personnel who can assist with particular needs such as administering vaccines or dispensing appropriate drugs, being present with patients in the same room may be the only way that the necessary assistance can currently be provided.

Notice that what people must be present to be able to do can change as technology changes. So the requirement to remain in a particular country may vary with current technological levels. As more advanced ways of delivering services are developed, what may be permissibly required of citizens (especially before they depart) may need to be reassessed. But until such time as we have successfully mastered beaming hologrammed versions of ourselves into far-away locations, Skyping our way to all the remote villages in which needy people live, or managing in other ways to build robust institutions or satisfy core human needs from remote locations, being present in the same space as the needs one is trying to meet will still be an important factor in eliminating obstacles for people without the essentials for a decent life.

We might again note that requiring presence—even quite coercively—has much precedence. Consider visa categories commonly used in the United States, such as the J1 visa, whereby many visa holders are subject to a two-year home country presence requirement before they will be allowed re-entry to the United States. Those who are required to return for two years are in that category because home countries believe that the visa holders are engaged in a process of acquiring skills which are in short supply in the home countries, and they would benefit from such citizens' return on completion of training. Under this arrangement, the US government allows visitors to study in the United States so long as they return to their countries of citizenship for a period of two years after study is completed. It also coercively enforces these requirements on behalf of other countries. These requirements are not commonly held to be impermissible, or at least are widely tolerated, and are no more coercive than the sorts of compulsory service programs for which I am arguing.

Another objection related to that of requiring presence is that it can lead to wasted talent (or "brain waste") if there are no jobs for skilled workers to fill in the country of origin and yet they are required to remain there. Objectors often point out that there are many who are currently unemployed in poor, developing countries.[3] Why add to the problem when emigrants might have better job prospects outside of the country and furthermore, if they send remittances back to citizens in countries of origin, would be of greater overall benefit to a poor country in that way?

In answering these reasonable concerns, I would make at least two points. There need to be appropriate job opportunities in the home country if the state can reasonably require citizens to perform service and delay departure. The state that requires service must, of course, make service opportunities available in those countries of origin and must be the employer of last resort if jobs are not readily available. A second response I would offer is that often unemployment is so high because of insufficient public funds to employ people to do the work that would target unmet need. However, if states could collect more revenue, for instance, through enlarging the tax base including emigrants in the pool, states would gain an important source of revenue to employ some of those who are currently unemployed or underemployed. Indeed, the current levels of unemployment are sometimes a quite direct result of waves of mass emigration of skilled workers and the subsequent loss of tax revenue (and flow on consequences such as diminished ability to grow the economy adequately). Far from this unemployment data casting doubt on my position, it shows instead the importance of designing robust public policy that can stop the vast uncompensated flow of valuable resources from poor developing countries, be it in the form of tax revenue or human skill sets.

Objection 6: What about those who are unskilled? If some are required to contribute through their taxes or perform compulsory service, does fairness not require this of all?

Developing countries may argue there is a consistency case for implementing compulsory service requirements on all their citizens, both skilled and unskilled. Alternatively, they may wish to tax both skilled and unskilled citizens. In entertaining the idea of such programs it will be relevant to consider the nature of people's talents and how they may best contribute to development in poor countries of origin. In tackling this objection, there are further questions that should be explored concerning whether unskilled workers contribute best through compulsory service or by working outside the source country and having a portion of their wages taxed to provide revenue to source country governments. Once the argument broadens out from the core group in focus, namely highly skilled workers who have largely acquired their skills in developing countries, further analysis may be needed.[4] So, it is plausible that unskilled citizens who leave should also be required to make a contribution to countries of origin, if skilled emigrants are so required. The form that contribution should take should track relevant benefits, harms, and ways in which they might contribute best. Unskilled workers who leave might assist best by working in foreign countries and having a portion of their wages taxed (rather than through performing compulsory service within the country before departure), thereby providing an important revenue stream for source country governments.

Objection 7: The programs that are being advocated are unusually coercive. Why think it is permissible to coerce people to labor for the benefit of others?

First, note that compulsory service practices are quite widespread: at least seventy countries around the world employ such programs currently, including the United States.[5] Mexico set up the first such program in 1936. Many countries have compulsory rural service, though the terms vary considerably. Singapore and Malaysia have a three-year compulsory service requirement for medical school training, while South Africa's compulsory service requirement is only one year. In India, one year of rural service is a precondition for a basic MD degree. Indirect forms of compulsory service are also widely practiced. In Ghana, MD degrees are awarded only one year after completion of requirements for graduation to discourage departure at least for one year, as newly trained doctors are effectively nudged into working in the country for a year. India has made a period of rural placement a requirement for post-graduate admission.

While many complain that compulsory service programs would involve an unusually high level of coercion, we have many precedents for practices involving similar levels or coercion. It is worth comparing compulsory service programs with other practices that are commonly thought permissible, though they may involve similar levels of coercion. Medical graduates are required to work for a few years as residents in order to gain professional certification. Programs of medical residency often involve a period of long hours of service, often in locations at others' discretion, and at low pay (at least by market rates), and these practices provide relatively inexpensive care to the community. The degree of coercion involved here seems similar to what is being proposed with the kinds of compulsory service programs that I would endorse.

More generally, coercion for the benefit of others can be justified as we see with the practice of redistributive taxation. Such redistributive practices might be considered mildly coercive and yet quite justified because of our ideals of social justice. Note that redistributive taxation involves, in effect, having to labor for the benefit of others (mostly in the form of foregoing some income for the benefit of others), and yet we accept that in liberal democracies these contributions can reasonably be required of us. In the context of this debate, Michael Blake and I agree that redistributive taxation is permissible. So we are in agreement that there are some defensible practices in which we can be required to labor for the benefit of others. That there are occasions in which we can be expected to labor for the benefit of others is not at issue, but whether we can be expected to do so in the case of compulsory service programs or by taxing non-resident citizens is.

It may also be worth noting that there are many countries (including liberal and social democracies) around the world that routinely require much greater levels of service and sacrifice from their citizens, notably in the case of compulsory military service. To name but a few, these include Norway, Switzerland, Indonesia, Denmark, Brazil, Finland, Greece, Mexico, Bermuda, Israel, and Austria. In such cases, one can routinely be expected to risk life and limb in service to one's fellow citizens. What I am arguing for here involves contributions far less onerous than that.

Objection 8: Why not think that the developed country has an important obligation to send its citizens to the poor, developing country rather than expecting poor citizens to remain?

I am sympathetic to the idea that it is typically more costly to ask someone to go to a new environment rather than expecting people to remain where they are.[6] But, someone might object, maybe the developed country citizen can be expected to absorb more costs given her state's contribution to sustaining global injustice? Though I think this point is reasonable, recall that my primary question is what poor, developing states may do to solve their own problems. So my focus is what defensible actions they may take that are under their control. They might ask developed countries to make a greater contribution in discharging global justice obligations, perhaps by sending some skilled citizens from developed countries to developing ones for a period of time. And they might be waiting a while before discussion about that even begins to happen. In the meantime, the core question remains salient, and developing countries can permissibly introduce measures (such as compulsory service or taxation) that will help them solve their own problems.

Objection 9: The issues under consideration here are an instance of a general problem of transitional justice: do we put constraints on those living now in order to benefit people in the future? The

(Popperian) skeptical counterargument is that we are so uncertain that we will actually be able to do any longer-term good by the constraints that there is a danger we simply lose twice over, by making the lives of the would-be emigrants and those who we are aiming to help through enhanced institution building worse. So it is better to let those who can find a good life now through migration enjoy the chance for that life (by not restricting their options). It seems that the burden of proof shifts to those who want to regulate emigration to show that restrictions will actually improve things for those who would otherwise be left behind.

I think this is an important objection. After all, it may be that the would-be emigrants are so unhappy about having to stay and fulfill a compulsory service requirement before departure that, even though they are physically present in the country, their presence does not have as good results for institutions as it could either because they engage in counterproductive activities or their resentment at having to stay blocks any motivation they would have had to contribute in more productive ways to their society.

I have two responses to this objection. The first response is to try to minimize this potential hazard and we could do so by ensuring that whatever restrictions on movement are finally endorsed in a particular country are the result of a process involving would-be emigrants (along with other relevant stakeholders). If potential emigrants are engaged in a deliberative process in which the arguments for and against restrictions are presented, where their views about fairness are also acknowledged and balanced against others' positions, they may feel more engaged in the process and willingly decide to be helpful in institution building while they fulfill the compulsory service requirement and possibly beyond. Having said that, to address this objection convincingly, more research about factors that facilitate the kind of institution building that promotes development when compulsory service programs are in play (and more generally) would be welcome.[7]

A second response to this objection might go like this. The policies we eventually endorse must track the available evidence. Even if there is not yet enough evidence that compulsory service programs fix institution-building problems, we can give limited support to the idea that such programs can help address another relevant and related harm which we have clearly identified: loss of service. We do not need to gather more evidence to know that asking someone trained at the tertiary level to provide services for a limited period in her field of expertise, where such services are in short supply, would constitute progress in addressing domains afflicted by serious loss of service because of a shortage of skilled persons. And this might well have a positive flow on effect for the institution-building problem. Attending to some core goods may be necessary precursors for good institutions to be able to take root, so providing core goods and services seems to have well-established good indirect effects on institution building as it brings into being more of the necessary preconditions.

NOTES

1. For further discussion of this issue, see Christopher Heath Wellman and Phillip Cole, *Debating the Ethics of Immigration: Is There a Right to Exclude?* (Oxford: Oxford University Press, 2011). Wellman also uses respect for

human rights as an important consideration in determining legitimacy.

2. Green, *From Poverty to Power*, p. 97; Duncan Green, *From Poverty to Power: How Active Citizens and Effective States Can Change the World* (Oxford: Oxfam International, 2008).

3. Javier Hidalgo, "The Active Recruitment of Health Workers: A Defence," *Journal of Medical Ethics* 39 (2013): 603–609; Christophe Lemier, Christopher H. Herbst, Negda Jahanshahi, et al., *Reducing Geographical Imbalances of Health Workers in Sub-Saharan Africa* (Washington, DC: The World Bank, 2011), 11; Josefine Volqvartz, "The Brain Drain," *The Guardian*, March 10, 2005.

4. Other concerns about consistency might be these: Why single out those who have developed their talents before leaving a country for special treatment? What about those who have "raw talent" but develop their skills elsewhere? While these two questions are not unimportant, they are not the core paradigm case for which I am concerned to develop reasonable policy. Once that case goes through, we may wish to consider developments to take account of variations and compexities not related to our central case.

5. A noteworthy program is the US National Health Service Corps (NHSC), which offers a conditional scholarship scheme: one year of service is to be undertaken for each year of scholarship received for training. These can involve terms of one to twenty-five years.

6. Kieran Oberman makes this point in "Can Brain Drain Justify Immigration Restrictions?," *Ethics* 123 (2013): 427–455.

7. In responding to this objection, it may be interesting to consider briefly some of the demonstrated impacts of such compulsory service programs that are in existence. There is a general problem in health services research with trying to show direct evidence of physician impact on population health. And this general problem affects proving the clinical efficacy outcomes of compulsory service programs. However, there are standard measures that indicate enhanced service provision is available, and these are taken as indicators of success. For instance, Mozambique can

report that all 148 districts in the country now have at least one physician, which was not the case prior to the compulsory service program. Similar results can be found around the world. Before compulsory service programs were introduced in Puerto Rico, there were no physicians in sixteen of seventy-eight municipalities, whereas after implementation, at least one doctor was employed in all seventy-eight municipalities. Studies show good results in Indonesia and Turkey, with South Africa showing "better staffing levels in rural hospitals, shorter patient wait times and more frequent visits to outlying clinics by health workers" (Seble Frehywot, Fitzhugh Mullan, Perry Payne, and Heather Ross, "Compulsory Service Programmes for Recruiting Health Workers in Remote and Rural Areas: Do They Work?," *Bulletin of the World Health Organization* 88 (2010): 364–370, at 366–367).

Programs are likely to be more effective when at least four conditions obtain: first, good planning such that individuals are trained for the procedures and conditions relevant to working in rural areas or underserved communities. Second, availability, both within the healthcare system and the community, of necessary support for people to function effectively. Third, there is transparency about how service is allocated and clear understanding of the rationale behind service programs. Fourth, community support can make a tremendous difference in how effective their presence is for community health. When healthcare workers feel that their services are highly valued, they often believe the work they do in these underserved areas is more valuable, and this can affect their willingness to remain in such communities. For more on such research, see Frehywot et al., "Compulsory Service Programmes: Do They Work?"; also S. J. Reid, "Compulsory Community Service for Doctors in South Africa—An Evaluation of the First Year," *South African Medical Journal* 91 (2001): 329–335; and Anthony Cavendar and Manuel Alban, "Compulsory Medical Service in Ecuador: The Physician's Perspective," *Social Science and Medicine* 47 (1998): 1937–1946. The latter two articles are particularly noteworthy in that they draw attention to the fact that the doctors themselves found the compulsory service they were required to perform was, overall, a rewarding experience. This feature is interesting since it can be raised in contexts where some complain that the programs are coercive. Even if they are coercive, they may still be quite rewarding. As Hamish Russell helpfully points out, this can go some way toward dissipating some of the concerns about coercion.

6

Summary of Conclusions from Part I

HERE IS A SUMMARY OF the core positions for which I have argued in Part I. A poor, legitimate developing state may defensibly regulate emigration of skilled workers—directly or indirectly—when certain conditions obtain. I summarize the conditions for the two principle programs on which I focused.

COMPULSORY SERVICE

A poor, legitimate developing state may defensibly introduce and maintain compulsory service programs when the following factors, labeled *background conditions, legitimacy, presence, responsibilities*, and *reasonableness*, all apply:

Background Conditions

(1) Evidence from the particular country suggests skilled citizens can provide important services for which there are severe shortages, and their departures considerably undermine efforts to meet citizens' needs. The ways in which citizens' departures exacerbate deprivation may be quite direct (such as failure to provide important services necessary to meeting basic needs) or more

indirect (such as when the institutional reforms necessary for development have been hampered by net losses resulting from migration of skilled citizens).

(2) Governments have invested in training skilled workers to provide for their citizens' needs and to promote beneficial development.

(3) Governments have made students aware of the fact that they will be expected to meet needs on completion of their training, at least for a short period, and have made this an explicit condition of student's accepting the opportunity for tertiary-level training in various significant courses of study.

(4) Losses that result from skilled workers' otherwise uncompensated departure are not adequately compensated for by benefits that result from those who leave.

Legitimacy

States exercise power legitimately when they make good-faith efforts to protect human rights. (That measure will serve as a concise proxy for the relevant issues, though legitimacy also includes making good-faith efforts to provide sufficient public goods, operating an impartial system of justice, collecting and spending public resources judiciously, and so on).

Presence

Being present in the country is important to remedying the deprivations.

Responsibilities

The skilled workers have important responsibilities to assist with need satisfaction. This is the case at least when all of the following considerations apply (in roughly descending order of importance):

(1) Governments have invested scarce resources in creating human capital to provide for the needs of citizens and are entitled to a fair return on their investment.

(2) By leaving without compensating for losses, emigrants thwart governments' attempts to discharge their duties.

(3) Citizens have received important benefits during their residence in the state of origin and failure to reciprocate for those past benefits involves taking advantage of others or free-riding unfairly.

(4) Citizens leaving without compensation creates important disadvantage for others from which they deserve to be protected.

(5) Uncompensated departures that result in governments being unable to discharge their duties undermine citizens' abilities to support their governments. Fair-minded citizens should not undermine fellow citizens' abilities to support legitimate governments that attempt to discharge their duties in good faith. We also have other grounds for helping compatriots to support their institutional schemes such as loyalty and a concern for unintended harmful side effects.

When all of these conditions obtain, citizens have a responsibility to repay accumulated moral debts.

Reasonableness

The compulsory service program does not require unreasonable sacrifices.
The costs of staying are not unreasonable.

TAXATION

A poor, legitimate developing state may defensibly introduce and maintain taxation programs on citizens residing in other countries when certain conditions obtain such as the following.

Legitimacy

States exercise power legitimately when they make good-faith efforts to protect human rights.[1]

Background Conditions

(1) Evidence from the particular country suggests skilled workers can provide important services for which there are severe shortages, and their departures considerably undermine efforts to meet citizens' needs. The ways in which citizens' departures exarcerbate deprivation may be quite

direct (such as failure to provide important services necessary to meeting basic needs) or more indirect (such as when the institutional reforms necessary for development have been hampered by net loss migration of skilled workers). Taxation of skilled citizens would assist in remedying deprivation.

(2) Governments have invested in training of skilled workers to provide for their citizens' needs and to promote beneficial development.

(3) Governments have made all high-skilled citizens (whether prospective migrants or not) aware of the need to tax such citizens to assist with remedying deprivation, and have made taxation expectations an explicit condition of student's accepting the opportunity for tertiary-level training in various significant courses of study.

(4) The losses that result from skilled workers' uncompensated departures are not fully compensated for by benefits that result from citizens who leave.

Responsibilities

The skilled citizens have important responsibilities to assist in remedying deprivation. These obtain when all of the following considerations apply in roughly descending order of importance:

(1) Governments have invested scarce resources in creating human capital to provide for the needs of citizens and are entitled to a fair return on their investment.

(2) By leaving without compensating for losses, emigrants thwart governments' attempts to discharge their duties.

(3) Citizens have received important benefits during their residence in the state of origin and failure to reciprocate for those past benefits involves taking advantage of others or free-riding unfairly.

(4) Citizens leaving without compensation creates important disadvantage for others from which they deserve to be protected.

(5) Uncompensated departures that result in governments being unable to discharge their duties undermine citizens' abilities to support their governments. Fair-minded citizens should not undermine fellow citizens' abilities to support legitimate governments that attempt to discharge their duties in good faith. We also have other grounds for helping compatriots to support their institutional schemes, such as loyalty and a concern for unintended harmful side effects.

When all of these conditions obtain, citizens have a responsibility to repay accumulated moral debts.

Reasonableness

The taxation program does not require unreasonable sacrifices.

NOTE

1. Again, that criterion will serve as a concise proxy for the relevant issues, though legitimacy includes also making good-faith efforts to provide sufficient public goods, operating an impartial system of justice, collecting and spending public resources judiciously, and so on.

PART II

MICHAEL BLAKE

7

The Right to Leave:
Looking Back

IT IS RARELY ENJOYABLE TO argue in favor of the status quo. Philosophers, like other people, like to think they make things better through their professional activities; they believe—or hope—that their arguments will make the world a more just place. It is professionally unsatisfying to argue that the institutions we have—here and now—are more or less the institutions we *ought* to have. We already have them, after all; why waste paper defending them?

I am going to argue, though, that the status quo actually embodies some significant moral wisdom. Not all parts of the status quo, of course; the world as we have built it is radically unjust, and the global economic relationships it contains are in need of substantial revision. On that much, Gillian Brock and I agree. What I want to defend, though, is the idea that all humans have a basic right to leave any country, including their own, and to form new political relationships with consenting other states. This basic proposition makes any attempt by a state to forcibly prevent people from leaving that state—to coercively insist upon allegiance and obligation, against the wishes of the would-be emigrant—fundamentally unjust, and a violation of the most basic norms of human rights. I therefore believe that we are severely limited in how we may legitimately deal with the issues arising under the broad heading of the "brain drain." States are not, most importantly, permitted to use coercive force to insist that their own citizens continue to reside within their borders.[1] They are not allowed to use coercion to prevent the departure of their own citizens; since many of the "compulsory service" proposals Brock defends do just that, they are unavailable for use by a liberal state, however useful it might be for that state to use them.[2] This limitation is a sort of liberal orthodoxy, to use a phrase from Anna Stilz; the Universal Declaration of Human Rights (UDHR) includes this limitation, and modern liberal philosophy tends to accept it as well.[3] "Managed migration," therefore, is as unavailable to liberal societies as "managed apostasy" might be; even if it were useful for us to prevent individuals from abandoning their religious affiliations, we would have no right to coercively seek to limit such abandonment.[4] The rights of persons prevent societies from interfering with the freedom to leave, whether what is left is a religious group or the state's territorial jurisdiction. Neither can liberal states condition the right to exit or impose delays upon those who want to use that right; even a day's delay is an injustice, just as a day's imprisonment is unjustified if used in the absence of a legitimate trial.[5] Those people who want to leave their own societies, for whatever reason, have the right to do so; Gérard Depardieu, who has left France to avoid its high taxes, is perhaps a bad Frenchman, but that is at worst a matter of his being less than fully virtuous— he has not wronged those who remain in France, and they cannot rightly compel him to return.[6] I want to defend these ideas, not because they are self-evident—despite their appeal, they are not—but because there are plausible arguments *against* these ideas, and because getting clearer on why these arguments fail might help us understand why these ideas should be defended.

I should start, though, by setting up the terms of my discussion. I will be discussing, to begin with, both a particular practice and a particular justification. I will focus for this chapter and the next on the use of force by states to prevent people from leaving their jurisdiction, where that force is justified with reference to the interests and rights of the other residents within that jurisdiction. I will therefore be assuming a very great deal that might otherwise be subject to legitimate criticism; I will be assuming that states continue to exist, that they rule over defined territorial spaces, and so on; the question of emigration is only interesting when there are countries from which one might emigrate. I will be assuming, most importantly, that states have a legal right to *exclude* unwanted would-be immigrants, and that this right is not morally indefensible.[7] I will be discussing these questions from within a general picture of liberal democratic rights that assumes that states must justify their actions with reference to individuals understood as equal in moral value. I accept, finally, that the moral equality of persons generally— what Brock calls the moral equality imperative—is a valid, and appropriate, starting point from which state powers might be subjected to ethical criticism. These assumptions, of course, are not immune from challenge—they would have appeared strange indeed to many people throughout history—but I believe them to be defensible, and they are at any rate shared by Brock and myself. So, let us proceed to ask a basic moral question: are we right to think that states should, consistent with the norms and values of liberal democracy, have no right to forcibly prevent their current residents from departing?

Before beginning to answer this question, I would like to briefly examine what I am defending: the right to leave. In my view, the right to leave contains two distinct elements, which ought to be disentangled:

(1) **The right to exit:** Individuals have a moral right to remove themselves from the territorial jurisdiction of any particular state. This right is codified in the UDHR, article 13(2), which states that all individuals have a right to leave any country, including their own.

(2) **The right to renunciation:** Individuals have a moral right to renounce, once outside that jurisdiction, any particularistic claim of justice—a claim, that is, unlike those incumbent upon all of humanity generally—toward the remaining inhabitants of that jurisdiction. This right is codified in the UDHR, article 15(2), which states that no individual shall be arbitrarily deprived of the right to change his or her nationality.[8]

These two rights are worth examining in more detail. The former, I should note, I understand to be a right similar in strength to the right to move about within a particular jurisdiction—and, like that right, it can on occasion be waived. Individuals who sign a contract to remain within a particular place, for example, might justly have to pay restitution when they violate the terms of their contracts. Individuals who commit crimes, moreover, may justly be held to have sacrificed their freedom to move about within physical space. These facts do not indicate that the right to move about has ceased to exist; they do, instead, indicate that this right is not absolute. We do not, however, take away the freedom of movement from individuals in the name of distributive justice; we cannot chain workers to their tools, even if their continued labor might produce a more just distribution for the rest of us. It takes something as morally central as violation of a free and informed contract or of the criminal law for us to take this liberty from a citizen of a liberal state.

The latter right, too, is morally significant in that it insists that the particular duties of citizenship must be synchronous, by which I mean that particular duties to support a particular set of others can only be judged to exist when some particular sorts of political relationships exist. Those of us who reside in the United States, for example, do not have the same duties toward French citizens resident abroad that we have toward our jurisdictional fellows. Specific sorts of shared institutions give rise to specific sorts of duties, and where those institutions are not shared, the duties fail as well. One who gives up being an American— who renounces citizenship and removes his person from the jurisdiction of the United States—is no longer a rightful subject of these particular moral duties, and the United States would wrong him if it treated him as if he were. I want to tread carefully here; I do not want to say that all programs of worldwide taxation of income, such as that created by the United States, are morally impermissible.[9] If American citizens expatriate themselves, but continue to enjoy American citizenship—and the right to return that this citizenship involves—then the government of the United States may legitimately insist upon regarding them as part of the political community of the country and therefore subject to that nation's particular obligations of citizenship. What I want to insist upon, though, is that such a status cannot be imposed unilaterally, against the will of the person who has left. The right to renunciation is an important one, simply because it allows us to make a full and final exit to an unwanted political affiliation; no state has a right to regard an émigré as its own, when that émigré has made it clear that he no longer regards himself as a member and no longer accepts the benefits of membership. The right to return, of course, may be legitimately sacrificed on such occasions; the individual, if he renounces any duties toward these particular others, no longer has a particular claim against them to return to their society. But the right to renounce itself should be regarded as part of the right to leave, and programs that propose to penalize renunciants with reference to their future earnings—such as the United States' HEART Act, which imposes an emigration tax with reference to the earnings they would have made within the jurisdiction of the United States—are unjust.[10]

This is, then, how I will understand the right to leave, and it will be this right that I will defend. Before I proceed to this defense, though, I want to separate out three questions that are sometimes conflated in our discussion of the brain drain:

(1) **Does the brain drain have negative consequences on some metric of expectations we have reason to value?** This is the most central empirical question to be asked, and we must ask it as a precursor to our normative evaluations. We

are asked, here, to evaluate the empirical consequences of various forms of policy proposal and to
use this information—when we are able to obtain
it—to ground our moral evaluation of those
policies.

(2) **If there are such negative consequences, do
we have a collective duty to eliminate those
negative consequences?** There are, of course,
bad things in the world we should not eliminate.
Some of them, as noted below, are not rightly
understood as appropriate goals for state coercion. Others, though, are bad things whose possibility is a necessary analogue of good things
we properly regard as moral necessities. Think,
for example, of the possibility of heartbreak; it
is undoubtedly a bad thing, but it could not even
conceivably be eliminated in a moral universe
containing humans as we know them. (We could,
I imagine, eliminate heartbreak only by ensuring either love's absence or that human beings
never made incompatible romantic choices; that
world might be a fine place for angels, but not
for us.) Heartbreak is a necessary part of a world
in which romantic love exists; we can only effectively prevent heartbreak by effectively annihi-
lating human hearts. These considerations are,
of course, somewhat far afield from discussions
of migration, but the point is the same in both
spheres: there may be bad things in the world that
are necessary parts of things we rightly prize—in
the case of both heartbreak and migration, a particular vision of human freedom.

(3) **If there are such duties, do we have the right to use state coercion to enforce compliance with those duties?** The state is, famously, an odd sort of social institution; it proposes to use physical coercion, in a manner largely prohibited to any other form of social institution, and it proposes to do that in the name of the people so coerced. There are many limitations on what that sort of institution might do, even in the name of moral duties that are properly understood as such. I believe, for example, that we have strong moral duties to treat store employees with respect during our times shopping; we act badly toward those employees when we treat them as mere adjuncts to the machines they wield to check out our purchases. I also believe, though, that these duties are not rightly within the province of the state to enforce. This is true for many reasons, of course. Some of them are homely and obvious: allowing the police to arrest the rude would likely create, through abuse and cost, a worse world than one in which the police lacked that power. Other reasons, though, are more principled. What we owe to one another can include some things that are rightly regarded, even apart from prudential worries, as matters of virtue, not properly brought within the space of reciprocal coercion. Contrary to Brock's suggestion, I am free to leave any university—or orchestra—without being rightly made the subject of coercive force. I might be a bad professor (or violinist), but I cannot be rightly forced to remain with my current job by those my departure would

inconvenience.[11] Again, the example is far afield from immigration but might be brought to bear upon it; we may have a variety of duties to our societies, some of which—like the duty, if there is one, to stay within a particular society—are best understood as duties of virtue rather than enforceable duties of justice.[12]

I believe the above questions are often inadequately distinguished from one another; we sometimes go directly from the fact of something's being a bad thing to the legitimacy of banning that thing. I want to resist this tendency. I will try to keep these questions separate in what follows. I want, further, to be up front with my own answers to these questions, regarding the brain drain as I have described it above. My answers to these questions are, in order, "perhaps," "sometimes," and "almost never." On the first question, I want to note my profound ignorance about the empirical consequences of actual policy interventions; I must necessarily rely on the (competing) ideas of more empirically minded scholars.[13] When I discuss this question, in Chapter 8, I will do so not to settle the issue of what such proposals will actually do; I will, instead, try simply to raise some questions about the causal story offered in support of such proposals. On the second question, I will try to argue that we have reason to think that some of the negative consequences that accompany the brain drain are, in fact, the sort of negative consequences that cannot be eliminated in a world that adequately respects human freedom. We cannot hope to make a world without loss and without pain; the exercise of human freedom—the building of new relationships with consenting others—necessarily has consequences we would not have independently chosen. These consequences, though, cannot be avoided without avoiding freedom itself. On the final question, I will argue that while we may have some duties of virtue to support our nations—and while we certainly have duties of justice to other members of our society *while we are resident within that society*—we cannot be thought to have any obligation of justice *to continue to be a part of that society*. We may be selfish, unvirtuous people when we abandon our national societies for greater advantages, but we are not rightly prevented from this unvirtuous action. What we owe, morally speaking, might be distinct from what we can be morally forced to provide. The result of all this is that the ability of developing societies to keep their own citizens from leaving will be rather small. I do not want to say those societies can *never* coercively prevent their own current members from leaving; as I will discuss in Chapter 9, they *might*— under some truly horrible circumstance—be morally permitted to suspend the moral rights of their inhabitants, just as we might think that some rights are permissibly suspended during an emergency. Catastrophe might conceivably allow us to deviate from moral rights, but only in the name of ultimately returning to a world in which those rights are protected. The right to leave, by this analysis, is much like the right to be free from torture—a right that could only be suspended under truly exceptional circumstances, and even then only with a due sense of the profound moral remainder that such suspension might entail. To say this, though, is not to say that the right ceases to exist, nor is it to say that the state has any standing right to keep their own current residents from leaving—and, as I will specify, the emergency would have to be of sufficient gravity that the kidnapping of outsiders would be similarly permissible. Given the comparative rarity of these circumstances, I will generally speak simply as if there were never any occasions when a state may legitimately prevent its own current residents from leaving.

With all that in mind, I can now proceed to make the case in favor of the right to leave. I will not directly argue in favor of the right in the present chapter; I will, instead, reserve that discussion for Chapter 9. In this chapter and the following, I will offer some criticisms of some plausible arguments against the right to leave. There are, I think, a number of possible arguments that might be offered against that supposed right—and in favor of the moral legitimacy of a state's use of coercion to prevent the exit of its current inhabitants. I believe these arguments can be divided, without too much distortion, into two categories: arguments that look *backward*, toward the nature of the institutions that have given rise to our present worries, and arguments that look *forward*, to the beneficial effects of restrictions on emigration. I should note at the outset that these groupings are not arguments but families of arguments; there are many different forms of argument that exist under each heading, and some arguments that combine aspects of both. Nevertheless, I believe these families represent a good way of differentiating argumentative form. I will therefore examine, in this chapter, arguments that look backward, and reserve discussion of forward-looking arguments for the next chapter.

Backward-looking arguments, then, look toward the historical process by which we arrive at our present circumstances. The emigration of skilled workers is wrong because of the circumstances—whether global or local—under which these workers obtained their skills. I believe there are at least two arguments that might be adduced of this type, which I will term the arguments from *reciprocity* and from *community*. Different authors, naturally, will present different versions of each, but there is enough similarity to discuss them as argumentative types without undue distortion. We can take the following as thumbnail sketches of each argument.

Reciprocity: Economic relationships, both global and local, produce benefits and burdens; for the institutions undergirding these relationship to be justified, the benefits and burdens they produce must be distributed fairly. We can consider this under the heading of reciprocity, since our goal is to find principles of distribution that could be reciprocally justifiable to all those whose interests are affected by the principles of distribution. This analysis, however, applies not only to physical capital but also to what is termed human capital. Justice requires a concern for fairness in the division of the advantages and disadvantages of the creation, use, and allocation of human capital resources. There are two, related, ways we might worry that the current distribution fails these tests of fairness. The distribution might fail at the global level: when high-talent and highly trained individuals depart from developing to more developed societies, their actions represent a net transfer of productive resources from the impoverished to the wealthy.[14] The distribution might also fail for reasons of local fairness: those individuals who sacrificed to help build those talents and skills—including the taxpayers of the low-development societies in which they were educated—have a right to expect a reasonable return on their investment.[15] Distributive justice requires that the benefits of this investment flow to the impoverished societies that made the investment rather than the already wealthy societies to which emigration is sought. Those societies that are poorly developed, then, have the right to maintain the human capital that arises and is developed within their borders. They are therefore permitted to use coercion to prevent high-talent individuals from exercising their purported right to leave.[16]

Community: Individuals do not come into the world as atomic individuals, unencumbered by duties toward particular others; they develop and live within communities and owe loyalty toward those communities. We may disagree about whether the community is best described in terms of identity or in terms of politics; the argument, however, proceeds in a similar manner regardless of our choice. Those individuals who grow within—and whose talents are developed within—a particular community have duties to preserve and promote that particular community. As such, that community is permitted to use coercion to prevent that individual from removing her talents and selling them to the highest bidder abroad.[17]

Either one of these arguments would—if valid—give a liberal state the right to engage in coercive actions against would-be emigrants. As I have said, I do not think these arguments work. They fail, in my view, for one central reason: they do not adequately understand the requirements of human freedom and the fact that productive human capital—however economically valuable it might be and however that capital has been produced—necessarily comes attached to *human beings*, with all the rights that status demands. Humans have a right to be subject to only certain specific forms of coercion, even when other sorts of coercion might effectively make the world a better place. The arguments from reciprocity and community—like the arguments to be considered in the next chapter—neglect this important moral truth.

I THE ARGUMENT FROM RECIPROCITY

We can begin, then, by examining the notion of fairness in the distribution of human capital. The appeal of the argument is obvious; the world right now is an extremely unfair place, on any theory of distributive justice you might choose. It is unfair, to begin with, in simple terms of economics. The wealthiest societies in the world, with around 16 percent of the global population, control more than four-fifths of its wealth.[18] The remaining 84 percent of the world's inhabitants control the remaining 20 percent of its wealth. This difference in economics is, of course, productive of an enormous difference in the forms of life one might expect to lead. The burdens of disease are radically distinct in developed and in developing societies. The average inhabitant of Japan (per-capita GDP: $36,000) can expect to live until eighty-four years of age; the average inhabitant of Malawi (per-capita GDP: $900) can expect only fifty two years of life.[19] The injustice of finances, here, is partly responsible for an injustice in longevity, and an injustice in the shape of the lives lived prior to death.

How to fix these problems is, of course, a matter of some controversy. The field of development economics exists precisely because these problems have no simple or obvious fixes. It is clear, though, that there is a relationship between these inequalities and the global distribution of human capital. Take the most frequently discussed example, that of medical and nursing practice; we might note that the transfer of highly trained nurses from developing to developed societies—as in the transfer of nurses from Ghana to the United States—represents a net transfer from the impoverished to the already wealthy. That human capital—the medical knowledge and skill—could be used to make truly blighted lives less blighted; it is, instead, being used to provide secondary and optional medical treatment to those already well blessed with medical infrastructure. As such, the transfer of medical personnel from the developing to the developed world is a net move away from whatever a just distribution would look like.[20] We could condemn this simply with reference to the global economic relationships involved, but those who deploy this argument generally also make reference to the legitimate expectations of the global poor who invested in the education giving rise to the human capital of the skilled worker who is seeking to emigrate. The global poor invest what money they have in the training of medical staff—only to see the newly trained depart, leaving behind them only depleted national accounts. Surely those left behind can regard this pattern of behavior as unjust, and rightly act against it! Kieran Oberman, for example, insists that the educated worker has an obligation of repayment: where a worker receives expensive training from an impoverished society and knows that there is an expectation he will use that training for his fellow workers, he is legitimately coerced into meeting those expectations.[21] We may not know how to make the world perfectly just, but we do know, according to this argument, how to stop something that is making it less just: prevent the migration of medical personnel from the developing world. This analysis permits, in the name of liberalism, developing states to prevent emigration of their highly talented and highly trained residents; distributive justice itself tells against the legitimacy of the purported right to leave.

This is a powerful argument. I do not think it is a correct one. I will begin the analysis with a simple theoretical note: inequalities are not always matters of injustice. A given inequality must be shown to be a matter of injustice; it cannot be simply assumed that what is unequal is unjust. To take a simple example: most of us believe that there is nothing unjust in the unequal nature of talents, or of sexual attractiveness.[22] Some people are born with lucky faces, and some are not. Justice may constrain what can be the result of these inequalities—we may want to constrain the effects of beauty on employment, for example—but we are not required to constrain the inequalities themselves.[23] Something similar may also be true about the spatial distribution of talents and human capital. Imagine a United States that is as just as you could possibly want; whatever theory of distributive fairness you like is now put into place. Would the distribution of human capital now be equal across the various states of the Union? I do not think that would be likely; I believe that Kansas would—even in a just world—likely have a less flourishing art scene than, for example, New York City. People go to different places for different reasons, not all of which are morally problematic. Sometimes people choose locations because of natural factors; it is easier to be a surfer in San Diego than in Chicago. More often, they choose locations because of who has already chosen that location; it is easier to be a visual artist in Brooklyn than in Topeka, if only because so many other artists have already settled in Brooklyn.[24] These inequalities in the distribution of talents, though, hardly seem to be the right sort of inequalities to count as unjust. They are, instead, the result of the exercise of human freedom, as people use that freedom to build lives for themselves with like-minded others. If Kansas were to ask for transfer payments from New York City for departing visual artists—or if Kansas were to propose the forcible transfer of artists from New York to Topeka—we would have to assume that Kansas had failed to understand the basics of liberal justice.[25]

I discuss this example only to show that we must argue in favor of the injustice of a given inequality; we cannot simply assume it. Malawi and Japan, of course, are not the same as Kansas and New York. Malawi's poverty is, to begin with, well outside whatever realm of distributive inequality a plausible theory of justice could permit. Malawi's poverty, moreover, is hardly a natural fact in the world, resulting from some especially unlucky endowment of natural resources or geography. Malawi is, instead, an impoverished African nation surrounded by other impoverished African nations, all of whom experienced a century or more of violent colonial exploitation and degradation.[26] Phillip Cole emphasizes, quite rightly, that we should avoid thinking of immigration without having this history of violent colonialism clearly in our mind.[27] We are, here, facing an inequality in human capital that emerges from a history of injustice and radical evil. This inequality in human capital, moreover, perpetuates and exacerbates the inequality in life chances that we currently see. Can we not take these facts as sufficient reason to think that we should work against the inequality of human capital? Can we not take economic justice as a sufficient reason to think that we should directly prevent emigration from those countries already suffering from the legacy of colonialism?

I do not believe we can. I do not, to begin with, think that the program of prevention of exit is necessarily likely to actually lead to better lives for the world's poor; because of the effects of remittances, cyclical migration, and prospective emigration, it is entirely possible that a world without exit restrictions is a better one for the world's poor than a world with such restrictions. I will discuss this, however, in the next chapter. I want now to focus only on the morality of working against injustice. We have, of course, a collective duty—all of us, especially those of us in wealthy Western societies—to create a new world in which these economic injustices no longer exist. The question we have to ask, though, is whether or not we are permitted to use *this* particular means to work toward *this* particular end. From the fact that a goal is required of us by justice, after all, does not mean that any and all moves toward that goal are morally praiseworthy; I cannot, for example, start assassinating the wealthy and uncharitable, even if my doing so would result in a more just distribution of resources. People have rights, even under unjust circumstances, to use their resources, their persons, and their talents to develop a life for themselves, and they are permitted in justice to develop lives other than those that are maximally helpful for others. We give to ourselves, quite rightly, the freedom to build lives that are chosen from the inside; we owe one another a social world that is minimally just, but we do not therefore think we have an enforceable obligation to sacrifice all we care about in the name of that goal. We give ourselves this freedom; we should hesitate before taking it from individuals born abroad, under terrible social and political circumstances, who seek the same for themselves. My general contention is that while we do have a strong duty to build and sustain just institutions, this duty should be regarded as distributed equally across the world's population; no individual should be made to bear a disproportionate share of that duty's burden. The duty should be so distributed, I believe, because its demands must be made compatible with the fundamental interest we have in developing a plan of life for ourselves, in conjunction with others who consent to build a life with us. The program of refusing exit, however, runs afoul of this requirement by forcing a duty onto the would-be emigrant that outsiders are not asked to pay. If we were to do this to any other population—or if we were able to make explicit the true burden that emigrant is being told to bear—we would be more clear about the moral impermissibility of what that emigrant is being asked to do.

I want to therefore discuss, in this context, the idea of fairness in the distribution of the burdens of compliance with global justice. I will argue here that the idea of fairness precludes asking individuals to bear a disproportionate share of these burdens. I will consider, in Chapter 9, the related thought that there are sometimes burdens we cannot impose on *anyone*, regardless of how others are treated. For the moment, I want to establish only that the burdens we share to make the world a more just place are themselves subject to the demands of justice. To see this, take four cases in which an individual is being asked to bear a disproportionate share of the burden of building a more just world.

Kidnapped foreigner: Malawi takes hold of an individual Japanese doctor and forcibly transports him for a year to Malawi. The doctor is talented and well trained, and will preserve the lives of untold numbers of Malawian citizens. These Malawian citizens have the right to medical care, and the doctor will help protect that right.

Prevented foreigner: Malawi refuses to allow the exit of a visiting Japanese tourist, until she has spent a year working for the health of Malawian citizens. The tourist is a physician, and her talents and training will allow her to preserve the lives of untold numbers of Malawian citizens. These Malawian citizens have the right to medical care, and the doctor will help protect that right.

Kidnapped local: Malawi forces one of its citizens, who has scarce medical training, to spend a year working for the health of Malawian citizens. The individual was trained in a publically funded university but has signed no contract accepting the duty to use her training. She has discovered she dislikes medicine and wants to spend her time working in her father's restaurant. The doctor is talented and well trained, and will preserve the lives of untold numbers of Malawian citizens. These Malawian citizens have the right to medical care, and the doctor will help protect that right.

Prevented local: Malawi refuses to allow the exit of a Malawian citizen, who has scarce medical training, until she first spends a year working for the health of Malawian citizens. The individual was trained in a publically funded university, but has signed no contract accepting the duty to use her training. The doctor is not interested in spending more time than she already has within Malawi; she is interested in the comparative freedom and professional opportunities offered elsewhere.[28] The doctor is talented and well trained, and will preserve the lives of untold numbers of Malawian citizens. These Malawian citizens have the right to medical care, and the doctor will help protect that right.

I take it for granted that we are unlikely to think any of the first three cases are morally permissible. The first two cases seem obviously and immediately wrong; even if we bracket the prudential worries involved in cross-border kidnapping, there is no moral right to use the persons of others in this way, even if we could thereby preserve some important moral good. The third case seems similarly problematic, if less obviously so. The doctor has been trained by her society, but having been so trained, she is rightly understood as a full person, who is entitled to the same range of freedoms as anyone else—including the freedom to choose a job other than the single most beneficial one for her fellows. These cases clearly impose an undue burden on an individual person to bear the costs of compliance with a duty of justice.[29] The individual Japanese citizen in "kidnapped foreigner" is simply asked to do too much in the name of justice; she has the same burdens as others to help make the world a just place, but she also has a significant interest in the development of her own life, and she is asked to sacrifice that when others are not.[30] Perhaps she is more talented than others; that fact, though, seems morally irrelevant in the justification of forced exile. She has a right, like others, to bear only a proportionate share of the costs of making the world just, but here she is being treated unequally, so much so that she is being made to give up a central interest in her own life, when others are not being asked to do anything like the same. Similar things can be said of the "prevented foreigner"; that individual is being asked, simply because she happens to have the right attributes—geographic and personal—to sacrifice herself for the rights of others. She would be, I think, a deeply admirable person—indeed, a moral saint—if she were to volunteer for this sacrifice; a just state, though, does not force that sacrifice upon the unwilling.

The fact that the doctor in "kidnapped local" has accepted benefits—and has done so with the knowledge that there is an expectation of future performance as a doctor—might be thought to make a moral difference. I do not think, though, that it does. Consider, in this context, John Williams's novel *Stoner*.[31] The eponymous character is sent by his impoverished parents, who can ill afford the tuition, to the University of Missouri, where he is expected to learn agriculture so as to help the family farm. He eventually falls in love with literature and instead chooses (after some time spent learning agriculture) to become a professor of English. We can disagree about the morality of Stoner's choice, of course, but it is worth noting that even though he meets Oberman's tests for legitimate coercion—his impoverished parents can ill afford the tuition, and clearly expect him to return to the farm—very few of us think his parents would even in principle be right in forcing him to act as a farmer.[32] Stoner is an adult and entitled to build a life for himself with consenting others; even though he has been trained in the ways of farming, that knowledge is *his*, and he cannot be forced to use it in the way others demand. If he had signed a contract with his parents, of course, things might be different; Stoner can, if the bargain is a fair and free one, sign away his future. He cannot be thought to have done so simply because others would find that supposition *useful*.

Oberman considers, and rejects, the idea that it is unfair for us to impose particularly demanding duties upon the talented and well trained. It is not wrong, in particular, for us to sometimes ask the skilled resident of a developing country to work for the benefit of that country.[33] He offers two reasons for this that I want to consider here: first, it is less costly for her to stay than for an outsider to come in, given her greater familiarity with the local context, and second, it is sometimes fair for those who have greater skills to be asked to do more.[34] The former seems problematic for empirical reasons; the latter, for reasons of liberal justice. It is not, I think, necessarily more costly to an individual to be made to stay where she is, when that place is one she is willing and otherwise able to leave; outsiders, moreover, may have resources that might enable them to avoid some of the problems that are part of the reason so many people want to leave. (Wealthy Westerners, for example, could purchase security services more easily than impoverished but skilled locals.) At a more fundamental level, though, why should we think that the obligation to perform a particular sort of action varies based upon skill? Individuals may be obligated to pay more in taxes when they make more money, of course; they are choosing to use their talents in a market setting and must pay a fair share for these talents.

Nothing in this, though, says that we are able to issue differential demands upon the talented and the untalented. When John Rawls spoke of the collective ownership of natural abilities, he meant only to invoke the idea that all those in society can expect to obtain a justifiable portion of what those talents produce within the basic structure.[35] He never meant that we would subject those talents themselves to collective decision-making; indeed, Rawls argued precisely that we cannot directly assign jobs to persons, since liberalism's basic commitments include the free choice of occupation.[36] To say that the talented owe a different *sort* of obligation comes terribly close to simply saying that the talented are *themselves* a resource subject to collective ownership.

This explains our disinclination to allow the sorts of coercion considered above. "Kidnapped local" involves a citizen being made, as a result of her talents and training, to bear a disproportionate share of the costs of compliance. We see this as especially damaging, I think, because we feel that the right to free choice of occupation is a central liberal right. The reluctant doctor has made the choice to build a life for herself, with her family, that does not involve medicine. To force her to labor specifically as a doctor is to make her develop a plan of life for herself fundamentally at odds with her own desires. None of us, of course, lives a life we regard as perfect—I am not currently playing shortstop for the Red Sox—but it is one thing for that life to be unavailable to me because of natural talents and training and quite another for it to be taken away from me by the state. This latter is a significant cost, and we should refuse to make an individual bear it when others do not have to bear anything like so much.

We might try to save the story of fairness, of course, by insisting that perhaps liberals should not be so quick to condemn forced labor. Lucas Stanczyk has recently argued as much.[37] I will discuss this view in the following chapter. For the moment, though, I would note simply this much: even if it is true that we might sometimes be obligated to sacrifice our freedom in the name of the common good, we cannot be told to do so when others are not being asked to do the same. Fairness demands no less. In the cases discussed above, fairness would seem to be utterly absent. We have an obligation to work for a new, more just global order. We do not have the right to sacrifice individual people in the name of this obligation, simply because they happen to be convenient means by which we might get closer to justice.

II THE ARGUMENT FROM GRATITUDE

We are, then, unlikely to find a justification for abandoning the right to leave in the idea of distributive fairness. Fairness affects both what the global economic system ought to look like, and how we ought to get closer to that system; we cannot abandon fairness to individual moral agents in our search for a globally fair system. Fairness also affects the rightful distribution of benefits and burdens within the society, but there are limits on what we can ask individuals to do for their societies. Fairness precludes forcing particular forms of life upon individual persons, even when that form of life would be effective at the preservation of important goods. But perhaps we have ignored something relevant in our discussions. After all, the key difference between the kidnapped foreigner and the kidnapped local was that the former—but not the latter—involved a Malawian person, someone who, presumably, was born and raised in Malawi and whose development as agent (and as a professional) was undertaken in conjunction with significant others who were themselves Malawian. Could we not build the right to prevent emigration from materials such as these? This would extend the considerations of national fairness away from a notion of reciprocity to something less individualistic; the nation, like the family, is a place within which people become who they are, and perhaps like the family it is a site of important obligations. The Malawian emigrant might seem, on this account, churlish at best, in that she abandons her fellows in the name of an individual goal of self-development; can we not prevent her plans, when she owes so very much to those she proposes to leave behind?

I should be clear, at this point, that I am not discussing the idea that a state might contract with an individual person to provide education in exchange for guaranteed residency and service; that is a separate idea and—to my thinking, as I will discuss in Chapter 9—sometimes, if rarely, permissible. On this, Brock and I are in agreement. What I want to discuss here is a distinct argument, one that proceeds simply from the fact that the individual has spent some significant time within a society and has developed her plan of life within the social world provided by that society. We might, from these materials, develop an argument that the individual in question owes a debt to that society—one that is of sufficient gravity that the society is permitted to prevent that individual's exit. There

are, moreover, at least two different versions of this argument, depending upon which particular vision of society
one finds most morally significant. The former begins with
the cultural nation and argues that the individual in question has an obligation to her fellow national members that
precludes her rightful exit, or at least her exit prior to some
notion of repayment of debt. The latter begins with the
political society and argues that membership within that
society is of sufficient moral gravity that the liberal state
may justly prevent individuals from exiting that society.
I will deal with these arguments in turn.

i National Identity

There is a long tradition, within political philosophy, of
emphasizing the importance of the local community for
moral self-development. (This tradition, of course, generally begins by condemning the other long tradition within
political philosophy, that of ignoring the importance of the
local tradition entirely.[38]) The tradition is generally called
communitarian, although that label obscures as much as
it reveals; different communitarians have different perspectives on what precisely it is about liberal equality, and
different communitarians differ about what ought to be
brought in to augment or replace liberal thought. For our
purposes, what these theorists share is a commitment to
the idea that the local community—whether understood
in linguistic, cultural, or ethnic terms—is morally central,
so much so that liberalism should be abandoned if it cannot offer some place for the demands of that community.
In particular, we ought to focus on the idea that the community here produces duties, rather than simply rights.

Charles Taylor, for example, argues strongly that being a member of Québécois culture produces an obligation to work for the preservation of Québécois identity and the French language in North America; we are not neutral, he says—speaking for the Québécois—between those who want to stay "true to the culture of our ancestors, and those who want to cut loose in the name of self-development."[39] Alasdair MacIntyre is equally adamant that the demands of national membership produce duties that are sufficient to trump the abstract demands of liberalism; his example is Adam von Trott, who contemplated the question of killing Adolf Hitler with reference to his own particular identity as a German, rather than the universal demands of liberal morality. MacIntyre argues that von Trott is a comprehensible, even admirable, thinker. We owe, by MacIntyre's account, a duty of support and preservation to the national community that produced us, and so ought to act in favor of that society—not in favor of abstract morality or our own desires.[40]

Neither of these thinkers discussed the morality of the brain drain. Versions of their ideas, though, are frequently seen in popular writings on the brain drain, particularly by political agents who are members of national communities facing emigration. African political leaders who condemn the effects of the brain drain do so with a simple refrain: we want *our own* to return to us.[41] The notion of *our own* is hard to cash out in other than communitarian terms; the people who have left, on this analysis, are people whose identities, skills, and talents were developed and nurtured by the communities they have now abandoned. Those emigrants, then, are violating a duty they had toward the national community; that community, in turn, would have had some right to prevent their leaving in the first place. Similar ideas are expressed by Sigfredo Barros, a Cuban journalist, discussing the immorality of those Cuban baseball players who have defected to the United States:

> But I think they have stolen our baseball players. Because what is important to say is that Orlando, Ordonez, Livan, Arrojo, all of them were trained here in Cuba, their coaches were Cuban, and their successes are in part the successes of Cuban baseball and Cuban trainers. No one in the United States taught Arrojo to throw a sinker; he was taught that here in Cuba. Or the slider to Orlando, or Livan's 93-mph fastball, or to field balls like Ordonez does. We taught them those things here. That they went there looking for money, well, what can we do to them. But it is the Cuban school of baseball that taught them.[42]

There are several ideas here worth considering. Barros's arguments cite something very much like reciprocity; the ability to throw a sinker is, after all, a learned skill, and it is taught by persons. The more central idea, though, is something rather simpler: it is the idea that these baseball players are Cuban, part of the Cuban tradition and Cuban nation, and by leaving betray a national ideal that is worth defending. They owe it to the Cuban nation to show their talents off to Cubans, and not to the highest bidder. This idea rests on a notion of identity—of being Cuban, or Ghanaian—and on the claim that that identity is the source of valid moral duties. The communitarian vision can thus provide foundation for the common thread that runs through much of the discussion of the brain drain: they— the outsiders—are taking what is ours, what we have developed.

This vision has a long history, in both philosophy and in practice. Socrates's invocation of the laws as something very much like parents was a central part of his argument in the *Crito*. This idea was developed in the *Laws* into an argument that the good subject could never rightly shrug off her duties to remain a subject. What right to travel there was existed only at the pleasure of the sovereign, who would not grant this right to anyone not already proven to be a virtuous and loyal citizen—and, emphatically, not to anyone under the age of forty.[43] Throughout most of history, moreover, the subject could expect the sovereign to insist upon an immutable and eternal claim over her body and her property; the subject was, in Blackstone's phrase, liable for "perpetual allegiance."[44] The source of these strong duties was in the organic union between the nation and the subject; the former gave rise to the latter, and grounded the latter's unshakable obligation. The difficulty, of course, is that this vision is difficult to regard as ethically defensible. Fully critiquing the nationalist vision is outside the scope of this chapter. I think we might, though, offer something like a demurrer: even if it is true—even if the nation is causally responsible for the existence of the person, her development, and her acquisition of skills—it is not true that the moral conclusions defended necessarily follow. The reason for this, I think, is that—for those of us who defend the liberal vision of equality—politically enforceable duties must be defended with reference to *politics* rather than simply with reference to the culture or the nation.[45] People, for liberal egalitarians, are conceived of as free and equal, entitled to develop lives for themselves, subject only to the demand that other persons are entitled to do exactly the same. As such, it is hard to know what to make of the demand that we be made—through the coercive structure of the political community—to live up to a supposed duty to our linguistic, ethnic, or cultural fellows. If we were to accept a duty that emerged from that community—and I will, here, be neutral about that possibility—I believe it is best understood as a duty of virtue rather than as an enforceable duty of politics. Think, in connection with this, about one's duties to one's family or to one's neighborhood. Both can make a case that they have played a role in one's development. If one is successful in developing a set of skills that proves to be marketable, it is not obviously implausible that one might have a duty to "give back"—to provide special consideration in providing goods that will aid one's family or one's neighborhood. (I am, of course, discussing only goods that go beyond those that ought to be provided by a just liberal regime; the duty to create a just society, after all, would fall on all of us, no matter what family or neighborhood has helped create us.) Our reaction to those who fail to do this, though, is instructive; we do not generally think ourselves entitled to regard such people as having violated the *rights* of that family, or that neighborhood. These people are, at worst, *unvirtuous* rather than unjust. The newly rich member of an impoverished community who chooses to avoid his old neighborhood is perhaps lacking in virtue—he is less praiseworthy than he might be—but few of us would regard him as *wronging* the members of that community, and fewer of us would think that we should bring the force of law to bear upon him for his choices.

To say the opposite, I think, is to run the risk of treating people as something entirely too much like property. They do, after all, share something with property: both people and things can be shaped by our creative efforts. We can work together to build people; educators and parents spend much of their time doing just that. The insight of John Locke, though—that people have a special moral relationship to what their own labor has created—may fail when what is made is a *person*. Even if I have built my daughter, what I have built is entitled to a vision of her own life that may be utterly distinct from what I would have it be. That is painful, but the alternative world would be vastly more painful. Laboring to build a person, then, creates something that is entitled to what mere property cannot have: rights against its creators. Children have duties of gratitude to (competent and decent) parents, and students have duties of gratitude to (competent and decent) teachers. In neither case, though, do those who create have rights to *own* what is created. Human capital comes necessarily attached to persons; those persons have the right to do what those creators may despise.[46]

To return to the case of the brain drain: those who have given rise to persons—those who have worked to bring about individual persons, and who have shaped them into the people they are—may legitimately expect certain things from those they have helped create. They may expect, most importantly, that those created are grateful for those that worked to create them. They may not expect obedience, however; they are not owners of property, since what has been created here is a person, who cannot justly be owned by anyone other than herself. They cannot, then, justify coercively preventing that person's exit with reference to these ideas of loyalty; loyalty may be a virtue, but it is not a sufficient justification for the use of political coercion.

ii Political Loyalty

The notion of loyalty, of course, is more capacious than the preceding use of it. The notion of loyalty might be used even by liberals, whose use of it would make reference to the demands and interests of liberal politics. Anna Stilz, most centrally, has developed this concept with reference to the demands of the liberal state. Stilz's vision is that the abstract demands of liberal morality—notably those given by a Kantian picture of morality—must be rendered specific and defended by a particular legal and political code, administered by a particular legal and political society. That particular society, then, is entitled to support from particular persons—namely, those whose rights it defends and whose entitlements it specifies with reference to its legal institutions.[47] These ideas, though, can be brought to bear upon the right to exit, and Stilz defends the idea that this right could be *qualified*—so that, for instance, the individual who proposed to exit could not rid herself of her duties to her fellow citizens simply be exiting. The reason for this, on Stilz's view, is that the individual who is seeking to leave has the obligation to support and defend just institutions, and that this obligation entails that he not treat the current members of that society unjustly through his exit. The other members of one's society, on this view, are entitled to a political society that treats them justly, and if they are materially disadvantaged by someone else's departure—as they will be, in many cases of high-talent emigration—they have a right to insist that the individual in question compensate them for the proposed exit. Individuals must, in other words, support just institutions, and they cannot escape these obligations through departure.

The right to exit, on this account, may be qualified, in that we might rightly insist upon some scheme
to ensure that the liberal rights of those left behind are
well-protected against the actions of the one departing.
Stilz acknowledges that freedom places a constraint on
what can be done in the name of justice; we cannot insist
on perpetual allegiance, for example, and must respect the
desire to depart. But we can, in Stilz's view, make departure
more costly. We can, for instance, insist upon the taxation
of worldwide income, as the United States and Eritrea both
do. We can tax exit itself. We can do all of this, in the end,
because exiting is just one more action taken within the
context of a domestic political society, and it is up to that
society to determine how this action should be regulated.[48]

This argument has many similarities to Brock's own
argument, as we shall see; it shares a concern that individuals who emigrate may be undermining the justice of
the societies from which they depart. Where they differ,
I think, is in how they understand the demands of justice.
Stilz begins with the idea that the duty to stay is a duty
that emerges from the duty to support just institutions,
while Brock begins with a duty to help *create* such institutions where they do not already exist. Stilz is thus limited
in what she can say about the rights of many states from
which the brain drain occurs today, few of which are best
described as democratically legitimate; this is, of course,
something Stilz accepts. Stilz is, moreover, not committed
to the idea that the border itself ought to be closed by force;
her central idea is that the obligations we have as citizens
ought to exist even after exit from the territorial jurisdiction of a just regime, given the interests and needs of the
other residents of that society.

It is with this fact, though, that I want to begin my analysis. Imagine that the society in which I live—which is a tolerably just society, we may imagine, although not especially equal in its distribution—would be rendered slightly less just because of my withdrawal from it. In Stilz's view, I am obligated to continue my association with that society, in that I am obligated to continue acting as if I were a part of it, paying my taxes and so on, even after I am outside of that society. The question, though, is why. I have physically removed myself from that society's jurisdiction and now form part of the mass of humanity outside that jurisdiction that has a collective duty to assist that society in becoming more just. Why should I have any greater duty toward that society than someone born and resident abroad? I am not obligated, after all, to support those institutions that would be most benefited by my support. Even if my tax payments would make a greater difference for Ghana than for the United States, I am not under a moral obligation (or permission) to pay Ghanaian taxes instead of American ones. Why, then, should the one who is outside the territorial jurisdiction in which she was educated, and who now seeks to renounce her citizenship in that jurisdiction, have any particular duty to support the institutions of that jurisdiction?

Stilz's answer is that we have a natural duty to support just institutions, and that this duty entails a particular duty to support our *own* society's institutions. That much, I accept. Imagine, though, that I were to say: I have done that, simply in virtue of obeying the law during my residency in that society. I paid my taxes faithfully, upheld the law, and did every other thing demanded of me. Now, though, I have *exited the society*; I have, we might imagine,

acquired some new society, within which I now live. It is
that society, not the first one, which will defend my rights;
that society, not the first one, which will give me a voice for
purposes of politics. What rationale can be offered for the
proposition that the first society is entitled to any particular form of loyalty from me now?

The problem, then, is that the natural duty to support
just institutions does not in itself tell us anything about
which institutions we are obligated to support. We can
imagine, I think, at least two different interpretations of
the duty: one of which looks at a person as a present agent
and one of which looks at her as temporally extended.

Synchronic: The natural duty to support just institutions is a duty to support those institutions which are *now*
engaged in the project of protecting our rights. The duty is
paid for in the currency of respect for law: the duty consists
in such common moral obligations as the prompt payment
of taxes, obedience to legal commands, and so forth.

Diachronic: The natural duty to support just institutions is a duty to support those institutions which have *in
the past* engaged in the project of protecting our rights. The
duty is paid for in a wider range of duties, including most
prominently distributive obligations toward those we have
left behind.

I want to emphasize that neither of these visions is
obviously implausible as an interpretation of the duty to
support just institutions. The latter version, though, has
some costs. Most importantly, it insists that the agent has
duties to some people in virtue of their history together,
and that the duty to support just institutions is a historic
duty. This seems, to me, deeply problematic. It seems as
if the source of our obligations is now not the familiar

territory of political justice but something more temporally extended and complex. Indeed, it seems now as if we are rightly held to have specific obligations *of justice* to a population with whom we are no longer in political association. (I am assuming, of course, that the individual in question has renounced his claim upon citizenship in her country of origin; if the individual retains citizenship and the right to return, then the argument I make here does not apply.) This seems morally problematic for a liberal. The liberal vision, I will argue in Chapter 9, proceeds from the idea that the authority of the state must involve justification to people considered as free and equal in the present; the liberal principle of legitimacy is one that tries to make the political project as near to a voluntary project as it can be.[49] The diachronic account, though, makes us liable for the support of institutions despite our own stated (and acted-upon) unwillingness to be supported by them. The diachronic account thus depends upon some moral relevance to history rather than to current political relationships. If the preceding section has established anything, it is that appeals to history of this sort are often better avoided.

We are, then, perhaps subject to duties of virtue to remain in particular places; I do not believe we are subject to duties of justice. Stilz argues that it is unjust for the wealthy elite of a society to exile themselves, thereby escaping their legitimate bill for the upkeep of their society's institutions. I do not think this is right; if Gérard Depardieu emigrates to Russia, he is a bad Frenchman, perhaps, but he cannot be thought to owe France particular duties once he is outside France and has abandoned his French citizenship. Imagine, after all, that an impoverished country tried—in a variant of tourist inclusion—to kidnap high-talent outsiders, citing its own principles of distributive justice as justification. (Perhaps French commandos simply force Depardieu to return to Paris from Moscow.) Those kidnapped would have any number of good replies, but one of them would surely be: "We were *outside* the scope of your laws, and so those principles did not apply to us. We were fully supporting the just institutions where we were living." Why can the one who has successfully exited not say the same thing?

Stilz would not, of course, endorse the commando raid, nor would she force Depardieu to remain within France's borders. She would, however, endorse a proposal that insisted upon a portion of Depardieu's earnings abroad, in the name of distributive justice. As is now clear, I do not think there is any basis for this proposal. Depardieu, if he is no longer protected by French institutions, is no longer subject to any particular obligation of justice to those institutions. I want to note, however, that what Stilz says here is powerful, both in its own right and because it raises the issue that institutions are relevant from the standpoint of justice; liberals therefore have good reason to examine carefully what institutions are required by justice, and to work to create them. Since this is the contention with which Brock is most concerned, I will therefore close this chapter, and proceed to analyze Brock's own account in the next.

NOTES

1. I understand a coercive act as one which serves to remove otherwise available options; it is a threat, rather than an offer. The gunman who forces me to choose between my

money and my life removes the otherwise available option in which I keep *both* my money *and* my life. I do not think that coercion is always morally wrong—modern states are thoroughly coercive institutions—but it always stands in need of justification. I discuss these matters more in Michael Blake, *Justice and Foreign Policy* (Oxford: Oxford University Press, 2013).

2. I would, therefore, argue that "compulsory service" types (1) through (3), as discussed by Brock, are morally prohibited. Types (4) through (7) seem much more like the sorts of regulation of an activity within a particular jurisdiction that do not involve restricting the right to exit; I do not believe that what I say here therefore condemns these patterns of state action.

3. Anna Stilz, "Is There an Unqualified Right to Leave?," in Sarah Fine and Lea Ypi (eds.), *Migration and Morality: The Ethics of Membership and Movement* (Oxford: Oxford University Press, forthcoming). See also John Rawls, *The Law of Peoples* (Cambridge, MA: Harvard University Press, 1999), 74. Even those generally in favor of revision of border controls tend to oppose exit controls. See, for instance, Joseph Carens, "Aliens and Citizens: The Right to Open Borders," *Review of Politics* 49 (1987): 258–259; Phillip Cole, *Philosophies of Exclusion* (Edinburgh: Edinburgh University Press, 2000). Cole is more open to the possibility of coercive inclusion in "The Right to Leave versus a Duty to Remain: Health-Care Workers and the 'Brain Drain,'" in Rebecca S. Shah (ed.), *The International Migration Of Health Workers: Ethics, Rights, and Justice* (New York: Palgrave, 2010), 118–129.

4. I will focus on the direct coercive prevention of exit in this book, but I think the arguments in favor of the right to leave might imply something stronger—that the state cannot rightly work to make the exercise of the right more costly. The prohibition on "substantially burdening" the exercise of rights might apply to the right to exit as much as it does to the rights of freedom of religion. On the idea of substantial burden, see, most centrally, Sherbert *v.* Verner, 274 US 398

(1963), and the Religious Freedom Restoration Act of 1993, Pub. L. 103–141.

5. See Robinson *v.* California, 370 US 660 (1962) at 667: "Even one day in prison would be a cruel and unusual punishment for the 'crime' of having a common cold."

6. Depardieu has set up residence in Russia to avoid France's new 75-percent "supertax" on the extremely wealthy. David M. Herszenhorn, "That Russian Movie Star, Gérard Depardieu," *The New York Times*, January 3, 2013.

7. I will not defend it here; see my "Immigration, Jurisdiction, and Exclusion," *Philosophy and Public Affairs* 41 (2013): 103–130.

8. The right, as stated, allows for some interpretive space, in that a non-arbitrary deprivation of the right might pass legal muster. I will ignore this legal complexity and argue for a right on which the only deprivation of the right that is morally defensible is one that could justify the deprivation of a basic liberty; conviction of a criminal act, as discussed above, might justify both imprisonment and a suspension of the right to leave.

9. The United States and Eritrea both impose tax on worldwide income; other countries tax only on territorial earnings. The Eritrean taxation scheme was condemned by the United Nations Security Council, in UNSCR 2023 (2011).

10. The Heroes Earning Assistance and Relief Tax Act of 2008 provides for exit taxation for citizens and long-term permanent residents upon expatriation from the United States. See Pub. L. No. 110-245, 122 Stat. 1624 (West 2008).

11. Specific performance of personal labor contracts is generally not an available remedy at law; we cannot, in short, be forced to do a particular job, although we might be subject to specific damages for contractual breach. See Restatement (Second) of Contracts §367(1): "[a] promise to render personal service will not be specifically enforced."

12. I understand duties of virtue, with Immanuel Kant, as a category of obligation that is not rightly made subject to coercive enforcement by the state. Kant includes such obligations as the duty of respect, by which we are obliged to

refrain from gratuitous insult and personal affront, and the duty of sympathy, by which we are obliged to work for the preservation of the agency of other persons. Neither of these duties are rightly made the subject of government enforcement. I am, of course, ignoring a very great deal of Kantian moral philosophy here; my own use of the concept of duties of virtue means only to invoke the idea that the duty is not rightly the subject of political coercion, rather than the wider framework of Kantian thought. For a discussion of this, see Arthur Ripstein, *Force and Freedom: Kant's Legal and Political Philosophy* (Cambridge, MA: Harvard University Press, 2009).

13. For a good discussion of this, see generally Devesh Kapur and John McHale, *Give Us Your Best and Brightest* (Washington, DC: Center for Global Development, 2005).

14. Kapur and McHale note that the departure of the highly educated from developing countries amounts to "the poor subsidizing the rich." Kapur and McHale, *Give Us Your Best and Brightest*, 29.

15. "If one consumes the resources of the poor in the knowledge that they expect reciprocation, one has a duty to reciprocate in the manner they desire or at least repay them the costs of the resources consumed." Kieran Oberman, "Can Brain Drain Justify Immigration Restrictions?," *Ethics* 123 (2013): 427–255, at 435.

16. Versions of this argument can be found in Kieran Oberman and in Anna Stilz. Stilz does not make it the foundation of her argument; she rests more weight on the duty to support just institutions.

17. This is, historically speaking, a popular argument, and political institutions in the early modern period tended to assume that the right to exit was conditioned upon the will of the sovereign—a view reiterated by the modern Soviet Union in response to the 1948 UDHR. See Frederick G. Whelan, "Citizenship and the Right to Leave," *American Political Science Review* 75 (1981): 636–653.

18. These figures come from the United Nations Development Report, as discussed by Thomas Pogge in his *World Poverty and Human Rights* (London: Polity Press, 2002).

19. Figures are from the CIA World Factbook, available at https://www.cia.gov/library/publications/the-world-factbook/.
20. This is emphasized in Kapur and McHale, *Give Us Your Best and Brightest.*
21. Kieran Oberman makes this more explicit, grounding an obligation to repay in the expectation of reciprocal service. See Oberman, "Can Brain Drain Justify Immigration Restrictions?"
22. The example is discussed in Elizabeth Anderson, "What is the Point of Equality?," *Ethics* 109 (1999): 287–337.
23. I discuss this in Michael Blake and Mathias Risse, "Two Models of Equality and Responsibility," *Canadian Journal of Philosophy* 38 (2008): 165–200.
24. Fernando Tesón notes, similarly, that people may move somewhere precisely because they are not receiving an adequate challenge where they are. Fernando Tesón, "Brain Drain," *San Diego Law Review* 45 (2008): 899–932.
25. But see Patrick J. Carr and Maria J. Kefalas, *Hollowing Out the Middle: The Rural Brain Drain and What It Means for America* (Boston: Beacon Press, 2010).
26. Thomas Pogge emphasizes that one plausible basis for our obligations to developing nations is in our shared and violent history. See Pogge, *World Poverty and Human Rights.*
27. Cole, *Philosophies of Exclusion.*
28. One recent analysis found that wage differentials were "overwhelmed by other determinants of nurse migration," including professional development, linguistic similarity, and presence of existing diaspora community. Sue J. Ross, Daniel Polsky, and Julie Sochalski, "Nursing Shortages and International Nurse Migration," *International Nursing Review* 52 (2005): 253–262, at 260. See also James Buchan, *Here to Stay? International Nurses in the UK* (London: Royal College of Nurses, 2003), which echoes the idea that wages were a comparatively minor determinant of migration patterns.
29. Lucas Stanczyk might disagree, as I will discuss in the next chapter. See Stanczyk, "Productive Justice," *Philosophy and Public Affairs* 40 (2012): 144–164.

30. Key to my argument, of course, is that there could be an adequate response to injustice that—if all parties were actually made to live up to their duties—would in fact lead to adequate justice. I accept the possibility that there might be cases in which that assumption will fail; I discuss this possibility in the next chapter.
31. John Williams, *Stoner* (New York: New York Review Books Classics, 2006).
32. Oberman's attitude is complex. He allows that agent-centered prerogatives place limits on what can be asked of us, but does not allow these prerogatives to displace his central argument, which is that individuals may be justly coerced when they violate the expectations of others that repayment is due. (Another layer of complexity is added in that Oberman focuses on immigration, rather than emigration; since I believe in a more general right to exclude than Oberman does, I am here focusing on his moral argument, in isolation from the uses to which he puts that argument.)
33. Oberman identifies two reasons for this: assistance to the poor, which is a general duty, and repayment of benefits received, which is a special duty. I here focus on the latter.
34. Oberman discusses this in the context of a special duty, based upon the local community. He allows that it might be permissible to compel outsiders.
35. See John Rawls, *A Theory of Justice* (Cambridge, MA: Harvard University Press, 1971), 179.
36. Rawls, *A Theory of Justice*, 276.
37. Stanczyk, "Productive Justice."
38. See Charles Taylor, "Atomism," in his *Philosophical Papers, Volume 2: Philosophy and the Human Sciences* (Cambridge: Cambridge University Press, 1985).
39. Charles Taylor, "Multiculturalism and 'The Politics of Recognition,'" in Amy Gutmann (ed.), *Multiculturalism: Examining the Politics of Recognition* (Princeton, NJ: Princeton University Press, 1994), 25–74.
40. Alisdair MacIntyre, "Is Patriotism a Virtue?," in Ronald Beiner (ed.), *Theorizing Citizenship* (Binghamton, NY: SUNY Press, 1995), 286–300.

41. See the speech of Thabo Mbeki, asking: "[D]o we not have need to recall Africa's hundreds of thousands of intellectuals back from their places of emigration in Western Europe and North America. To rejoin those who remain still within our shores!" Thabo Mbeki, The African Renaissance Statement of Deputy President, cited in Tesón, "Brain Drain," p. 900.

42. Available at http://www.pbs.org/stealinghome/debate/defections.html#def.

43. "First, no permission of foreign travel shall, in any circumstances, be granted to any person under the age of forty." *Laws* 950d. See generally *Laws* 950d-951c.

44. See Whelan, "Citizenship and the Right to Leave," pp. 644–645.

45. The nation may prove relevant for justice, of course; Will Kymlicka argues that liberals can be robbed of their liberal rights when the nation is treated with insufficient respect. See Kymlicka, *Liberalism, Community, and Culture* (Oxford: Clarendon Press, 1991).

46. This argument is similar to that of Fernando Tesón, who grounds the prohibition on coercion on self-ownership. I ground my own argument on related, but distinct, ideas, such as the idea that a liberal government can only justify its powers with reference to the protection of the rights of those it coerces; these ideas might be grounded in self-ownership, but should be appealing even to people who do not believe in robust property rights in the self. See Tesón, "Brain Drain," p. 899.

47. See Anna Stilz, *Liberal Loyalty* (Princeton, NJ: Princeton University Press, 2010).

48. Whelan notes that this argument was the one taken by the Soviet Union in response to the inclusion of the right to exit within the UDHR; the Soviet delegation insisted that the right to exit was within the sovereign right of the domestic political society to regulate. See F. G. Whelan, "Citizenship and the Right to Exit," pp. 642.

49. Rawls, in his early work, argued that a society satisfying the constraints of justice would come "as close as a society can to being a voluntary scheme." John Rawls, *A Theory of Justice*, p. 13.

8

The Right to Leave: Looking Forward

THE PRECEDING CHAPTER DEALT WITH arguments that looked back, toward the social world in which a prospective migrant grew and developed her skills; it dealt with ideas such as gratitude and loyalty, which are best understood in terms of the shared history of the migrant and her (current) fellow nationals. These ideas are powerful, but they are not the only sorts of ideas we might use to ground the idea that the state can rightly prevent (or condition) exit from its territory. We might, instead, examine ideas that begin with the idea that those who want to leave sometimes make things worse for these fellow nationals when they depart. These arguments look forward, to the good consequences of having these would-be migrants remain where they are, but the arguments are not best understood as consequentialist arguments. The good consequences envisioned include values, such as rights-protecting institutions, that all liberals have reason to prize. The core of these arguments is that the would-be migrant, in leaving, would abandon her fellow nationals to some status we have reason to think is morally wrongful, and that the state is therefore rightful in preventing her from leaving. This argument comes in more than one form. We might emphasize that the bad consequences envisioned are simply bad outcomes, such as someone's having inadequate healthcare; alternatively, we might imagine that the bad consequences are institutional, and that the one who leaves undermines the institutions that are required by justice.

I believe that Gillian Brock is best read as defending a variant of the latter approach, and a recent argument by Lucas Stanczyk can be understood as a version of the former. This chapter will discuss these ideas. I will begin with Brock's arguments. Both types of arguments, of course, are ones with which the defender of the status quo must come to terms. What I say below, then, is intended primarily as a means by which we might begin this task; it is emphatically not to say that arguments such as Brock's are not worthy of our respect. They are, and I am grateful to Brock for having made me—and, of course, the rest of us—come to terms with these ideas.

I GILLIAN BROCK: THE INSTITUTIONAL TURN

I think, in a book like this, it is perhaps unnecessary for me to summarize Brock's view; that view is presented, with more clarity than I could muster, in Chapters 1 through 6 of this book. I will open my critical remarks by noting a few aspects of the view which are both especially important, and with which I stand in agreement.

(1) **Institutions are sites of liberal justice.** Individuals exist not simply as social atoms, engaging in one-to-one relationships; they exist against

a backdrop of social institutions, which collectively define the expectations of those individuals. These institutions, moreover, must do an adequate job of defending these expectations, or the social world within which those individuals live is one they have rights to have changed. John Rawls's idea that the basic structure is the site of political justice seems relevant here; for Rawls, as for Brock, our analysis of justice must make reference to the institutions we have developed to define and defend the rights upon which liberalism insists.

(2) **Institutions are sites for economic development.** This aspect of the view focuses on the relevance of institutions for economic well-being; societies with flourishing institutions are likely to have individuals flourish within them as well. The wealth and poverty of nations, in this view, is related not simply to economic resources or favorable geography; it demands responsive and transparent institutions as well. If development is part of what liberalism demands—as, Brock and I agree, it must be—then institutions are relevant for liberal thought.

(3) **Institutions are not natural, but social.** This idea may seem obvious but should be emphasized: there is nothing natural, or inevitable, about the institutional set that exists within any society. These institutions are built by persons, and—as importantly—can be changed by persons as well. Institutions, in other words, are legitimately subject to alteration when they fail to perform the functions that justify those institutions.

(4) **Individual persons have the duty to preserve such institutions when they exist, and to help create them where they do not.** This idea follows on from the above; if liberalism is a thesis about what persons deserve, and if what people deserve includes institutional sets that adequately defend their rights, then all of us—collectively—are legitimately subject to a duty to defend those institutions. What this duty demands, of course, may be subject to some disagreement; the duty may, for example, take different forms for those currently subject to a state's authority than for those who are not. The duty itself, though, seems universal in scope. If all humans matter, and matter equally, then all humans are obligated to build a world within which the moral status of humanity is given adequate respect.

I make all four of these explicit to specify the ground over which Brock and I agree. Our disagreement, of course, comes about in what implications we take the above vision to entail. Brock views these materials as sufficient to permit a state to engage in some forms of action designed to prevent the exit of its current residents. The justification for this, of course, is that individuals with high human capital—the well trained, highly talented, and highly motivated—would be well positioned to build institutions within those societies that currently suffer from underdevelopment in both their economic and institutional lives. If liberalism contains a duty to work for justice and just institutions, then those who propose to leave have a duty to stay. This duty, in turn, may be legitimately subject to enforcement by the state. Brock has emphasized, of course, that this use of coercion is limited; the right to exit is conditioned, and exit is postponed rather than precluded. What is key, though, is that the one who proposes to leave *right now* is legitimately subject to coercion precluding her exit. Brock believes that liberalism can be made compatible with that use of coercion. I disagree.

Why, though, do I disagree? The full answer to that question awaits the discussion, in the next chapter, of the moral centrality of the right to leave. For the moment, though, I want to discuss only the ways in which I am not convinced by Brock's arguments. My disagreements here fall into two categories: the empirical and the theoretical. I will go over these in turn.

I will start my discussion of the empirical worries, though, with a caution: I am not an empirical scholar. What I say here is not intended to say what *is* true about the likely consequences of the right to forcibly prevent exit; it is, instead, designed to point out what *might be* true about such consequences. Political philosophers have reason to be modest about the extent to which they can do the jobs associated with empirical social sciences.[1] This means, of course, that any full discussion of the morality of the brain drain cannot be had solely between philosophers; it must include specialists in development interventions as well. Since I cannot provide this discussion here, I will limit myself to a few areas in which I believe Brock's account of the likely consequences of her proposal are perhaps subject to empirical dispute. Since neither Brock nor I are development economists, our discussion here is necessarily little more than a suggestion for others—with more empirical training than ourselves—to follow up.

With that caveat in place, we might proceed to the consequences of a state proposing to prevent its current residents from departing. Brock has given us some reasons to think that such a policy might lead to a more just world, in which institutions are more responsive and in which liberal rights are more protected. Her emphasis is on the effects upon a state of the absence of particular persons: their absence, in her view, is a bad thing, and it is bad enough to permit the state to prevent that exit. While she acknowledges the empirical complexity of the issues and the ways in which emigration may sometimes help the country of emigration, I want to give these factors more stress than she does in her own analysis. I will here borrow from the ideas of Devesh Kapur and John McHale. Kapur and McHale agree with her that the absence of this human capital can undermine the viability of important institution; they caution, though, that there are other effects of the emigration of skilled workers, not all of which are best understood as negative.[2] Kapur and McHale therefore note that the net effects of the brain drain are difficult to pin down with any degree of confidence. While Brock emphasizes the negative effects of the absence of human capital, Kapur and McHale note three other effects of the right to leave that might balance these negative effects:

(1) **Prospective migration:** Simply put, the awareness that education tends to lead to greater possibilities—to the right to leave a less developed society, and enter a more developed one—tends to increase the number of people who want that education. The ability to leave provides a powerful set of incentives. It should be noted, though, that

these incentives apply even for those who do not, in the end, have the ability to leave the country; they may lack the wealth to leave, might not find a willing employer, and so on. The net result of this is that there may be, under some circumstances, a *reduction* in the number of people obtaining a particular qualification, when those with that qualification are prevented from leaving. We may, perhaps, think of the right to exit from a less developed country to a more developed one as a sort of lottery, entry into which comes in the form of a particular form of skills acquisition— say, medical training. Some of those who obtain this training will leave, having won (on this analogy) the lottery; others will want to leave, but will be unable to do so. Those latter individuals, though, do not lose their training simply because they have not been able to use it abroad. The net result of all this is that a lottery with exit as a prize may in fact be more effective at producing a skilled domestic labor force than a prohibition on exit; this phenomenon is sufficiently common that economists have given it the name "brain gain."[3] We might regard this as unfair, perhaps— why should other countries be so well off that exit to them is analogized to a lottery prize?—but our present concern is not with fairness but with consequences. One consequence of Brock's proposal, if the "brain gain" phenomenon holds true, is that the net human capital of the domestic labor force might go *down*, if that labor force is prevented from leaving.

(2) **Diaspora effects:** The existence of foreign-born workers resident abroad has a number of powerful effects upon the home country, simply in virtue of the fact that there are now people with the linguistic and social competences required to mediate between different societies. Kapur and McHale refer to these persons as "reputational intermediaries," able to facilitate economic and knowledge exchanges between societies because of the ways in which they participate in the lives of both societies. There are at least three ways in which these diaspora effects may assist in the development of low-income societies:

a. **Trade:** Trading links between societies are made more robust when there are individuals who are able to navigate the perilous waters between cultures; economic exchange, after all, is exchange between persons, and those who remain home may find themselves better able to navigate the waters of foreign investment when they are able to deal with those who have left. To put this in the simplest terms, having a diaspora community abroad tends to increase the economic opportunities for those who do not go abroad, and this economic benefit is a powerful engine for human development.

b. **Knowledge:** Those who have left a particular place do not thereby abandon their social ties to that place. They are, instead, often keen to continue social relationships to their places of origin, and these social relationships may

include the transmission of beneficial knowledge. The skills that have led an individual
to leave her home may be supplemented by
skills acquired abroad, and these skills may
be transmitted through informal channels of
social and familial relationship. The effects of
this are most powerful when the individual
returns, as discussed below; they occur, however, even when the individual's departure
is permanent. As a result, to preclude exit is
sometimes to foreclose valuable channels of
skills-based development.

c. **Remittances:** The notion that remittances
are a central engine of development is a controversial one. What is not controversial is
that the scope of remittances is enormous;
the World Bank estimates that over half a
trillion dollars will be sent to the developing world in remittances by 2016.[4] Brock
quite rightly questions whether remittances
are adequate for the development of social
institutions. I want to emphasize, though,
that the *absence* of these remittances might
well *impede* the development of these institutions. If, as seems true, poverty is both
cause and result of malign or corrupt political systems, then cutting off a powerful
engine of wealth may delay significantly the
development of adequate institutional sets.
Lant Pritchett has recently estimated that
allowing three thousand more Bangladeshi
emigrants to enter the United States would

generate more income *in Bangladesh* than the annual income of Grameen, one of the most important microfinance banks working today in Bangladesh.[5] To put this in the simplest terms: remittances cannot do *everything*, but we should not therefore take them to do *nothing*—and to reduce the incentives to individuals to develop scarce skills, by making it more difficult for them to use those abroad and earn greater wealth, is to run the risk of destroying one of the few channels through which money flows into impoverished societies.

(3) **Return effects:** When people leave a place, they do not always stay abroad. Kapur and McHale estimate that between 30 and 50 percent of people who leave for employment abroad will eventually return. This fact holds true for those coming from developing societies, who often maintain cultural and affective links to their countries of origin. Those who develop sufficient capital abroad to become economically secure in their countries of origin may choose to return to those countries of origin. This fact, though, brings with it benefits to that country; those who return have new skills and habits that may help build new institutions in their societies of origin. Pearl Esuah-Mensah, the deputy managing director of a Ghanaian bank, recently urged expatriate Ghanaians to return to Ghana—not because of loyalty, or solidarity, but because those Ghanaians who have worked in

other countries have experienced different social norms and institutions, which may be of benefit to Ghana:

> [Customer service in Ghana is] notoriously bad . . . We need people to teach us in Ghana what customer service means. . . . [T]he more of you who come home to Ghana and demand proper customer service, the better.[6]

This is a simple example, but instructive; social institutions include social norms, and there is undoubted value in Ghanaians developing better practices in dealing with their publics. To prevent exit, then, might be to prevent the eventual development of better institutions within developing countries themselves.

I believe these ideas are sufficient to cast doubt on the idea that the absence of human capital from a developing society is an unequivocally bad thing. I do not, of course, claim it to be a good thing overall; to say that requires more skills in empirical science than I have. I cite these ideas only to emphasize the ways in which the overall story may be more complex than it at first appears. I would close by adding two more ways in which the effects of emigration restrictions might be more complex than we think:

(4) **Substitutability of human capital:** Human capital is a capacious term, encompassing any number of valuable human skills and capacities. It is not clear, though, what sorts of human capital are best suited to assist in the development of institutions with adequate capacity

to protect liberal rights. To see this, note that one of the most powerful drivers for nurses to exit developing countries is not simply the wage differential but violence in the country of origin; to think that precluding the exit of nurses would reduce violence, though, requires us to think that a nursing degree will assist in building an adequate police and judicial infrastructure.[7] This, I think, is not always true. What makes a person attractive abroad is a particular sort of human capital; it may not be directly of use in the complex sets of problems involved in setting up a responsive political society. Michael Clemens notes, in connection with this, that those who emigrate from African countries often studied and worked in African cities rather than in the dramatically underserved rural areas; as such, the skills that allow these emigrants to work internationally may translate poorly to the development of infrastructure appropriate for rural society.[8] Brock may, of course, justly note that it is often the young and energetic who emigrate; energy, if not skill, might indeed be useful in a variety of contexts. That is true, of course, but it is worth asking whether those who are now energetic will continue to be so after being precluded from following their professional desires. Again, this is an empirical question; it may well be true that Brock's analysis is right. I do, however, think there are plausible stories that might tell against that analysis. While nurses are undoubtedly well equipped to treat the sick, it is far from clear that they are therefore necessarily well equipped to build responsive political institutions.

(5) **Effectiveness of coercion:** Humans do not like being coerced. They especially do not like being coerced to remain in places they do not want to be; the number of undocumented residents in the world, from the United States to the United Arab Emirates, is testimony to that.[9] This is not to say that such coercion is necessarily illegitimate; it is instead to say that—if such coercion is to be justified with reference to its results— we should not assume that such results include a complete absence of migration. If, as seems to be true, some emigrants are motivated by poor conditions within their own societies, they may well cross borders even if told they are not allowed to do so. The result of this is costly, both in terms of the human lives affected by the coercive violence and the training that is often sacrificed in the name of emigration. Ghana has, for example, recently begun withholding nursing certificates from those who do not practice for some time within Ghana. This program may lead to some Ghanaian nurses remaining within Ghana; it may also lead to some nurses fleeing Ghana to work elsewhere outside the medical field. This problem—referred to as "brain waste" in the economic literature—should warn us against any easy confidence that our coercive interventions will always produce the results we desire.[10]

I introduce all this because I want to note that Brock's justification ultimately demands that prevention of exit lead to good results—and that this is an empirical result that may not always hold true. We cannot be confident—at least, not without some empirical work—that preventing the talented from departing will actually make the institutions of the coercing society more justifiable.

What I want to discuss in more detail, though, is the moral theory undergirding Brock's proposal. As I have said, I agree with a very great deal of Brock's political philosophy. I believe, though, that the right to leave is morally central, which she denies; as a result, I believe her proposal is fundamentally misguided. I will defend the former proposition only in the next chapter; in the present, I will try only to demonstrate that we have reason to think—even if we do not (yet) defend the right to leave—that the proposal she has made is unfair. To see why this is so, though, we may return to the examples from the previous chapter.

In the example of the kidnapped tourist, Malawi refuses to allow the exit of a visiting Japanese tourist until she has spent a year building institutions of medicine within Malawi. That tourist is sufficiently talented at the building of infrastructure that she will make medical practice within Malawi significantly better for all Malawians.

I believe our reaction to this example is instructive; we are unlikely to think that the government of Malawi is within its rights to do this, and we are likely to think that at least one reason for this is that it is treating the Japanese visitor *unfairly*. Assume, as is true, that Malawi's medical infrastructure is inadequate; globally, we all—collectively—have some part of the responsibility for making that infrastructure better. The tourist, though, can say

that she is being singled out and made to bear a disproportionate share of the burden of compliance here. While she,
along with all others resident in wealthy and developed
societies, should have to pay some part of the cost, she
should not have to pay these *particular* costs. She is being
treated, we think, in an illiberal way, even if the goal for
which she is being used is a valid one for a liberal to defend.

What is true of the kidnapped tourist, though, seems
equally true for the prevented emigrant. Assume, now, that
the Malawian is prevented from leaving. Assume, again,
that the justification for this is not one of actual contract,
in which the Malawian bargained for specific training in
the name of a specific duty to remain. Instead, the government of Malawi simply says, "You'll make Malawian
institutions better by remaining, and so we will make
you stay." I think the government is wrong to say this,
and the character of this wrong is identical to that of the
kidnapped tourist. While the Malawian has some obligation to help make Malawian institutions responsive, she
has no more or less of a responsibility than that held by
any other person. Whereas those people are being asked
to sacrifice comparatively little, this person is being made
to bear a significant cost, one which directly implicates the
course of her life and her own evaluations of what makes
that life go well or poorly. This is, to put it bluntly, morally perverse. We cannot balance our moral ledgers by placing such a strong duty precisely on those people who have
the least protection, the worst institutions, and the lowest
prospects. They would be, perhaps, noble for choosing to
remain; they would be saints, who sacrifice their own lives
in the name of others. But we cannot force sainthood upon
them. Their governments, more to the point, should not

think that liberalism gives them a pass to demand such sacrifices. Even if the goal is noble, the path is prohibited.

This is, I believe, a grave difficulty with Brock's proposal. I believe she has some resources with which to deal with this difficulty; I would like to examine four possible responses here. The first two responses try to show that the kidnapped Japanese resident is distinct from the Malawian resident prevented from leaving; the latter two try to make us more comfortable with the idea that liberalism might sometimes legitimately allow states to place differential burdens upon their subjects.

One first response, then, is to begin with the relevance of history. The Malawian citizen has a history within the society of Malawi; the Japanese citizen has nothing similar. (We might imagine she has visited for a while, on a tourist visa, and now wishes to depart.) The Malawian, then, has taken some benefits from the Malawian people; they have sacrificed to create her skills, and have worked together to make a world within which she has flourished. Can we not cite these facts in showing that the Malawian resident—but not the Japanese resident—may be justly prevented from departing?

I do not think we can; at least, I do not believe Brock can, if she wants to preserve the core of her moral argument. This response, after all, turns a forward-looking argument about institutions into a different sort of argument, one about gratitude or loyalty. Those arguments, as discussed in the last chapter, are common but are not easy to harmonize with the moral universalism that makes liberalism attractive. If Brock wishes to say that Malawian residents have particular duties to work for Malawian institutions, simply because they grew up in Malawi and learned to be themselves within a Malawian society, then her argument collapses into a communitarian argument about social identity and duty. She does not want her argument to be read that way, though; she understands herself as a cosmopolitan liberal. As such, though, the history of the Malawian is likely a difficult factor to introduce into the discussion. The Malawian may have been born into the society in question, but that brute fact may tell us nothing about how much she must sacrifice by comparison with other human persons. The Malawian may justly complain that the burden placed on her cannot be justified with reference to the simple fact of birthplace.

We might try a second tactic, then, and note that the Malawian is simply better situated to respond to the injustice within Malawi than the Japanese citizen. The Malawian, we might imagine, knows the language, social customs, and normative structure of Malawi better than someone who grew up abroad could ever hope to do. She will simply do a *better job* at making institutions work, and she will do this because those who do not have her attributes could not hope to do what she does. Can we not thereby justify a difference between the Japanese and Malawian cases?

Again, I think this will prove difficult to do. We might, to begin with, simply change the hypothetical, so that our Japanese tourist is so absurdly skilled that she could do a better job than any Malawian citizen might; that change, though, would not alter our sense that the Malawian government wrongs the Japanese resident by preventing her exit. Our disquiet here cannot simply be explained away through factors like these. More to the point, though, I think it might be difficult for us to defend the idea that *obligations* increase with *ability*. There are at least two reasons for this. The first is that we might sometimes have reason to ask *why it is* that someone has greater skills than someone else, and whether or not that allocation of skills reflects facts we have reason to accept. It might well be the case, for example, that it is easier for a woman than for a man to be a stay-at-home parent in the United States: there is less of a social stigma attached to full-time parenting for women, perhaps, and much of the social machinery attached to parenting assumes female parents will take the dominant role. (I say this as a male participant in several "Mommy and Me" classes.) Our response to this should not stop with the fact that it is more difficult for men than for women; we should instead recognize that we ought to allocate the burden of parenting fairly, rather than simply placing the burden upon the one currently able to bear it most cheaply.

The second reason why we should not think that burdens rise with ability is more abstract and goes to the relationship between *skills* and *plans of life*. We rightly believe that all people should have a significant freedom to develop a life for themselves from the inside; the idea of autonomy holds a (rightly) important place within political philosophy. We should therefore be hesitant before we start assigning stringent duties to individuals simply in virtue of what skills they happen to have. Imagine, for example, a mountain community, in which all inhabitants must take turns acting as lookout against the wily mountain goat. (The wily mountain goat, perhaps, tends to eat our crops, making everyone in our community that much more hungry.) Imagine further that one inhabitant is exceptionally skilled at the job of acting as mountain goat: she can do it better than others, so much so that the village would be considerably safer if he was simply forced to stand watch during the entirety of his waking life. Would the village be justified in forcing him to do this? Some might say yes—Lucas Stanczyk, as discussed below, might accept the result—but most of us would say no; from the fact that we can do a thing better than others, we should not infer a duty to do that very thing. The fact that the Malawian person happens to have a rare set of talents—here, the combination of medical skills and knowledge of Malawian traditions—does not oblige her to use *that* set of talents. Our lookout might prefer to be a professor; our Malawian might prefer to use her medical training elsewhere. In both cases, the state acts wrongly in preventing her from developing her chosen talents with particular chosen others. The fact that it is coercing her to do what she is good at doing does not make a moral difference.

This leads, though, to the third response, which is to assert that we should be more comfortable than I clearly am with differential burdens. We do, after all, create differential burdens all the time; the wealthy pay more taxes than the rest of us, and they sometimes do so in virtue of their greater talents. This, though, is a differential burden; if I am complaining that we are not allowed to force would-be emigrants to bear a disproportionate share of the burdens of justice, should I not also condemn the greater tax bills of the domestic wealthy? On this strategy, we would use the fact that the wealthy must pay more in taxes to establish the general principle that an unequal bill is not inherently unjust; having done so, we could establish that the burden borne by the would-be emigrant is not, itself, an injustice toward that individual.

I would note, in passing, that Brock's response to this issue does not seem quite right: Brock notes that we are comfortable with redistributive taxation, which seems very much like an insistence that some may be made to perform labor for others—so why not simply become comfortable with making some work for the benefit of others? This is the inverse of an argument made by Robert Nozick, that taxation for the purposes of redistribution is tantamount to forced labor—although, where Nozick wanted us to become less comfortable with taxation, Brock wants us to become more comfortable with forced labor.[11] For my part, I think the reply to Nozick might suffice as a reply to Brock: we should regard redistributive taxation as akin to forced labor *only if* we think that people are fully entitled to whatever property they can acquire in the open market through the use of their talents. Those of us who are of a Rawlsian disposition, though, do not think that we have any reason to do that. Redistribution is not the taking of what is owned, but a recognition that when it comes to fungible property—to, bluntly, the making and owning of *stuff*—we are rightly able to develop different principles of ownership in response to the needs of social justice. We have the right to decide what to do with our persons and our talents; we do not have the right to whatever proceeds our talents might bring us in the open market. Nozick's argument then—and Brock's now—ignore this relevant moral difference. Nothing here, therefore, should make us feel comfortable with forced labor, since redistributive taxation should not be thought to resemble forced labor.

Imagine, then, that the justification for the greater tax burdens of the wealthy is that those are needed to create a just social and political world; one in which, perhaps, there is the continuing possibility of political community between the wealthy and the poor. We should, on this account, be sure that there is some sort of distributive justice within the society, which would require working against the sorts of inequality that might make democratic life impossible.[12] This rationale, though, seems hard to apply to an act that is, by its very nature, designed to alter the political community so that one member is outside that community. To use the principles of justice within a community to govern who may leave that community seems to get things back to front in a particularly pernicious way. The principles that govern justice within a society cannot be thought to be directly applicable to the rights and interests of one who seeks to *exit* that society.

We should also note, finally, that there is a difference between coercively affecting the distribution of *fungible* goods and coercively insisting upon *relationships and plans directly*. The two are linked, of course; what I can do depends upon how much money I have. But we have, rightly, differentiated between principles telling us how much money we will earn with our talents and how we must use our talents. The latter seems to many of us more dangerous and difficult as a site of coercion, and therefore interventions that propose to prevent actions are often more difficult to justify than those that affect earnings. We think, accordingly, that it is one thing for us to have inadequate funds to go on a pilgrimage and another thing entirely for the government to prevent our pilgrimage when we would otherwise have the means to go. This distinction might be justified with reference to the work of John Rawls, of course, but we might as easily just take it as a part of our ordinary moral experience: it is one thing to offer differential tax burdens and another thing entirely to impose differential degrees of freedom.[13]

We might, in light of this, simply bite the bullet and say that we should be willing to think that differential degrees of freedom are compatible with liberalism. Stanczyk chooses this route, asserting that liberalism imposes constraints on employment all the time: doctors, after all, must engage in professional education, which counts as forcing them to act in a particular way they might not have independently chosen. Brock, in contrast, might deploy the analogy of marriage. According to this analogy, those who have married have placed themselves in a situation in which they are rightly responsible for the well-being of their spouses, even if they might prefer to exit the relationship. Both theorists, then, might argue that we ought not to be quite so hesitant to demand forced actions in the name of liberalism. What specific people have chosen to do makes them legitimately subject to differential burdens; those who have chosen to acquire medical knowledge, then, might have a special duty to use it to develop medical institutions.

This is, I think, the best response that might be made here. I do not think it ultimately works. The reason for this is simple: individuals can rightly be coerced for a variety of reasons, but none of these reasons easily translates to the case of the would-be emigrant. Look at Stanczyk's case of the doctor who must labor to keep his practice current; we are regulating here to ensure that what is going to be done—namely, medical practice—*will be done well*. This is a far less controversial ground than coercing someone in order to preclude their doing a thing (and, we may assume, doing it well) in a disfavored location. We are rightly hesitant before we think that the permission to regulate labor extends to a permission to pursue social ends more generally; think, in connection with this, of the use of regulatory language by the state of Texas to make it more or less impossible to run an abortion clinic.[14] We find this cynical, I think, because we understand the point of regulation as protecting people from *bad* agents—not promotion of a particular vision of social justice (here, one without reproductive rights). The fact that we can regulate doctors to be good doctors, in other words, doesn't easily extend to a permission to coerce them to be good doctors *here.*

I think this general point recurs in our discussion of marriage. Why, upon the dissolution of a marriage, does each party have an obligation to support the other party's standard of living? There are a variety of reasons, of course—we are, most importantly, right to think that equality within the marriage would suffer if one party could destroy the other by leaving—but all these reasons are to be understood against the backdrop that the marriage itself is *chosen.* We do not apply these relationships of coercion to other, unchosen forms of human affiliation; even if my neighborhood would have been made worse off by my going off to college, that neighborhood could not coercively keep me simply because I happened to have been born there. We are, in general, more willing to defend specific duties when they are triggered by specific actions, voluntarily undertaken; it is comparatively more difficult to think that we have such duties simply because of luck.

Even if the analogy to marriage were to work, it is not clear that it would provide any basis to argue against the right to exit. When a marriage ends, there are two competing needs that must be addressed: the needs of the parties to have a just distribution of marital assets and the needs of the parties to be free to *leave*. The latter has generally been taken, in law, as being important; we cannot be made to stay in a bad relationship, and the financial needs of others cannot fully trump our right to exit that relationship. Thus, the US Supreme Court has asserted, when there is no ability to pay a settlement, the state has no right to use coercion to enforce that settlement; the individual cannot be forced, directly or in virtue of poverty, to continue the unwanted association.[15] Brock's proposal, in contrast, would be that the departing spouse must condition her exit upon the consent of the remaining spouse—and that the latter might be able to insist that the former stay, for some indefinite period of time, within the relationship. This is, understandably, a view that courts have generally been unwilling to defend.

We might proceed to examine Stanczyk's argument more directly. I have been assuming that there is a valid liberal prohibition on forced labor; I have used this assumption to ground my rejection of the proposal in the case of the kidnapped tourist. Stanczyk's argument urges us to rethink this quick rejection of the idea that we are not permitted to force others to work for us. Stanczyk's argument is distinct from Brock's own on one important point: he is not concerned directly with the right to exit, focusing instead on the question of justice in the allocation of jobs to persons. As such, he is agnostic about whether or not a proposal such as Brock's is morally justifiable. His view is, however, an interesting alternative to Brock's own, since we might use it as an alternative basis on which to construct some proposal in favor of coercive inclusion. We should, then, examine what Stanczyk's argument actually says.

II LUCAS STANCZYK: LABOR AND LIBERAL RIGHTS

Stanczyk's argument can be summarized rather neatly:

1. Justice does not directly constrain occupational choice.
2. Justice forbids forcibly assigning jobs except where liberties are at risk.
3. Justice requires society to ensure more than merely liberties.

These three propositions are mutually incompatible because the final proposition demands the existence of an institutional scheme of sufficient strength and scope to defend the various entitlements to which liberal egalitarians believe we are entitled—and the first two propositions preclude the use of coercion in getting us toward this institutional scheme.[16] The result, of course, is that we might arrive at a world in which we are forced to choose between these apparently incompatible values. In Stanczyk's view, we ought to jettison our instinctive opposition to the idea that a legitimate government might directly and coercively assign jobs to persons. If a world emerges in which we have to sacrifice the value of free choice of occupation, or in which our liberal entitlements are respected, we should choose the latter. On this construal, of course, it is possible for us to directly assign persons to jobs. Having done so, we might insist (although Stanczyk does not) that the right to exit itself should fall as a result. Again, while Stanczyk would not necessarily accept this application of his view, it is at least possible for us to use his ideas to think that both precluding an emigrant and kidnapping a tourist might be defensible actions by a liberal government.

I want to begin my discussion of Stanczyk by emphasizing something he also emphasizes: we are living in a deeply non-ideal world. Stanczyk accepts that his principle would not suspend the right to free choice of occupational choice in a well-ordered society. I believe that Stanczyk has underemphasized the importance of this fact for his theory. It means, to begin with, that we are now dealing not with what liberalism allows, simpliciter; we are dealing with how we ought to move from a deeply disordered world to one in which liberalism itself might hold sway.

We should, I think, pay attention to this fact in our examination of how we are entitled to act. If we are, indeed, under deeply non-ideal circumstances, then at least two things are true:

(1) The otherwise illiberal action we propose to take must be the *best* way to leave those unjust circumstances.

(2) The otherwise illiberal action we propose to take must be *proportional* to the injustice we face.

I believe these considerations may make Stanczyk's solution less attractive than it might at first appear.

To see this, note the following similar arguments:

(1) We are entitled to medical infrastructure, as part of our liberal guarantees. Therefore, individuals may be justly forced by the state to work within that infrastructure.

(2) We are entitled to an adequate supply of food, as part of our liberal guarantees. Therefore, individuals may be justly forced by the state to grow food.

(3) We are entitled to a flourishing and diverse media, as part of our liberal guarantees. Therefore, individuals may be justly forced by the state to produce political commentary.

Even if we were in sympathy with the first argument, I take it we begin to get nervous at the second and third. The reason for this, I think, is that it is not clear that directly coercing people to do an important thing is a good, or even permissible, path to a world in which that important thing is done well. Sometimes, what is produced by coercion is different, and lesser, than what is produced freely. To be forced by a government to produce articles and books *about* that government is simply different—from the inside— than doing that as a result of one's own choices. The feeling is different, of course, but the result is too. A flourishing and diverse media is, I believe, part of what we are entitled to as a part of our liberal guarantees, but it does not follow that it can—even in principle—be produced by means of coercion.

I note this not because I think medical practice is the same as journalism—although I believe the two might not be wholly unrelated, especially when we discuss the creation of new medical infrastructure.[17] I note this only because I want to get us away from thinking that coercion is the best means to get us to any particular desired state of affairs. Sometimes, there exist required states of affairs that might be best produced—or only capable of being produced—by indirect means. Look, then, at the case of food. It is undoubtedly true that we have a right to food; that is hardly controversial, either within liberalism or within human rights more generally. But this right is hardly sufficient to act as a justification for forcing liberal citizens to work on farms. What the right to food means is a right to live in a social world in which markets in things like food will emerge and persist. When we use the locution of a right to food, I take it we mean this much—and, of course, that the market is constrained so that no one is unable to purchase adequate food. We believe, moreover, that under conditions of freedom, a market in food will emerge; indeed, Amartya Sen seems to have proven quite well that famines exist only when malign governments have created the circumstances under which markets in food begin to fail.[18] When we face an absence of food, then, our first response should not be to simply move around food; nor should it be the forcible collectivization of the farm system. We should instead ask why the farm system has failed and take steps to correct that problem. The coercive imposition of food production on unwilling citizens could only even in principle be justified after this methodology had been exhausted.[19]

I say all this because I think something similar might hold true in the case of medical practice. Before we are willing to suspend or eliminate the right to develop a plan of life from the inside, in conjunction with consenting others, we would have to ask why we are in a world that is so deeply second-best. We cannot force others to grow our food until we have discovered why markets in food have not emerged; we will, I think, discover that political malfeasance is often lurking in the background, and it is that malfeasance that we should deal with first. Similarly, a society cannot force others to remain until it has discovered why so much of that society wants to flee. It might discover that there is no solution other than forcing the would-be migrant to stay; that is an open possibility. But we should be hesitant to use this means to obtain this result, and suspicious of leaders who claim it is the only way. An analogy might be made to torture: many of us accept that we would permit torture where the alternative would be utter catastrophe. But we had damned well better make sure that the alternative *is* catastrophe rather than inconvenience.

And, of course, there may be some things we cannot do even in the face of catastrophe. Think, in this connection, of slavery. Rawls's project began with a discomfort with the morality of utilitarianism: he noted that there could be, under some circumstances, a utilitarian rationale for slavery, and that this was—for him—a sufficient reason to seek a replacement for utilitarian thought. The idea that slavery could ever be justifiable was so abhorrent that we ought to abandon any methodology that endorsed it. Rawls therefore took the prohibition on slavery as a provisional fixed point in his methodology and sought to develop a political philosophy that explained and extended our horror at forced labor. I am attracted to Rawls's methodology and share his conviction that slavery can never—even if useful—be morally rightful. I think what Stanczyk defends here is not slavery—chattel slavery, after all, was the extinction of all rights, rather than simple forced labor.[20] But slavery begins with forced labor, and constitutional amendments that (in the United States) ended slavery did so by ending forced labor. This prohibition on slavery has been extended, in American law, to a standing prohibition even on specific performance of personal service as a remedy for contractual breach; we cannot be made to labor for another, on pain of state coercion, even when we have contracted to do so.[21] I believe we are right to be horrified at the possibility of forced labor, and am more convinced than Stanczyk is that forced labor is never compatible with liberalism. If we were to arrive at a circumstance in which we would have to enslave in order to have a liberal society, I believe we would have arrived at a genuinely tragic state of affairs—we would, that is, face a world in which liberalism itself were not capable of guiding our politics. If moral tragedy is understandable as emerging from circumstances in which there are no just moves away from injustice, then the world imagined here might be a world of tragedy.

In the next chapter, I will discuss my belief that the international world is itself a site of moral tragedy.[22] For the moment, I will reiterate my contention that liberalism has an implicit range of applicability. It applies within the social worlds in which the three principles he identifies are, indeed, capable of being jointly satisfied. Outside of that realm, we have reason to amend our circumstances, so that we return to the world in which liberal rights are possible. We do not abandon the three propositions, but we seek a world in which they are possible, and even on the road to that world, there are some things we cannot do. Forced labor may be among them.

In response to this, Stanczyk may argue that we do, in fact, insist upon forced labor all the time: many states, including most self-described liberal ones, have at one point created systems of mandatory conscription into the military. I believe this argument confuses what states *have* done with what they *may* do. I do not want to argue that conscription is always morally prohibited. I do want to insist, though, that if it were defensible, it would have to be because of a set of circumstances that made conscription a permissible response to a particular emergency set of circumstances. We can take Rawls's own discussion of conscription as instructive here: conscription, to be morally permissible, would have to be a temporary restriction of liberty, justified with reference to a set of circumstances that threatened the continued survival of the just state itself.[23] The restriction of liberty, for Rawls, could only be justified with reference to the continued preservation of liberty. I would emphasize two things that Rawls does not: first, only the otherwise rights-protecting state has a legitimate right to conscript, and second, conscription must have some good chance at actually succeeding and returning the society in question to the status quo within which rights are protected. The first amendment is necessary, since only the state that protects basic liberties can justify its actions with reference to these liberties. The second amendment is needed to emphasize that the restriction on liberty must be an emergency concession, justified only as a temporary deviation from liberal justice; it cannot become a way of life. I believe both of these clauses make it difficult for us to accept the idea that the forced labor of doctors in sub-Saharan Africa can be morally rightful. In the first place, I do not think many of these states are able to rightfully coerce in the first instance; in the second, I believe it is important to note that the pathway between exit restrictions and a flourishing liberal society is, at best, a long and winding one.[24] The existence of forced military labor in the world should not blind us to the extraordinary nature of such a practice, and it should offer us no comfort in the justification of forced labor generally.

I have, in the present chapter, offered only my negative conclusions; I have argued that the claims of Brock and Stanczyk are subject to some important worries. I have not tried to defend the proposition that the right to exit is itself morally important, nor have I tried to get any sense of what the acceptable sorts of policy response to these worries might be. It is to these tasks that I now turn.

NOTES

1. I defend this view in Michael Blake, "Global Distributive Justice: Why Political Philosophy Needs Political Science," *Annual Review of Political Science* 15 (2012): 121–136.
2. See Kapur and McHale, *Give Us Your Best and Brightest* (Washington, DC: Center for Global Development, 2005).
3. See, on this, Michael Clemens, "Do Visas Kill? Health Effects of African Health Professional Emigration," *Center for Global Development Working Paper 114*, (Washington, DC: Center for Global Development, 2007); and Mari Kangasniemi, L. Alan Winters, and Simon Commander, "Is the Medical Brain Drain Beneficial? Evidence from Overseas Doctors in the UK," *Social Science and Medicine* 65 (2007): 915–923. See also Kapur and McHale, *Give Us Your Best and Brightest*, 73–86.
4. World Bank press release of October 2, 2013, available at http://www.worldbank.org/en/news/press-release/2013/10/02/developing-countries-remittances-2013-world-bank.
5. Cited in Dilip Ratha, "Dollars Without Borders: Can the Flow of Remittances Survive the Crisis?," *Foreign Affairs*, October 16, 2009, available at http://www.foreignaffairs.com/articles/65448/dilip-ratha/dollars-without-borders. See also Lant Pritchett, *Let Their People Come: Breaking the Deadlock on Global Labor Mobility* (Washington, DC: Center for Global Development, 2006).

6. Cited at http://www.recruiter.co.uk/news/2013/07/come-home-to-ghana-work-and-bring-your-customer-service-demands-with-you/.

7. Sue J. Ross, Daniel Polsky, and Julie Sochalski, "Nursing Shortages and International Nurse Migration" *International Nursing Review* 52 (2005): 252–262.

8. Clemens, "Do Visas Kill?" 37.

9. The United Nations estimates that, as of 2000, there were 175 million migrants in the world, of which approximately 15 percent were irregular migrants. See *World Migration Report 2005: Costs and Benefits of International Migration*, report of the International Organization for Migration, available at http://publications.iom.int/bookstore/free/wmr_2005.pdf.

10. See generally Martine Rutten, "The Economic Impact of Medical Migration: An Overview of the Literature," *The World Economy* 32 (2009): 291–325.

11. Robert Nozick, *Anarchy, State, and Utopia* (New York: Basic Books, 1974).

12. See generally Michael Blake, *Justice and Foreign Policy* (Oxford: Oxford University Press, 2013).

13. Rawls, in his early work, distinguishes between liberty and the worth of liberty; states are obligated to equalize liberty, but not the value to the individual of what that liberty allows him to do. Thus a state is required to equalize freedom of worship, but does not have to subsidize expensive pilgrimages, even if those are indeed required for religious practice. See John Rawls, *A Theory of Justice* (Cambridge, MA: Harvard University Press, 1971), 204.

14. The law requires doctors providing abortion to have admitting privilege at a hospital—a significant burden, and one that effectively closed several abortion clinics within Texas. The law was found constitutional by a sharply divided Supreme Court in 2013. See Adam Liptak, "Justices Reject Bid to Block Texas Law on Abortions," *New York Times*, November 19, 2013.

15. "A court may not impose punishment in a civil contempt proceeding when it is clearly established that the alleged

contemnor is unable to comply with the terms of the order." Turner *v.* Rogers et al., 564 US—(2011), citing Hicks *v.* Feiock, 485 US 625, 638, n. 9 (1988).

16. Lucas Stanczyk, "Productive Justice," *Philosophy and Public Affairs* 40 (2012): 144–164.

17. It might, for that matter, also be true of medical practice; as one anesthetist recently noted, we might well be hesitant to accepting an anesthetist who is doing his job because of coercion. See G. Keith Smith, "If I Point a Gun at My Doctor, Will He Still Care?," *Association of American Physicians and Surgeons Newsletter*, November 24, 2013.

18. Amartya Sen, *Poverty and Famines: An Essay on Entitlement and Deprivation* (Oxford: Oxford University Press, 1983).

19. It is instructive, I think, that the primary examples Stanczyk uses are those of the townships in South Africa, and of the non-rights-respecting regimes of central Africa. Both of these contexts involve either current injustice, the legacy of injustice, or both. I believe our responses here should be to examine this injustice directly, rather than revising liberalism's self-conception. Stanczyk also discusses the rural United States, and here his arguments may have more force—although, as I will explain, I continue to disagree with his analysis of what we are permitted to do in response to these problems.

20. For a discussion of some of the wrongs of slavery that go beyond mere servitude, see Orlando Patterson, *Slavery and Social Death: A Comparative Study* (Cambridge, MA: Harvard University Press, 1985).

21. See Restatement (Second) of Contracts §367.

22. This conception of moral tragedy was one that emerged from discussions with Patrick Taylor Smith, to whom I am grateful.

23. Rawls, *A Theory of Justice*, 377–382.

24. Michael Clemens, for instance, has argued that even if exit restrictions could effectively raise the Democratic Republic of Congo's real per-capita growth rate to 4 percent—which is a dramatic improvement over the current rate of zero— it would take approximately 250 years before we could

expect the standard of living in the two countries to equalize. While neither Brock nor I focus on standard of living,
it is important to note that the restrictions on mobility she
imagines might—even under the best of circumstances—
be required for a very long time indeed. See Michael
Clemens, "Economics and Emigration: Trillion-Dollar
Bills on the Sidewalk?," *Journal of Economic Perspectives* 25
(2011): 83–106, at 91–92.

9

The Right to Leave and What Remains

IT IS PERHAPS TIME TO take stock. If what I have said in the previous two chapters is correct, there are some potential weaknesses in the arguments in defense of a state's right to restrict exit from its territory. These arguments have generally begun with the demands of global justice and the importance of working against that injustice in our current (deeply unjust) world. What they have tended to ignore, though, is the moral importance of treating people fairly in the task of working against injustice. To presume the right to preclude exit—even temporarily—is to impose a deep burden on people, and to press these burdens against some of the global poor is a deep unfairness. Neither can we ground the right to preclude exit in the past relationships between the would-be emigrant and her society of origin; to be rightful sources of enforceable obligation, the burdens we accept must be accepted under conditions of fairness, and such does not seem to be the case with the relationships we are here considering. However attractive the policy of refusing exit rights might seem, we are therefore unable to ground it in arguments such as these. We have an obligation to work against injustice; we do not thereby have a right to do anything we might think effective in this task.

What this response does not address, though, is whether there is indeed something special about the right to leave—something that makes it an especially important interest that a person might have. If we did not have that interest, we might be less concerned than we are about the inequity involved in preventing people from leaving developing societies. (We could, perhaps, seek to make the burden of supporting and creating just institutions more equitable; we might imagine that *all* persons should be subject to some sort of global duty to work in developing societies.) To deal with these issues, we ought to ask the most basic question of all: why is the right to leave a basic liberal right?

This chapter will attempt to answer this question—and will then seek to show what can, consistent with the right to leave, be done about the brain drain. I therefore have two tasks in what space remains. I will first attempt to give some positive defense of the right to leave, to show that this right is in fact morally significant. The second is to discuss what policy levers and instruments might nonetheless be possible responses to the continuing inequalities exacerbated by the brain drain. Those who defend the right to leave, after all, are not thereby committed to the conclusion that the current world is a just one; we are, instead, committed to the idea that justice constrains both what a just world might look like *and* pathways toward that world we might legitimately choose.

I IN DEFENSE OF THE RIGHT TO LEAVE

Recall that the right to leave contains two distinct elements:

(1) **The right to exit**: Individuals have a moral right to remove their persons from the jurisdiction of the state in which they currently reside.

(2) **The right to renunciation**: Individuals have a moral right, once outside the jurisdiction of a state, to renounce particular obligations of justice toward the inhabitants of that state.

Why, though, should these two rights be thought important? Why should just states act as if people had these two rights? There are, to this question, three broad answers I would like to introduce. I will describe them as the arguments from *practice*, from *interests*, and from the *separateness of persons*; I will present them in this order, from most applied to most theoretical.

i The Argument from Practice

It is one thing to say that, in a particular case, a given act might produce laudable results; it is entirely another to think that the right to do that thing should be generally endorsed, with the associated state apparatus set up to allow acts of that type. Think, in conjunction here, with the act of torture. Many of us would be willing to accept that in certain ticking-bomb hypotheticals the act of torturing would be permissible. (I do not think all of us would; some of us would be absolutists about torture, as many of us are about slavery.) To say this much is emphatically *not* to say that the government should set up the apparatus to allow state torture, to hire efficient torturers, to create an infrastructure of torturing sites, and so on. The reason for this is fairly simple: when one has a hammer, one is tempted to go out looking for nails.

This is Henry Shue's argument against torture, but I believe it applies with equal force to the right to coercively prevent the exit of one's own citizens.[1] It is one thing to say that such preclusion would, in a given case, bring the society closer to justice. It is quite another to say that this right is, in the general case, one justly held by all (or even by all "responsible, but poor") governments. Even if we are confident in the initial case, we are not—and should not be—confident in the results that would follow from acknowledging the right to act in this case. The right to keep one's own citizens from exiting is simply a right that would predictably lead to bad results if announced as a general right under international law. To allow the guns of the border to be turned toward one's own citizens so as to prevent their exit is always bad policy, however benign the circumstances under which the desire to do it emerges.

Support for this might emerge from the circumstances under which the right to exit was first articulated as a norm of international human rights. The right was created, in 1946, as a response to the atrocities of Nazi Germany.[2] The general failure of the global community to adequately respond to the suffering of the European Jewish population gave rise to the modern conception of asylum and refugee laws; it also gave rise to the idea that the citizen could, as a matter of right, remove himself from those circumstances that threatened to destroy him. In both the right of exit and the right of asylum, the same conceptual idea can be used as moral support: we have the right to have rights, and to live in a political society in which that fact is respected.[3] The idea of the right to exit as a right to enter into a new world, one in which one is adequately protected in one's basic moral entitlements, is a settled one in international law, and the right to exit is a necessary part of that moral protection.

It is important to note, in connection with this, that in our post-1946 experience, the countries most likely to engage in systematic human rights abuses have been the ones most hostile to the right to exit. When the UDHR was being drafted, the Soviet Union was enormously hostile to the right to exit, claiming that it was a right that should be a matter for the local jurisdiction; states had the right to condition exit on the needs of those citizens remaining. They therefore abstained during the voting on the UDHR's clauses defending the right to exit.[4] The Soviet Union, of course, was hostile to the right to exit throughout its existence, and was particularly ruthless in its refusal to allow Jewish citizens to emigrate to Israel; the term *refusenik* remains in English largely as a result of the Soviet refusal to allow these citizens to depart. The *refuseniks* were, as a result of their desire to leave, painted as anti-Soviet traitors and subjected to enormous social and political discrimination within Soviet society.[5] East Germany, of course, built the Berlin Wall to prevent emigration. Ostensibly a barrier against undocumented immigration (the Wall's official name was *antifaschistischer Schutzwall*, the "Anti-Fascist Protection Rampart"), the Wall actually served to prevent the emigration of East Germans. This emigration, notably, was painted by the East German hierarchy as a deviation from the duty held by citizens to the East German state. *Republikflucht*, as it was termed, was a crime akin to military desertion, and (in the words of the government) a "betrayal of the GDR's working people."[6] Walter Ulbricht, the primary agent responsible for the building of the Wall, justified the violent coercion of would-be emigrants by arguing that the West was engaging in "systematic recruitment" of needed East German citizens: "West Berlin," he argued, "represents a great hole in the middle of our Republic, costing us more than a billion marks a year."[7] East Germany, in short, insisted that it had a right to expect its citizens to remain where they were and justified the use of sanctions with reference to that right. Similar sanctions are imposed today by Cuba upon those citizens who want to emigrate to the United States; North Korea, of course, treats their would-be emigrants most brutally of all, imprisoning not only them but their entire families, often under circumstances that are tantamount to death sentences.[8]

The point I want to draw here is a general one: *states from which one has to defect are, without exception, bad states.* The states that have sought to forcibly maintain a relationship with their own citizens are states that are either indifferent or hostile to the most basic rights of persons. This fact should, I think, give us pause before thinking that a state right to forcibly prevent exit is something liberal theory should support.

This might seem, of course, rather unfair; Brock's proposal, after all, gives a right only insofar as that right is able to preserve or support just institutions—it is not a general right to suspend the norms articulated in the UDHR. My worry, though, is that the *announcement* that the rights of the UDHR are capable of being suspended does several deeply problematic things. First, it sends the signal to malign states that the right of exit is not, after all, such an important international norm; it provides aid and comfort to those who want to treat their own citizens as a resource pool, rather than as sources of moral claims. Second, and perhaps more worrying, it is not clear that such a right, even if used only by legitimate and decent states, will always be used by them in a legitimate and decent way—nor that such states will always *stay* legitimate and decent. When states start to tip into human rights abuses, or begin to fail the dictates of liberalism, individuals often respond by seeking to exit those states. Bosnia-Herzegovina, for example, is facing a widespread exodus of its most educated citizens, as they tire of the widespread corruption that forms an increasing part of life in that country.[9] If Bosnia-Herzegovina were able to suspend the right to exit, as proposals like Brock's imagine, then can we really suppose they would not want to do so? Indeed, Albert Hirschman has argued that emigration from East Germany was one of the most powerful goads that forced some degree of reform onto the East German leadership. Widespread emigration of skilled Germans led those left behind to begin thinking critically about their government; pressure for reform mounted as skilled emigration rose—precisely the opposite effect to that described in Brock's argument.[10] Most skilled emigration, it seems, is the result of dissatisfaction with where one is, more than envy over where one is not; we flee bad places, rather than simply desire good ones.[11] If places that were starting to become bad, though, are able to simply suspend the right of exit, then they are likely to do so and save themselves the embarrassment of widespread exit. This, though, would seem to have bad consequences for both the would-be emigrants and for the society itself. The consequences for the former are obvious: they will have to remain where they are, in a society falling into corruption and illiberalism. The consequences for society, though, are worth noting as well: a society that faces the widespread exit of its most talented citizens is a society that is, at the very least, facing a standing pressure for reform. A society that can force those citizens to remain is a society that has no such pressure. Instead of earning the allegiance and energy of its citizens, it can simply claim them at the point of a gun.

I do not want to overstate my claim here; I imagine that it is *possible*—though unlikely—that a state could develop a program such as Brock defends, and use it for only the purposes Brock allows. I do think, though, that our experience suggests that it is vastly more likely that such a state will preclude exit more often, and for worse reasons, than justice would ever allow. I also believe, quite strongly, that to announce such permission would weaken a norm of international human rights law that is worth preserving. Taken together, I think these practical concerns—however mundane from the standpoint of liberal theory—are sufficient to make any proposal like Brock's worthy of rejection.

ii The Argument from Interests

Being precluded from leaving involves an interference with the forming of new relationships. That much is obvious; the one who is prevented from moving to the United States is thereby prevented from forming new personal, professional, and political relationships with and in the United States. She is also made to continue relationships—again, personal, professional, and political—against her will. I believe these are significant facts, and that they stand in the way of any right to suspend or condition exit from political society. There are two particular aspects of these ideas I want to discuss here, each of which rests upon the value of these *chosen* relationships. Violations of the right to leave involve, first, interference with voluntary acquisition of new forms of relationship, and second, the continued maintenance of an unwanted form of political relationship. I will discuss these in turn.

The first idea begins with a simple notion: when one moves to a new place, one forms new relationships. These relationships are social, of course, but also political. There is value to such relationships; our lives are given value, from the inside, from the things we build together with consenting other people. When one proposes to do a thing with some consenting other set of people, the state has to be very careful before it thinks it has the right to use force to prevent that thing from happening. It does not, of course, have no right to get involved; people's right to build things with others is not unlimited. But to say that we are unable to freely associate with others, in terms that are acceptable to both sides, is a significant cost. Christopher Heath Wellman uses ideas such as these to ground a general right to exclude unwanted would-be immigrants; those to whose presence we do not consent have no right to entry into our territory, simply in virtue of our lack of consent to their social presence.[12] I do not think these ideas are entirely right as the basis of the right to exclude; I want to focus on political association, rather than on social relationships. The basis of Wellman's view, though, seems correct to me; there is value in what is done with the consent of all parties, and we should be hesitant indeed before interfering with this process by which value is created.

I think we understand this quite well when it comes to intimate relationships. If a state were to prevent a person from marrying a consenting other person, we would rightly be outraged. Interference with the right to marry might be justifiable were the world to take a particular consequential shape, but the burden should be on the state to explain its decision. The same is true with the decision to form a new political relationship with some other state. The bond is not intimate, perhaps, as it is with marriage—although the political relationship is perhaps just as pervasive as that of marriage. The political bond is part of what creates the identity of the person, just as the bond of marriage does; naturalized citizens generally experience the process of naturalization as an emotionally significant event. To prevent this process from occurring—to insist that a person cannot leave what is unchosen in the name of what is chosen—is to rob some value from the world, for the person who desires to leave. To put this in the most abstract and bland terms: the state should not regard itself as licensed to interfere in the creation of new sources of value by interfering with the freedom to form consensual forms of relationship with others.

One response to this, of course, is to say that the state does this all the time, and does so in the name of justice; the state prevents racists from forming racist terror cells, prevents the Jaycees from meeting in single-sex groups, and so on.[13] The difficulty, of course, is in taking these examples as giving us a general right to prevent voluntary association. These cases seek to balance the right to association with the right of society to create justice for its residents. As mentioned, the decision to exit is not quite the same as a decision made within a particular society. Even if we can stop Americans from using their freedoms to undermine the freedom of Americans, we cannot think that we have thereby acquired the freedom to stop Americans from leaving America. The latter decision is, significantly, one that ends with the absence of any political relationship between the person and those who are still resident within America. The limited freedom of the government to preclude the associative freedom of Americans, in other words, should not be taken as a blanket permission to prevent new forms of association; the right of any American to leave cannot be so easily defeated. More to the point though, even if we are willing to prevent these sorts of association from existing, we ought to be aware that we are even here interfering with freedom; we ought to be very careful before we trample on such freedoms in the name of liberalism. All I want to establish here is that the freedom to exit is important in precisely the same manner as other freedoms, in that it represents a vehicle by which value might be brought into the world. From the fact that this freedom might sometimes be overridden, we should not infer that it no longer exists—nor, I believe, that it is generally capable of being overridden in the case of the right to exit.

The final moral notion I want to discuss, though, is the inverse of this idea: it is the idea that we should not, in general, be forced to remain within a relationship by a party to that relationship. If there is a way in which I can cease to be a party to that relationship, then the other party to that relationship commits a *pro tanto wrong* by coercing me into remaining. Nothing I say here prevents states from regulating, for example, the terms on which a marriage ends. In entering into a marriage, I have—explicitly or implicitly—accepted certain contractual (and statutory) terms, which preclude my exercise of my freedom to leave. I have waived my right to exit, simply in virtue of my free choice to enter into a particular form of voluntary relationship. The state, though, is not such a relationship—or, rather, it is not always such; most people are resident in a state in which they were born and accordingly had very little say in the matter of their citizenship. For such a state to prevent them from exiting is for that state to maintain a particular relationship against the wishes of one party to the relationship. This is, I believe, morally wrong; it may sometimes, as with the right to form new relationships, be overridden, but the showing of why it may be overridden *here* must be made. We are, in general, hostile toward the idea that persons may be made to play roles, or perform jobs, that they would not in general choose to do. Most states, for example, are very hesitant to award specific performance as a remedy for contractual breach; the United States, as discussed in the previous chapters, grounds this antipathy toward specific performance in the anti-slavery provisions of the Constitution. In other words, we are hostile toward the idea that one part of a relationship may coercively ensure that it continue, when the other party is willing and—apart from that coercion—able to abandon it.

I want to be fairly careful here; I do not think that there is an absolute right to leave a state, if by that we mean a duty on the part of other states to allow us to enter. Some thinkers—notably Phillip Cole and Lea Ypi—have argued that we have no reason to value the right to exit, when we do not have an equivalent right to enter some other state.[14] Those who are forced to remain in a particular place because that place will not let them leave, under this argument, are in no different situation than those who cannot depart because no other state will let them enter. Cole intends for this argument to ground a right to enter, but we might reverse its intention: why should we not abandon the right to exit, since that right is useless in a world without a right to enter?

The argument against this is simple: rights are not reducible to the states of affairs they make possible. We are, in general, concerned not just with what a particular state of affairs brings about but also with the relationship between the parties in question. Think, in connection with this, of the death of Hermann Goering. Goering was supplied with a cyanide capsule by Private Herbert Stivers, who believed it was needed medicine. Goering committed suicide on the night before he was to have been hanged. Stivers later expressed profound regret at his role in helping Goering "cheat the hangman."[15] If we are concerned only with the results of actions, Stivers's regret is mysterious; whether he acted or not, the result would have been the same—a dead Hermann Goering. Stivers's regret, though, is entirely comprehensible. The Allies wanted Goering dead, true, but they wanted to be the ones to *kill* him; Goering's decision to act as his own executioner placed an illegitimate agent (himself) in charge of the process of death. What is of interest in a right's validity, then, might be not simply the results that it brings about but the relationship between the parties to that right. Goering was not the right agent to bring about his own death; his act in killing Goering was different in kind from the Allies' act in killing Goering. So it is with emigration. A liberal state cannot rightly act to prevent an agent from leaving; it is not the right agent to bring about the result in which that agent remains *in situ*. That state's act is different in kind from the act of another state that refuses to allow the would-be emigrant from acquiring a new status within that latter society.

The acts are different in the same way that my decision not to let you *into* my house differs from my decision not to let you *leave* my house. The former is, generally, a valid use of my discretion; the latter is, generally, a felony.

It is one thing, then, for me to be denied the right to leave because no other state will have me—and quite another for me to be denied the right to leave because my own state wants to continue its relationship with me. The simple idea here is that we may not reduce the right to its results. If I am prevented from marrying Melissa because she finds me repulsive, the result is similar to that produced when I cannot marry Melissa because the state prevents my marriage. The latter, though, rightly strikes us as morally much more problematic than the former. So too, I think, with a state's decision to maintain a political relationship with me against my wishes. Even if the net result of its action is unexceptional—I cannot leave—it is not the right sort of agent to produce this right. Agents should not, in general, be allowed to perpetuate a relationship with those able and willing to leave. The interests of the person in developing their own forms of life are too central to liberal thought for this state right to be permitted.

iii The Argument from the Separateness of Persons

The final argument I want to consider here is the most theoretical, and it begins with a very basic question of liberal political philosophy: what is it that justifies a state in having, and exercising, a particular sort of coercive power? Different theorists, of course, have had different answers to this question. Utilitarian thought, for example, regards it as a sufficient justification for the use of coercion that it maximize social benefit. Utilitarians would therefore feel unashamed, in justifying coercion of a given individual, about citing greater benefits to others. Imagine an impoverished citizen, who asks of a utilitarian society: why am I so poor, relative to the other members of society? In that society, it is a sufficient reply for us to say: you are poor, because the rest of us benefit from your poverty. The overall consequences for *us* are so good, that it is justifiable for *you* to be poor.

Rawls's work began with the rejection of this methodology.[16] (Indeed, I think it would be fair to say that much of Rawls's early work consists in the attempt to come up with a better reply to that impoverished citizen.) What was wrong with this methodology was that it required the individual to identify with the others in his society so strongly that he did not regard his own welfare, his own self-development or moral personality, as a distinct category of reasons. Rawls's criticism of utilitarianism thus amounted to the claim that it could not adequately respect the *separateness of persons*. The idea here is that justification of a particular sort of coercive policy would have to be made to the person, considered as an individual, with a certain sort of veto power over being used as a mere means for other citizens' benefit. What this veto required, of course, was enormously complex; Rawls's own work identifies a particular sort of choice situation, from within which people are able to decide fairly which rights and principles of distribution shall be used to evaluate society. Inequality, most centrally, must be justified as being in the interests of the one against whom that inequality is pressed. We need not be concerned directly with the specifics at present. What we should note, though, is that Rawls insisted—rightly, in my view—that some such veto would be required. People cannot be coerced simply because their being so coerced would be *useful*. This is true even if the coercion would effectively lead to results we would all have reason to value; people have the right not to be so used, even in the name of what is rightly regarded as morally valuable.

How does all this relate to emigration? The answer to this question, I think, begins by looking at the different sorts of justification offered to the impoverished for Rawls, and for the utilitarian. The utilitarian says, "You are (relatively) poor, because it is useful to all of us for you to be so." The Rawlsian says, "You are (relatively) poor, because *you* have reason to accept this world in which you are poor." Rawls's difference principle entails this result; we are able to say to the worst off that she has a reason to accept, as an individual, a world in which she is worst off. Were the gap between her and the wealthier individuals of her society to be lessened, she herself would be made more poor. The details here need not concern us; the key is that the justification is made to the individual herself, conceived of as a creature with her own motivations, her own interests, and a non-infinite capacity for altruism. The Rawlsian justification demands that we do not coerce the individual except when we can, in some specific way, say, "We do this for *your* benefit, and not simply that of others."[17]

What, then, can the Rawlsian say to the would-be emigrant? Imagine that someone is crossing from Ghana into the United Kingdom. Assume, for the moment, that both the United Kingdom and Ghana are rights-protecting states, capable of imposing moral duties. Assume, further, that Ghana would like the power to coercively prevent the exit of its citizens. Based upon what can it justify this power to those over whom it is exercised? I cannot see any way in which it can do so.[18] The emigrant is, by definition, going to have her rights adequately protected within the United Kingdom; none of her rights are at stake here. The *only* thing that can be said to her is some variant on the theme of "You are *useful*, for others, and we will coerce you so as to extract this benefit." If Rawls is right, though, this is precisely what a liberal state cannot say. The liberal state is precluded from regarding its own citizens as a resource for others in this way. Justification, if it is pressed against a particular individual, must be made with reference *to* that individual, to her rights and to her interests—and our would-be emigrant, who would have her rights adequately protected in the United Kingdom, can only be coercively prevented from leaving for the United Kingdom if she is viewed as a resource, rather than as a person.[19]

I believe full development of this line of argumentation might require some more Rawlsian analysis than we can in the present context entertain. We might ask, for instance, why the wealthy within society can be coerced to pay taxes, while the wealthy who want to leave society cannot be coerced into staying. I believe there are answers to such criticisms: the wealthy who live in society, after all, have their properties and persons protected by the coercive institutions of that society, while the most that can be said about the would-be emigrant is that she *once received* such protection from that society; the cases seem relevantly distinct. I believe, though, that the general frame of the argument is enough: we ought to reject the right to prevent exit, since any justification of that supposed right would seem to violate the moral constraints Rawls identified. This is, I think, why Rawls himself, when he discusses the right to exit, assumes that such a right is obvious, and discusses only whether liberal states must *assist* their would-be emigrants in leaving—a complication I gladly leave aside here.[20]

All the above, of course, only goes some way toward establishing the moral centrality of the right to leave. I believe that these ideas may, with some degree of refinement, ground a human right to leave of the same strength as the international human right to leave one's own country. The moral right, in other words, is powerful and central; even if it may be overcome in some circumstances, it is in general a standing right worthy of our respect. This right, further, should in general be respected by states, even if there might emerge cases in which the state could produce good results by ignoring the right. To violate this right would require the creation of institutions that would eventually produce bad results likely to outweigh the momentary good we have desired. And, finally, even if all these considerations were to be ignored, we would have to face up to the fact that to refuse the right to exit would be to impose a disproportionate cost on those who seek to exit—that is, it would be to treat the residents of developing societies unfairly in the shared task of responding to injustice. These considerations, put together, would seem to me to represent a fairly significant bar in the face of any proposal to coercively restrict exit from developing societies.

Even after this, though, we still have a problem. The problem is that nothing Brock has said about the problems of the brain drain is false; she is entirely right to say that the brain drain sometimes exacerbates the difficulties of development and represents a way in which the impoverished countries are brought further away from what justice would insist they deserve. What, then, should be our response? What can be done about the brain drain, if we are no longer able to simply coercively stop it from happening? The final section of this chapter will survey some possible responses to these questions. My conclusions, I am afraid, are not very hopeful. There are some things that can be justly done in response to the brain drain, but these responses will not adequately address the problem. In the end, I will suggest that the brain drain represents a sort of moral tragedy; we have a truly unjust world, and there are no solutions that are simultaneously effective and just.

II RESPONDING TO THE BRAIN DRAIN

In classifying responses to the brain drain, it is perhaps helpful to consider the agent charged with making that response. We might think that at least three agents could be charged with the response. First, the developing society—the country of emigration—might want to work against the brain drain. Second, we might want to consider actions that could be taken by the developed society—the country that receives migrants. Finally, we might consider responses that could be taken by the world community as a whole. I will consider these possibilities in turn.

i What Can the Developing World Do?

If what has gone before is correct, the states of the developing world are morally precluded from preventing the exit of their own citizens. The state cannot seek to prevent an individual leaving the state any more than it may seek to prevent apostasy from a particular religion. The action of the state, in prohibiting the would-be emigrant from leaving, is morally equal to preventing a useful tourist from departing; the cases of kidnapped tourist and prevented emigrant are equally morally prohibited. What is true of simple coercion, I think, is true whether that coercion is for a day or for a year: the state cannot rightly prevent those within its jurisdiction from leaving.

This fact will, I think, place a significant constraint on what developing societies can do. However useful it might be to prevent someone from exiting our society, we are morally unable to do so while regarding ourselves as *liberal*. In what follows, I want to discuss four ways in which a society might work against the pernicious effects of the brain drain, while still accepting this result. The first is the most powerful and involves the declaration that the present world is in an emergency situation—one in which liberalism's demands must be suspended. The final three are ways in which a state, even if precluded from preventing exit, might work against the effects of the brain drain.

A ETHICAL EMERGENCIES
It is always possible, of course, for a state to say it would, under some emergency circumstances, prevent a useful tourist from departing. This would be done in full

knowledge that it is *unfair* to that tourist—she is made to pay a disproportionate share of the burdens of compliance. The state does this even though that tourist has the right, under liberalism, to depart. The state, however, faces a true emergency circumstance and had the right to suspend liberal rights in the face of such an emergency. The equation between the kidnapped tourist and prevented emigrant, then, could be made to serve a different purpose; a state might be willing to say that, in face of an ongoing catastrophic emergency, the right to leave generally might be suspended. If it were willing to say this, it might be true that the state would be, at the very least, less guilty of treating its own human capital as its property in an objectionable way. The state here is willing to suspend the right to leave generally and is able to cite the ongoing emergency as a reason to do so.

If there is a case in which such action is plausible, I suspect it is the current situation in Africa as regards medical personnel. I do not want to say the case is, in fact, one in which such an emergency declaration is appropriate; as I discuss below, there is much that would have to be established before that declaration can be rightly made. But, as Brock has detailed, the case is dire; medical personnel are leaving some African societies more quickly than they can be trained—and those people, once trained, will tend to leave for developed societies as well. Can we not, then, simply declare that this set of circumstances is a true emergency, and that the liberal rights I have defended simply fail to apply during such circumstances?

I think we might be able to do this—*if* certain things hold true about the circumstances in which we make the declaration. An emergency, after all, is not a moral blank check. Building on our earlier discussion of conscription, let us say that an emergency suspension of liberty would only potentially be justifiable when four facts hold true. First, we would have to face an emergency of sufficient gravity that we could justify the wrong we propose to do. Second, we would have to show that the rights violation we propose to do is likely to lead, within some reasonable period of time, to a significantly better world—one in which, most centrally, the rights of persons are significantly better protected than they currently are. Third, we would have to be able to ensure that there is no other pathway toward a just world. These three tests, of course, echo the earlier discussion of conscription. I want, though, to emphasize now something that I did not emphasize there. Fourth—and finally—we would have to be able to somehow later compensate those we wrong for the evil we have made them experience. It is one thing to do what one has no right to do, and quite another thing to do so without any compensation after the fact.[21]

These points, of course, are collectively rather demanding; indeed, I am not sure that any of the latter three tests can be met. For reasons I have discussed, I am not sure that the program will work, nor that competing programs will work more poorly, nor that we will ever be in a position to adequately compensate the kidnapped tourist or the prevented emigrant for what we have done to them. The declaration of emergency, in short, is not always an easy way out of the demands of morality.

So, if the developing state is unable to use coercive force and cite the emergency circumstances under which it is operating, what is it able to do? There are at least three possible levers by which the state might be able to work against the worst effects of the brain drain: it might seek a program of worldwide taxation on emigrants; it might employ conditional repayment schemes for education, which are conditioned on continued residence; or it might engage in some renovation of medical practice. I will consider these in turn. I believe all of them are, under some circumstances, permissible; none of them, however, is without some significant drawbacks.

B WORLDWIDE TAXATION OF EMIGRANTS

Taxation of an emigrant's worldwide income is a long-standing idea, and has a lengthy history within development economics. The Bhagwati tax is grounded in the idea that the emigrant, while resident abroad, owes some financial duty to her compatriots back home; it insists that the state from which the emigrant comes may rightly tax the income she makes abroad.[22] Whether or not such taxation programs are likely to produce good results is questionable; we have need not only to ask where money is taken from, but also where money is likely to go. We also need to ask whether such taxation, since it depresses the wage differential between the society of origin and the foreign society, might not reduce the demand for educational training in the country of origin. Assume, however, that all these worries have been eliminated and the state is able to acquire through global taxation some pot of money it is likely to use well. Is the program of global taxation morally legitimate?

I believe whether it is or is not depends entirely upon what relationship that emigrant has toward her society of origin. An emigrant, after all, has two rights: the right to remove herself from the physical jurisdiction of her society

of origin and the right to renounce any ties to that jurisdiction. If an emigrant has exercised both of those rights,
then I believe it is illegitimate for that society to insist
upon any continued specific relationship with that emigrant. To say otherwise would be to insist upon something
entirely too much like the "permanent allegiance" of a previous century; political allegiance, for liberalism, depends
upon actual engagement with particular political institutions, and this emigrant no longer engages in any way with
her society of origin. There is, for reasons discussed in this
and previous chapters, no right on the part of a state to
exercise coercive authority over one who is no longer resident or citizen of that state. The justification of coercion
must make reference to facts involving the protections of
the rights of that individual; these facts are, in the present
case, no longer true.

A more interesting case, though, is more common.
What if the individual in question wants to maintain her
citizenship, and hence a right to return to her country
of origin? I believe, under these circumstances, that the
worldwide taxation of income is not inappropriate; the
taxation in question can be conceived of as something
like a voluntary transaction—here, the right to return to
the jurisdiction is conditioned on the maintenance and
support for that jurisdiction's political infrastructure. If
I can renounce my Canadian citizenship, I can become—
as far as Canada is concerned—simply one more foreign
citizen, with no particular claim to entry or settlement
within Canada. If I choose to do this, then Canada would
have no right to regard me as under a particular obligation to support Canadian political society. If I choose not
to do this, though, I am taking advantage of a particular

obligation upon the part of other Canadians—namely, the obligation to let me into their political society and to protect my rights once I am within that society—that they do not have toward persons generally. The continued holding of Canadian citizenship abroad, in short, is not a benefit in the past; it is, rather, the provision of a benefit in the present, and as such it might be justly made the subject of collective decision-making by the Canadian polity. I have the right to exit, and the right to renounce my Canadian citizenship; if I do the former but not the latter, then my fellow Canadians may rightly insist that they should be compensated for the continued benefit they provide me.

I think, therefore, that any question about the moral justifiability of proposals of worldwide taxation is one that awaits the specific details of those proposals. I am talking about moral justification, not wisdom. It is, after all, potentially counterproductive to give high-skilled persons incentives to renounce their citizenships. If Kapur and McHale are right about the powerful effects of return migration, we might hesitate before making such round-trip migration less likely. At the very least, though, we can say that some such proposals are not in themselves unjust.

C CONTRACTUAL OBLIGATIONS TO REMAIN

An alternative proposal—and one that is frequently employed within societies, both developing and developed—is to make educational provision contingent upon the signing of a contract. Such a contract might specify an enforceable obligation to remain within a particular jurisdiction for some particular length of time. I should note, to begin with, that Brock is quite right about the numerous variants of this proposal, some of which appear only to be non-coercive or, at the very most, coercive ways of regulating domestic medical practice.[23] Some of this, in my analysis, is morally permissible; a just state, or at the very least a "responsible, but poor" one, has some (limited) freedom to decide how medicine shall be done within the borders of that state.[24] I am here focusing only on a separate issue: can the state use its coercive machinery to prevent someone from exiting that state, and cite a contractual basis for this coercion? Could developing societies not take greater advantage of this methodology and use contracts to constrain the exit rights of those they educate?

The answer, I think, is a very qualified yes. It is obviously permissible to bargain away our rights; we can accept an obligation to avoid exercising any particular right, and under the right circumstances such an obligation is morally binding. The difficulty, of course, comes about in the problematic phrase "the right circumstances." Not all things that have the shape of contracts actually succeed in creating moral obligation. If the circumstances in which an individual makes her contract are morally impermissible, the contract that emerges may not be morally enforceable.

Think, in this context, of the case of Jesse Dimmick. Dimmick, fleeing from the police, took a newlywed couple hostage, threatening them with a knife. He made them promise not to give him up to the police; they gave him their word that they would not contact the police. When they breached that promise and contacted the police once he fell asleep, he sued them for breach of contract.[25] His lawsuit failed, of course, because one who makes a contract under duress of that sort is not held to the consequences of making a contract under conditions of freedom.[26] You cannot be held to have agreed, from within a morally illegitimate set of circumstances, to remain within those circumstances. Someone who agrees to stay in a society that is not rights protecting, though, is making a contract to do just that; they are agreeing, from within a society in which their rights are not protected, to remain within that society. Can they, in fact, be held to have fairly bargained away their rights to leave? I fail to see how. Just like the newlyweds in Dimmick's case, the one who agrees to stay in a society in which she is subject to illegitimate forms of violence and poverty is making that agreement against a backdrop of a lack of freedom; she is facing duress, in that the other party to the agreement is essentially saying that she must agree to remain within that society in order for her to be provided with a particular benefit.[27] That she makes the agreement and takes the benefit does not make that other party rightful in insisting upon compliance.[28]

What this means, in practice, is that not every state that might want to make use of conditional repayment schemes is legitimately able to do so. There would seem to be some minimal level of state adequacy that is required for the state to legitimately enforce a contract to remain. A state that permits—or causes—widespread human rights abuses is not one that is able to legitimately enforce such contracts. I suspect this means that some of the places most in need of physician services will not be able to use this methodology to acquire them. This does, however, not seem to be entirely unreasonable; we are—and should be—more deferential to the coercive authority of a democracy than to a tyranny. I cannot here describe which societies would have which permission with any degree of certainty, but I believe that Ghana's proposals stand some chance of being permissible; those that come out of Sudan are likely less morally defensible.[29] These specific conclusions, though, await a great deal more work on both the nature of human rights and the specifics of rights-protection within these two societies.

D RETHINKING MEDICAL PRACTICE

There are, I think, many things that developing states can do to make it less likely that those with scarce medical skills will be able and willing to leave that society. We can divide these into two categories; the first deals with making medical practice at home more attractive and the second with making medical practice abroad less available. We can deal with these in turn.

Developing states might, to begin with, improve the conditions under which people labor in the country of emigration. As I have said, people who leave more often flee bad professional conditions, in which violence and corruption are rife, than simply seek higher wages. It is open to a state, then, to remove these push factors. This is, of course, a bit too easy for me to say; the actual causes of corruption and violence in developing societies are complex, and responding to these has proven enormously difficult. It is, moreover, somewhat akin to blaming the victim, when we insist that a developing state should clean up its own house first. All this is true. Nevertheless, it is open to a developing society to make things marginally better for the talented and well trained by working steadily to make professional life less unpleasant for those who remain. To say that this is impossible is rather patronizing—as patronizing, perhaps, as saying that a developing society could easily respond to the issues of corruption and violence but is choosing not to. States are able to reduce push factors but not eliminate them; in our world, there will likely be any number of reasons why people emigrate, not all of them within the control of any state. Improving working conditions, then, is incrementalism and tinkering at the edges of an unjust world. It is not, however, without value or impossible; there may be reason to value such small changes, when the larger ones we might try are either impermissible or ineffective.

More controversially, we might try to make it more difficult for medical practitioners educated at home to use their skills abroad. There are at least two proposals here worth discussing: Nir Eyal and Samia Hurst have proposed that developing societies can focus their training upon those skills that are most likely to be of direct use only within developing societies—upon, that is, the diseases of the inhabitants within developing societies. This seems entirely within the moral rights of the society in question; Eyal and Hurst conceive of this as a coercive restriction of the liberty of the medical student, but I believe it is best understood as a different sort of offer.[30] If the state in question is under no obligation to provide medical training to any individual in the first place, is it actually coercive for the training that is offered to be of most use within the domestic context? The state is, after all, under no particular duty to enable its citizens to be maximally attractive to foreigners. While an insufficiently rights-protecting state is unable to bind its citizens by morally obligatory contracts, I do not think it follows that it cannot alter its medical curriculum so as to maximally benefit the local population. A related proposal, from Staffan Bergström, would work for the training of non-physician surgeons, or *técnicos de cirurgia*; given that not all medical problems require physician intervention, increased outlays on non-physician medical personnel would seem to be of benefit to health-care in developing societies.[31]

All these ideas, of course, amount to meliorist tinker-ing at the edges. What else, consistent with justice, can be done? One answer is to shift the burden from the devel-oping world to the developed world. What can those of us who live in wealthy societies do in response to the brain drain?

ii What Can the Developed World Do?

The developed world represents a set of people who ben-efit from the brain drain; those of us resident in wealthy societies have greater access to medical treatment than those resident in developing societies, and we have that access in large part because of immigration. What should the response of wealthy states to these facts be? The first—and most obvious—response is to exclude highly talented people from our own societies.[32] This is politically unpalat-able to most parties except for the furthest right wing, but it would at the very least stop some of the worst injustices of the brain drain. Or so we might think.

I think there are at least three grave difficulties with this proposal. The first is that the right to exclude is lim-ited at best. There are some individuals who have the right to enter into our society, and they may include some of the people considered under the heading of the brain drain. Many of us, after all, believe that there are rights to be admitted into a functioning liberal democratic state that are held by those suffering under a non-representative regime, and a state that interfered with that right in the name of global justice would be a perverse one indeed. The second is that this exclusion might produce underemployment and undocumented migration rather than increased foreign skills acquisition. When people want to depart and are prevented from doing so, they may sometimes choose to leave and work in the informal economy—wasting, in most cases, their skills—rather than deploy those skills in their own societies. The final worry, of course, is that this program is objectionably paternalistic. It involves a wealthy society saying to a would-be immigrant: stay where you are, for the sake of social justice. I have emphasized that such a response cannot be used by a state to preserve a relationship with its own citizens, against the wishes of those citizens. There is, however, something equally disturbing—something that presupposes more wisdom about poverty than anyone, let alone someone in a wealthy society, has—about a wealthy society saying it to the foreign poor.

So, simple exclusion is probably not a good response to the issue. What about ethical recruitment? This tool is, I think, perhaps one of the most promising ones with which to respond to the issue of the brain drain. It reflects the idea that simply because we believe a transaction is morally legitimate, we are not thereby committed to making as many instances of that transaction occur as possible. We may regulate the ways in which offers are made to "nudge"—to use Cass Sunstein's memorable term—consumers into making good choices.[33] So, perhaps, with medical recruitment. Even if those who want to leave Africa have the right to do so, we might justly regulate recruiters from wealthy societies, so as to "nudge" those who are wavering in their decision-making into choosing to use their talents at home. Recruiters who wade into African teaching hospitals, making elaborate promises about wealth and living conditions abroad, might be justly prevented from doing so; this sort of restriction is no more objectionable, I think, than other forms of restriction on advertising. Indeed, a group of physicians recently wrote an article for *The Lancet* proposing that the active recruitment of physicians from Africa should be treated as a crime under international law.[34] While I do not here take a position on their proposal, I would note that they focus on restrictions on *recruitment*, rather than on mobility; the proposal explicitly recognizes that health workers have a moral and political right to emigrate. These restrictions on recruitment, moreover, look equally valid when undertaken by wealthy societies as when undertaken by developing societies. In either case, the freedom to leave is not negated; all that is affected is the freedom of others to engage in commercial speech about the benefits of departure. We have to tread lightly here, of course; individuals have the right to leave their own societies, and we cannot justly prohibit other individuals from welcoming them into new lives in new places. What we can do is something much like what we already do in the regulation of cigarette advertising: we cannot—and should not—prevent the activity of smoking, but we can make it more difficult for those who profit from smoking to make the practice of smoking seem attractive. So, perhaps, with recruitment: we cannot—and should not—stop individuals from emigrating, but we might at least place some limits on what sorts of promises and imagery can be employed to induce emigration.

What about directly dealing with the injustice between societies? If Ghana has so few nurses and the United States so many, why should we not directly engage in transfer payments from the United States to Ghana? We could imagine at least two forms of such payments: financial and in kind. On the former, perhaps it is time to engage in some financial instrument designed to repay Ghana and similar states for their medical investment. The issue here is not immediately ethical, but empirical. There is nothing wrong, I think, with a nation deciding—in the name of justice— to fund another society, to repay that latter society for its contributions. The only difficulty that emerges is what the likely result of that program would be. The proposal would raise the price of hiring foreign-trained workers, with the result that fewer of them would be hired; this might be considered a net positive, since we are trying to improve medical practice abroad, but we cannot assume that all those not hired abroad would be hired at home. The world is not quite that simple. Again, those who are refused legal admission may sometimes choose undocumented migration, with the result that brain waste may be the result of our well-meaning policy. Simple financial transfers, then, are potentially useful but not necessarily effective. Similar things may be said about in-kind transfers, in which medical schools in the developed world partner with those in the developing world to create knowledge transfers and training opportunities that are able to build up infrastructure within the developing society. Done well, this is likely to be of use to those developing societies. Although the programs will not solve all issues of the brain drain, they will perhaps make it more likely that highly skilled individuals will choose to remain within their own societies. The worry, of course, is whether or not we are able to do this well. Done poorly, the programs can amount to mere medical tourism—a brief, self-serving vacation for the medical elite from developed societies; this sort of tourism can be worse than nothing, as medical institutions are turned from promising development pathways toward those that are most appealing to visiting wealthy physicians. As with financial transfers, the net results of such programs will depend upon avoiding such untoward results.

The most important thing that can be done, though, is something that can be done solely as a matter of domestic politics: the developed countries of the world can stop underinvesting in their own medical and nursing educational capacity. This is the heart of the draft WHO Code on Ethical Recruitment: the developed states of the world are called upon to avoid relying upon the developing world as a source of cheap education.[35] The problem of the brain drain has emerged not simply because there are many countries in the world that people want to leave, and others they want to get to; it has emerged because the rich countries of the world have effectively outsourced much of the obligation to train medical personnel to developing countries, and have avoided investing in the expensive job of medical training. The single most important thing that the developed world can do here is, as a matter of ethics, uncontroversial: stop relying upon others to do the job of training the nurses and doctors of the future.

The conclusions to be drawn here, as above, are largely negative. There are means by which developing societies can bring themselves closer to justice—but there are no easy pathways, and no final victories. The most they can do is develop incremental and partial solutions, and even there the most powerful levers may be morally impermissible. It is time for us to think that the problem of the brain drain is not itself a problem, if by that term we mean something with its own solution; it is instead an epiphenomenon of global injustice generally, and we have an obligation to solve the problem of global justice before we can consider the problem of the brain drain. We can, therefore, turn to this perspective, and see what we can— as a global community—do to make the brain drain less problematic.

iii What Can We Do Together?

The brain drain emerges from, and exacerbates, global distributive injustice. Those fleeing objectionable circumstances are fleeing horrors that are fostered, in part, by global resource practices set up to benefit the world's wealthiest societies. Our focus, then, might be not upon the brain drain itself but upon the circumstances which have created it. We ought to avoid thinking that the brain drain is a problem that can be solved; instead, it is one facet of a broader problem—that of global economic injustice. Once this latter problem is solved, the problem of the brain drain may itself fade away—or, at any rate, would become no more problematic than the movement of persons within and between developed societies.[36]

I believe something like this is probably the right approach to the brain drain. It emerges as a problem under spectacularly unjust circumstances, in which global inequality is rife, and in which global institutions have failed to develop adequate responses to these inequalities. If we were to fix these inequalities, we would be able to avoid the particular inequalities that emerge from the brain drain. More importantly, though, I believe that dealing with the brain drain *without* addressing these more central forms of inequality is likely to prove futile. To force those resident in developing societies to bear the costs of development is likely to be unfair, illiberal, ineffective, or all three; we should, instead, seek to make the world in which people migrate more just.

This is right, but it is also deeply unsatisfying. The reason it is unsatisfying is that it tells us, essentially, to wait for a just world before dealing with the inequalities in human capital detailed in Chapter 1. Doing this, though, will mean ignoring those inequalities for the foreseeable future. We are unlikely to have any easy road between our own world and a just world. There are some things we can avoid doing, perhaps, in our search for justice.[37] There are, moreover, some things we could start doing that would make our world less objectionably unjust.[38] But we do not have any particularly great stock of knowledge about how to make impoverished societies wealthy. The interventions that we will have to use to undermine global injustice necessarily involve trial and error, and we are likely going to make enormous errors along the way.[39] We are, then, facing a long pathway, and we do not have clarity in how to move forward.

This approach to the brain drain, then, is likely to leave us somewhat in the dark. We want to eliminate this injustice, but we find we cannot do so until injustice itself is eliminated. This, in turn, is something we will find enormously difficult, if not impossible, to do. I believe, though, that this is precisely what we are facing. While there are some things we could do to make the world more just— we might, perhaps, adopt some version of Thomas Pogge's principles for recognitional legitimacy, on which we do not allow malign states to trade in resources and borrow in the name of their inhabitants—there is a vast panorama of ignorance behind these few bits of moral knowledge.[40]

We must move forward, and we must do so while focusing on global justice generally, and we must do that while being aware of our profound ignorance. What, then, can we say about the brain drain? In the end, I believe that the brain drain is an example of what might be rightly called a morally tragic result. There can be occasions on which we face significant injustice, and yet we cannot move away from that injustice without deploying means that are themselves unjust. I believe John Rawls's analysis of the family takes this shape: while the family exists, we are unable to achieve equality of opportunity. We cannot, however, eliminate the family, since to do that would be to violate basic moral rights—as well as, of course, create a world that is likely worse than even a fairly inegalitarian world of families. We are stuck, as it were, in a world in which we cannot escape from an unjust result through just means.

Much the same is true, I think, for the brain drain. Proper responses to that phenomenon would require that we work—all of us, together—to build a more just global economy. But we cannot work, in our own inegalitarian world, directly against the brain drain. We cannot—if I am right—effectively and justly respond to the phenomenon by coercion against would-be emigrants. Nor do we have access to any other means by which the problems exacerbated by the brain drain might be easily and finally eliminated. The most we can do is tinker at the edges of the phenomenon, by making the world less unjust tomorrow than it is today. The brain drain is unlike the family, of course, in that a just world would probably have families,

while that world would—we hope—have fewer of the negative results gathered under the heading of the brain drain.
The two cases are alike, though, in that both represent
cases in which human freedom makes the direct pursuit
of justice more difficult. We cannot—and should not—
directly eliminate the family; we cannot—and should
not—directly work to prevent voluntary emigration. This
fact will leave a great deal of emigration unchecked, and
the result will be that an unjust world will have a standing
pressure toward more injustice. We cannot work against
this injustice through justified means; we are in a world
that is not simply unjust, but tragic.

All of this, moreover, happens in a world of economic
relationships that make any simple response difficult to
accept. Our ignorance is profound, and we cannot move
quickly from injustice to justice. We cannot directly work
against the choices that are constitutive of the brain drain,
without thereby attacking the rights that liberalism prizes.
This is why, for me, the brain drain is a tragedy rather than
simply a problem. The brain drain involves a set of injustices that liberal politics cannot justly overcome.

My conclusions here are less than stirring; an exhorta-
tion to marginal improvement is always less rousing than
one for revolutionary change. I believe marginal improvement is all that is open to us. We may want to move to a
world without the brain drain, and do so directly. I do not
think we can, morally speaking, make that voyage. We can
make the situation better, but we cannot make it right—at
least until we have found a way to make the world itself
a realm of justice. In considering the justice of the brain
drain, prior to that blessed eventuality, we must conclude
that the best we can do is make a bad world slightly better;

we cannot hope to obtain justice in migration independently of justice more generally. We must, instead, work quietly and at the edges, respecting the freedom to exit; these quiet steps are, in the end, all that liberalism allows. These incremental movements toward justice are less dramatic than revolutionary alterations in legal and moral rights; they are, however, the limits of our legitimate hopes.

NOTES

1. See Henry Shue, "Torture," *Philosophy and Public Affairs*, 7 (1978): 124–143.
2. Frederick G. Whelan, "Citizenship and the Right to Leave," 75 (3) *American Political Science Review* (1981).
3. The origins of this concept are in Hannah Arendt; see Arendt, *The Origins of Totalitarianism* (New York: Harcourt, Brace and Jovanovich, 1968).
4. Whelan, "Citizenship and the Right to Leave," 642. Note also that the Soviet Union sought, prior to the abstention, to change the UDHR to allow freedom of exit *only* when that exit was in accordance with the laws of the country of emigration—an amendment, Whelan notes, that would have made the right to exit an empty formalism.
5. For a brief discussion of this, see David Newman, "Borderline Views: Remembering the Soviet Refuseniks," *Jerusalem Post*, April 22, 2012.
6. Patrick Major, *Behind the Berlin Wall: East Germany and the Frontiers of Power* (Oxford: Oxford University Press, 2005), 56.
7. Norman Gelb, *Berlin Wall* (London: Michael Joseph, 1986), 65. Cited in Major, *Behind the Berlin Wall*, 109.
8. On the latter, see David Hawk, *The Hidden Gulag: The Lives and Voices of "Those Who are Sent to the Mountains,"* 2nd edition (Washington DC: US Committee for Human Rights

in North Korea, 2012). On the former, see *World Report 2012: Cuba*, Human Rights Watch, available at http://www. hrw.org/world-report-2012/world-report-2012-cuba.

9. Laura Silber, "Dayton, 10 Years After," *New York Times*, November 21, 2005.

10. Albert O. Hirschman, "Exit, Voice, and the Fate of the German Democratic Republic: An Essay in Conceptual History," *World Politics* 45 (1993): 173–202.

11. Sue J. Ross, Daniel Polsky, and Julie Sochalski, "Nursing Shortages and International Nurse Migration," *International Nursing Review* 52 (2005): 253–262, at 260. See also James Buchan, *Here to Stay? International Nurses in the UK* (London: Royal College of Nurses, 2003).

12. Christopher Heath Wellman and Phillip Cole, *Debating the Ethics of Immigration: Is There a Right to Exclude?* (Oxford: Oxford University Press, 2011).

13. See Michael Blake, "Immigration, Association, and Anti-discrimination," *Ethics* 122 (2012): 748–762.

14. See Phillip Cole, *Philosophies of Exclusion* (Edinburgh: Edinburgh University Press, 2000); and Lea L. Ypi, "Justice in Migration: A Closed Border Utopia?" *Journal of Political Philosophy* 16 (2008): 391–418. I discuss these in Michael Blake, "The Right to Exclude," forthcoming in *Critical Review of International Social and Political Philosophy*.

15. Norbert Ehrenfreund, *The Nuremberg Legacy: How the Nazi War Crimes Trials Changed the Course of History* (New York: Palgrave MacMillan, 2007), 91.

16. I am focusing here upon Rawls's methods in *A Theory of Justice* (Cambridge, MA: Harvard University Press, 1971); I believe, however, that nothing I say here would stand in tension with what Rawls said in his later work.

17. See, for instance, the following passage: "One is not allowed to justify differences in income or organizational powers on the ground that the disadvantages of those in one position are outweighed by the greater advantages of those in another. Much less can infringements of liberty be counterbalanced in this way." Rawls, *A Theory of Justice*, 64–65.

18. One possible defense would be to note that Rawls allows a lesser liberty, when that reduction in liberty strengthens the system of liberty shared by all. The difficulty, though, is that the restriction in question—since it keeps the would-be emigrant from being protected by another, foreign set of political institutions—does not, in fact protect her liberty at all; by definition, it constrains her to protect the liberty of *others*. See Rawls, *A Theory of Justice*, 250.

19. It is worth mentioning, in this context, Rawls's idea of the strains of commitment: we are to propose principles only when we can be sure that we can, in fact, live with the demands those principles would place upon us were we to face those demands. This idea echoes the concerns discussed above; we are not permitted to simply propose principles that are useful—we must accept that persons have a limited capacity for altruism, and propose only those principles that can be justified to such limited persons. See Rawls, *A Theory of Justice*, §69.

20. John Rawls, *The Law of Peoples* (Cambridge, MA: Harvard University Press, 1999), 74.

21. In the legal context, we may have an obligation to repay those we have damaged, even when we were all things considered morally right in the actions we chose to perform. The classic case on this is *Vincent v. Lake Erie and Co.*, 109 Minn. 456, 124 N.W. 221 (Minn. 1910).

22. For a general discussion of the tax, including its history and some variants, see Jagish N. Bhagwati and John D. Wilson (eds.), *Income Taxation and International Mobility* (Cambridge, MA: M.I.T. Press, 1989).

23. Thus, Brock's cases 4 through 7 seem, to my thinking, to be cases in which the state in question is simply affecting how medicine shall be done within the domestic context; they do not represent cases in which the state insists that medicine shall be done within that context by preventing exit. It might, of course, be true that such states do not have the standing to rule at all; if Rawls is right that only some countries can be rightly thought of as imposing moral duties through legislation, then the citizens of other countries

might have no moral reason to regard domestic legislation as giving rise to such duties. I ignore this latter complication at present, however. See Rawls, *The Law of Peoples*.

24. Thus, the United States administers programs that condition the payment of tuition in medical school on an agreement to work in an underserved area after graduation for some numbers of years. The University of Washington is a party to the WWAMI Program, which does this for physicians in underserved areas of the western United States. In the view I defend, there is nothing in principle wrong about this arrangement—so long as the bargain is made under conditions of fairness, and so long as it does not insist upon the right to coercively prevent those students from exiting the United States. See http://www.uwmedicine.org/Education/WWAMI/About-WWAMI/Pages/default.aspx.

25. Joey Bunch, "Kidnapper Sues Hostages for Leaving Him," *Denver Post*, November 30, 2011.

26. Thus, Restatement (Second) of Contracts, §175(1): a contract is void when "a party's manifestation of assent is induced by an improper threat by the other party that leaves the victim no reasonable alternative, the contract is voidable by the victim."

27. Alex Lenferna has suggested to me that a state facing truly dire circumstances might be justified in making such an offer; unlike Dimmick, the state might be a victim of its malign circumstances, or wrongful international institutions. I agree that this would change our perception of the moral character of the one making the offer; Dimmick is a bad actor, and he compounds his wrong in his offer, while the impoverished state might not be wrongful at all. None of this, however, can go to the question of whether or not the one receiving the offer has an obligation to fulfill her supposed duties under that offer. If my consent is made under duress, my consent is not valid, even if the one making the offer is not himself the cause of that duress.

28. I should emphasize here that her condition is sufficiently wrongful that she has a right not only to leave her current state, but a right to enter into another, rights-protecting

state. See Michael Blake, "Immigration, Jurisdiction, and Exclusion," *Philosophy and Public Affairs* 41 (2013): 103–130.

29. These conclusions are, of course, tentative ones; I derive them from the analysis provided by Freedom House, which in 2013 described Ghana as a "free" state, with significant provision given for civil liberties and political rights; Sudan, in contrast, was described as "not free," with a ranking for civil liberties and political rights equal to that of North Korea. See http://freedomhouse.org/report/freedom-world/ freedom-world-2013.

30. See Nir Eyal and Samia A. Hurst, "Coercion in the Fights Against Medical Brain Drain," in Rebecca S. Shah (ed.), *The International Migration of Health Workers: Ethics, Rights and Justice* (London: Palgrave MacMillan, 2010), 137–158.

31. Staffan Bergström, "Maternal Survival and the Crisis in Human Resources for Health in Africa: Impact of the Brain Drain," in Rebecca S. Shah (ed.), *The International Migration of Health Workers: Ethics, Rights and Justice* (London: Palgrave MacMillan, 2010), 159–174.

32. Despite my discussion of him in connection with emigration, this is the focus of Kieran Oberman, in "Can Brain Drain Justify Immigration Restrictions?" *Ethics* 123 (2013): 427–455; his discussion is worth exploring, despite my criticisms of his view.

33. Richard H. Thaler and Cass R. Sunstein, *Nudge: Improving Decisions About Heath, Wealth, and Happiness* (London: Penguin Books, 2009).

34. Edward Mills, William A. Schaba, Jimmy Volmink, et al., "Should Active Recruitment of Health Workers from sub-Saharan Africa Be Viewed as a Crime?" *Lancet* 371 (2008): 685–688.

35. See WHO Code article 3.6: "Member States should strive, to the extent possible, to create a sustainable health workforce and work towards establishing effective health workforce planning, education and training, and retention strategies that will reduce their need to recruit migrant health personnel." WHO Global Code of Practice on the Ethical

Recruitment of Health Personnel, May 2010. Available at http://www.who.int/hrh/migration/code/code_en.pdf.

36. I echo here some conclusions of Alex Sager; he agrees that the brain drain is not capable of being solved in isolation from global distributive justice—although he may be more optimistic than I am about our ability to effectively solve the latter problem. See Alex Sager, "Brain Drain, Health and Global Justice," in Rebecca S. Shah (ed.), *The International Migration of Health Workers: Ethics, Rights and Justice* (London: Palgrave MacMillan, 2010); see also Alex Sager, "Reframing the Brain Drain," forthcoming in *Critical Review of International Social and Political Philosophy*.

37. See generally Thomas Pogge, *World Poverty and Human Rights* (Cambridge: Polity Press, 2008).

38. See generally Gillian Brock, *Global Justice: A Cosmopolitan Account* (Oxford: Oxford University Press, 2009).

39. For a history of how good intentions have led to bad results in development, see William Easterly, *The White Man's Burden: Why the West's Efforts to Aid the Rest Have Done So Much Ill and So Little Good* (London: Penguin Books, 2007).

40. Thomas Pogge, *World Poverty and Human Rights*.

PART III

RESPONSES

GILLIAN BROCK AND
MICHAEL BLAKE

10

Brock Responds to Blake

MICHAEL BLAKE OFFERS AN IMPORTANT contrary perspective to the one I explore in Part I. While he believes that it would be noble for departing citizens to stay and serve fellow citizens, this is not a matter of discharging moral duties. Rather, introducing policies aimed at requiring emigrants to give back to the societies they wish to leave would be forcing sainthood upon people. In this chapter I respond to some of the robust challenges Blake offers and, in doing so, further defend the position that poor developing countries may require skilled citizens to contribute to development through reasonable taxation or service programs and so may specify conditions that apply to citizens' exit. I defend the view against some core lines of attack, addressing concerns about the connections between skilled workers' activities and institution building (in section 10.1), whether enhanced obligations can track greater capacity (section 10.2), whether delaying freedom to depart constitutes an important denial of freedom of movement (section 10.3), and clarifying when coercion may be justified (section 10.4). I then make some cautionary remarks about the empirical literature and how we should view it in the context of this debate (section 10.5) before considering the issue of how to respond to brain drain if it is rightly viewed as a moral tragedy (section 10.6). Finally, I discuss how there is some convergence on particular policy proposals that might be justified here and now, despite the very different perspectives that Blake and I offer (section 10.7).

10.1 GOVERNMENTS' DUTIES TO PROVIDE FOR THEIR CITIZENS' NEEDS: THE IMPORTANCE OF INSTITUTIONS

Highly skilled citizens are able to deliver core goods and services that governments have duties to provide. Providing these essentials is important for creating the right conditions in which good institutions (so greatly needed for reducing domestic poverty and promoting development) can flourish. In particular, those institutions that promote accountability foster an environment conducive to innovation and investment in education, health, and infrastructure—all key ingredients for lifting people out of poverty. One of the most worrisome setbacks developing countries can suffer from emigration is damage to institutions or the ingredients that are necessary to establish good institutions, and therefore the loss that is sustained in opportunities for development and poverty reduction. Helping developing countries retain their most skilled citizens is therefore often a key issue in building the better institutions crucial to prosperity. Given the importance of skilled citizens to creating the kinds of societies conducive to justice, policy options aimed at retaining such citizens deserve consideration.

Is it permissible to tax emigrants or destination country citizens to compensate for losses? Are compulsory service programs defensible? In Part I, I examined the normative case for there being important responsibilities that need to be discharged, especially on the part of the emigrant and the destination country, though my focus was largely on what policy options under the control of poor, developing countries are permissible. I identified several central arguments as to why the emigrant has responsibilities, but one important line of argument involves governments' duties. When governments invest scarce resources in creating human capital to provide for the needs of their citizens, they are entitled to fair returns on their investment and so they are entitled to claim compensation from those who would benefit from their investment (such as emigrants and developed country citizens); indeed, not to do so would be to squander public resources and they clearly have responsibilities not to do *that*. I considered four policy variants on how that reasonable expectation could be implemented in the form of attaching compulsory service requirements to acceptance of places on tertiary-level courses or accepting subsidies for training, both at public and private institutions. I argued that all these policies were reasonable ones for a poor, developing country to implement. In addition, I argued that certain kinds of taxation programs may be justified as part of fair terms of exiting a community that has importantly subsidized or funded the creation of human capital. In general, then, I argued that states are permitted to specify certain conditions that have implications for skilled citizens' movement across borders. I have not argued for the state's unconditional right to prohibit freedom of movement, nor for the state's right to suspend people's rights to free movement. Rather, in Part I, I have explored some of the content of our right to freedom of movement, noting when and how it might be justly constrained by other weighty considerations, and thus when it is permissible for states to regulate exit.

Blake has a number of worries about my arguments and in this section I consider some concerning institutions and what people may be coerced into doing to build them. Blake objects that forcing nurses to remain in countries of origin on the grounds that doing so would help build institutions is unjustified. He notes that one of the most powerful drivers of emigration for nurses is the level of violence in the country of origin. But it is not clear that nursing activities will do anything to assist in building an adequate law enforcement infrastructure. That nurses are good at nursing implies nothing about their competence at institution building. So forcing nurses to stay is unjustified.

While I understand the worry Blake raises, the connections he draws between someone providing service in their field of training and direct institution building are too tight. Recall that when we surveyed the different losses that departing emigrants can facilitate for those who remain, I differentiated among at least the following three classes: purely financial losses, loss of skills and services, and loss of institution-building assets. I also noted that some of these types of losses may have important direct or indirect effects on others. For instance, loss of tax revenue can have a role to play in a state's effectiveness and capacity to build relevant institutions. And some goods need to be supplied at a threshold level as necessary precursors for growing or strengthening the right kinds of institutions. Nurses are not required to build institutions that involve skills for which they were not trained. But the nurse's contributions to healthcare or tax revenue do have important implications for effective and robust institutions in that state. We need to understand better the many mechanisms by which skilled citizens can contribute to a more desirable place to live. Healthcare provision can help stabilize and strengthen society in beneficial ways that can reduce violence. So, nurses do not have to directly address violence to have a valuable role to play in countries of origin.

One might also wonder in this case whether it is really violence that is the problem or rather inadequate enforcement capabilities in the face of violence? (Violence, after all, exists to some extent in all, even the most desirable, societies.) If the latter, as seems likely, such capabilities could be strengthened with more public resources that could be derived from additional fiscal contributions. The nurse's taxes may therefore be an important contribution to reducing violence.

Even if we have obligations to contribute to strong institutions, according to Blake this obligation must be distributed equally. He says that "even if it is true that we might sometimes be obligated to sacrifice our freedom in the name of the common good, we cannot be told to do so when others are not being asked to do the same. Fairness demands no less. . . . We have an obligation to work for a new, more just global order. We do not have the right to sacrifice individual people in the name of this obligation, simply because they happen to be convenient means by which we might get closer to justice" (p. 135). The worries Blake expresses here could be addressed by imposing a uniform service requirement on everyone. Several European countries do exactly this.[1] No one could then complain that they were being treated differently. Another plausible response to this worry is to point out that those who remain are providing the service expected of them (through their lifetime of service in the community and payment of taxes), so there is equal expectation in what people are expected to do. It is those who depart who are expecting different treatment from those who remain, if we do not mandate some contribution.

As I argue in the next section, greater capacity can entail that one may reasonably be expected to take up a greater share of responsibilities. This does not entail that one can be expected to sacrifice one's entire life—how could that be reasonable?—but rather to make a greater contribution than those not similarly able.

10.2 CAPACITY AND FAIRNESS

Blake does not share my view that greater capacity to assist can, in relevant circumstances and conjoined with other grounding factors, mean that the more capable have greater obligations. Instead he believes fair treatment requires that all have equal obligations, and the capable should not be expected to take up more than an equal share of any burdens associated with securing distributive justice. Blake argues that "while we do have a strong duty to build and sustain just institutions, this duty should be regarded as distributed equally across the world's population; no individual should be made to bear a disproportionate share of that duty's burden" (p. 126). In defense of such claims he invokes the example of someone who is especially talented at vigilantly spotting and deterring wily mountain goats. Even though all inhabitants usually take turns keeping watch, there is one person who is so much better than anyone else at this activity. Should he be required to sacrifice his life for the sake of the village, in virtue of his superior capacity? The kind of worry Blake presses through this creative example is likely to be widely shared, so is worth careful attention.

First of all, we could challenge whether this particular example is apt. One reason why I do not believe that the case can be used to rebut my central argument is that built into its set-up is the assumption that there is a minimal level of competence that we all have such that it makes sense to divide the chores equally among many people, at least in the absence of gifted goat spotters. Sharing duties equally makes sense as a principle for distributing burdens when no specialized skills are involved in performing the tasks. This seems to be the case here. But it would not make sense to assign chores equally if specialized skills are involved in doing the job well, for instance where surgery, engineering, or nursing activities are required.

Furthermore, in the case I make in Part I, capacity is only *one* of three important factors on which the grounds for differential obligations rest. The receipt of benefits under severe resource constraints, the contributions to exacerbating problems, the existence of responsible governance structures and people in governance roles attempting to perform their duties responsibly, along with other features of the case mean that the assignment of additional responsibilities may be quite reasonable. So to adapt Blake's case to these relevant considerations, we would have to add a few more features to his example, such as these two. First, mountain goat spotting is a highly skilled activity that requires many years of training and support from the community, so that the spotter can acquire the necessary skills. Second, lookouts are trained at the village's expense. Third, poor villages only have sufficient resources to invest in the training of a few individuals each year. Now we can ask the parallel question: could we reasonably require of those who undertake the necessary training that they assume extra duties keeping watch in those villages under such conditions? I believe we can.

I should add that greater capacity by itself may or may not justify differential responsibilities, depending on the case at issue. The only person who is able to swim who witnesses another drowning and can assist the person drowning at low risk to himself may, in virtue of capacity, be obligated to perform the rescue. Similarly, the only person trained in first aid at the scene of an accident also has a duty to assist that is not shared with those who lack the relevant skills. But now consider someone who is exceptionally capable at cleaning. She performs cleaning tasks at a superior level to everyone else in her family. Her capacity might be one relevant issue, but other factors might certainly crowd out exclusive reliance on superior ability as the criterion for distributing housework. Maintaining equal relationships within the family unit and ensuring that all take up an equal share of routine tasks are also important, so an egalitarian distribution is often a more appropriate way of distributing these chores than one that greatly weights superior capacity. I believe the weight we can place on capacity as a principle of distributing burdens may track when specialized skills are necessary to get the job done compared with whether competence at an ordinary level of skill is sufficient, but we need not take a stand on that issue here.

At any rate, we recognize that those with greater capacity can reasonably be expected to make a greater contribution to community projects and this is a perfectly familiar principle of social justice. Different capacity levels often feature as an important reason why different contributions to promoting social justice can reasonably be expected. Consider progressive taxation. We tax those who have greater earning capacity (which tracks larger income) at a higher rate than those who have a lower income. In this way, we do often think it fair to treat people differently on the basis of the varying ways in which they can contribute to promoting justice.

Blake, of course, acknowledges this. While he recognizes that progressive taxation within societies is a common example of where we do distribute differential burdens based on capacity to pay, he believes there is a difference between actions we may take within a society and those we may take when people want to leave that society. While he concedes that progressive taxation is defensible, and so that differential burdens based on capacity for those citizens within a system may be appropriate, he denies that differential burdens based on capacity can apply to those who wish to leave a political system.

What should we make of this argument? Should different rules apply to people who no longer wish to be part of a particular society? Would this create a moral hazard that should be taken into account? Would this create, for instance, perverse incentives for people to leave societies aiming at more social justice (perhaps through higher tax rates) in favor of those aiming at less? I imagine Blake would be happy to simply bite this bullet. People should be free to join associations whose terms appeal to them and if that means more socially just societies retain fewer members, that is unproblematic from the perspective of liberal justice.

When should the same rules be thrust upon people even when they wish to leave? The same rules should apply at least in the case where they have made an agreement to do so. And they have done just that in the case of "responsible, but poor." When their contribution is required to discharge social justice obligations (that they have also willingly and knowingly undertaken) we should not release them from the agreements they have made.

10.3 IS FREEDOM EVER SO SLIGHTLY DELAYED, FREEDOM DENIED?

For Blake, we cannot avoid some of the problems of brain drain "without avoiding freedom itself" (p. 120). In several places, Blake seems to assume that the slightest constraint on freedom means we no longer have enough of the core idea of freedom retained so that it makes sense to say we still have freedom.[2] But this seems implausible.

In Blake's view, even the temporary "suspension of the right to exit is impermissible" (p. 291). Now, to be clear, when I argue for a slight delay in exiting countries of origin, I do not believe that the right has been *suspended*. Rather, all rights have certain constraints built into them and I believe I am simply clarifying what some of those defensible ones are. Consider our rights to freedom of expression. We cannot all speak freely at the same time and hope to be heard. When we ask our students to raise their hands if they would like to speak in class, we are laying out some procedures so that the right to freedom of expression can be meaningfully exercised in certain contexts. Similarly, we prohibit many kinds of speech activities without this entailing that the right to free speech does not exist. You may not enter my house to express your views or set up a speaker system at my place of work, even if you would like me to listen to what you have to say. It is not a violation of your right to free speech to have such restrictions in place. Rather, it further clarifies the domain in which you are able to speak freely. This clarificatory work is important in a context of multiple claims, interests, and rights. The exercise of almost any right often bumps up against other important considerations, such as others' rights, interests, and harms. We have to figure out how these should be weighed. That we make considered judgments about how that balance plays out helps define the limits on the exercise of the right. The judgment in favor of others' rights or interests in certain cases does not entail that the right to freedom of speech is not important or that it can be suspended.

The idea of restricting freedom to ensure it is compatible with others' freedoms can be entirely freedom enhancing—traffic regulations are of this kind. When we constrain freedom of movement to ensure traffic flows freely, we might think of this as contributing to effective freedom of movement for all rather than as an impediment to the freedom that we recognize as important. So, I do not see that anyone is having their rights suspended so much as that we are clarifying what is involved in exercising the right permissibly, in a context in which others have rights too.

There are many cases where our freedoms are ever so slightly delayed or constrained which do not importantly undermine freedom. Blake rightly notes that "we are, in general, more willing to defend specific duties when they are triggered by specific actions, voluntarily undertaken; it is comparatively more difficult to think that we have such duties simply because of luck" (p. 177). While we generally think voluntarily entered-into relationships and associations are a stronger trigger for certain kinds of duties, I do not think these are always necessary to trigger all duties, even quite important ones. (I imagine Blake might concede this point, but I will anyhow illustrate here with some freedom-of-exit-related examples.) I do not choose my flying companions on airplanes, but when we disembark, I may have an obligation to delay my departure from my row slightly, for various reasons such as because others need to disembark first or we have a practice of delaying departure until all preceding rows are cleared. This is not a suspension of my right to exit. That right is constrained and defined by other practices and interests. Similarly, slow drivers delay my exit from the car park, but that is not an interference with my right to exit either.

Notice that it can be permissible to introduce various limits on freedom of movement whether or not voluntary actions on our part or memberships in relevant associations are relevant triggers. It is quite rightly permissible to restrict the freedom of movement of tourists, visiting dignitaries, or citizens when we try to protect various habitats or enforce rules of the road that restrict freedom of movement, so it is not the case that all important restrictions on movement are justified only when we are members of associations or when they are triggered by sufficiently voluntary acts.

Furthermore, there are forms of unchosen human affiliation that do generate some duties. I do not typically choose my neighbors, but because we are geographically proximate I have duties to check on them when we suffer civil emergencies, such as floods, severe weather, or earthquakes. And more to the point, when we are backing out of our driveways, we might have to delay exit to allow others to cross our path. That hardly counts as an important constraint on my freedom of exit. Consider also that children do not typically choose their parents. Despite this failure of voluntariness, sufficiently competent parents who perform their duties admirably are owed certain things from their children, including a certain *basic* concern for their well-being.

10.4 WHEN IS COERCION JUSTIFIED?

10.4.1 Some Clarifications

While I agree that coercing people into doing certain jobs is not always, or even usually, the best way to get them done, it can be permissible in the face of certain unfavorable conditions, when normal processes and market incentives are insufficient to attract the numbers required to do necessary jobs. This is especially justifiable when the state has an obligation to provide some of the goods and services involved.[3]

Recall that for Blake a coercive act is "one which serves to remove otherwise available options; it is a threat, rather than an offer. The gunman who forces me to choose between my money and my life removes the otherwise available option in which I keep both my money and my life" (pp. 148–148). He also says that coercion is not always wrong, "but it always stands in need of justification" (p. 149). I largely agree with Blake's views as expressed here. To underscore especially: *coercion is not always wrong, but it is always in need of justification*. And I have argued why I believe coercion is justified in the primary cases that are our focus. Because the issue of when coercion is permissible is a core area of disagreement between us, I summarize the key points of that argument next.

A poor, legitimate developing state may defensibly regulate emigration of skilled citizens—directly or indirectly—when certain conditions obtain. Importantly, states must be legitimate, background conditions must hold, and citizens must have relevant responsibilities. States exercise power legitimately when they make good-faith efforts to protect human rights.[4] The following background conditions must apply.

(1) Evidence from the particular country indicates that skilled citizens can provide important services for which there are severe shortages, and their departure considerably undermines efforts to meet citizens' needs. The ways in which citizens' departure exacerbates deprivation may be quite direct (such as failure to provide important services necessary to meeting basic needs) or more indirect (such as when the institutional reforms

necessary for development have been hampered by net losses resulting from migration of skilled workers).

(2) Governments have invested appropriately in training skilled workers to provide for their citizens' needs and to promote beneficial development.

(3) Losses that result from skilled workers' otherwise uncompensated departure would not adequately be compensated for by benefits that result from citizens who leave.

The skilled citizens have important responsibilities to assist with need satisfaction when all of the following considerations apply (in roughly descending order of importance):

(1) Governments have invested scarce resources in creating human capital to provide for the needs of citizens and are entitled to a fair return on their investment.

(2) By leaving without compensating for losses, emigrants thwart governments' attempts to discharge their duties.

(3) Citizens have received important benefits during their residence in the state of origin and failure to reciprocate for those past benefits involves taking advantage of others or free-riding unfairly.

(4) Citizens' leaving without compensation creates important disadvantages for others from which they deserve to be protected.

(5) Uncompensated departures that result in governments being unable to discharge their duties

undermine citizens' abilities to support their governments. Fair-minded citizens should not undermine fellow citizens' abilities to support legitimate governments that attempt to discharge their duties in good faith. We also have other grounds for helping compatriots to support their institutional schemes, such as loyalty and a concern for unintended harmful side effects.

When all of these conditions obtain, citizens have a responsibility to repay accumulated moral debts.

For compulsory service programs to be justified, governments must, in addition to the conditions outlined above, have made students aware of the fact that they will be expected to meet needs on completion of their training, at least for a short period, and have made this an explicit condition of student's accepting the opportunity for tertiary-level training in various courses of study. In addition, being present in the country must be important to remedying the deprivations. The compulsory service program should not require unreasonable sacrifices, and the costs of staying should not be unreasonable.

For taxation programs to be justified, in addition to the state being legitimate, and the relevant background conditions and moral responsibilities applying, it must be the case that taxation of those skilled citizens would assist in remedying deprivation. Governments should have made all high-skilled citizens (whether prospective migrants or not) aware of their need to tax such citizens to assist with remedying deprivation, and have made this an explicit condition of student's accepting the opportunity for tertiary-level training in various significant courses of study. The taxation program should not require unreasonable sacrifices.

I believe that the conjunction of these considerations is sufficient to make the case that what coercion there may be in such arrangements is justified.[5]

10.4.2 Blake's Cases

Recall the primary cases that Blake uses in order to make his central argument. Malawi kidnaps a Japanese doctor to assist Malawian citizens for one year (kidnapped foreigner); Malawi prevents a visiting Japanese doctor from leaving Malawi for one year (prevented foreigner); Malawi forces a citizen who is a doctor to assist needy Malawians though she would prefer to work in a restaurant (kidnapped local); and Malawi refuses to permit a citizen who is doctor from leaving Malawi for one year and presses her into serving needy Malawians (prevented local).

In none of these cases do I think the state acts permissibly. No agreements have been forged in any of these cases; thus, it would not be reasonable to expect any to be in play, nor would it be reasonable to impose such terms retrospectively. All these state actions are described in such a way that suggests no warning is given for such policies. The state acts justly in enforcing agreements or imposing arrangements only in certain kinds of cases, such as where fair terms have been proposed and people have agreed to them, thus willingly and knowingly entering certain arrangements under appropriate conditions. In non-emergency cases, the state may not retroactively enforce terms—such as service or taxation arrangements—without a considerable period of notice, preferably given before people make major life decisions.[6]

Notice also that Blake's four main cases have in common a characterization of being forcibly held against one's will. The cases are akin to forms of kidnap or slavery. But the compulsory service programs I defend are more accurately described as cases of having to wait a bit. Moreover the persons who have to exercise patience have willingly and knowingly agreed to such arrangements, so asking for their patience is entirely reasonable.

Consider these cases:

(1) Having to wait until one is 18 in order to get a driving license.

(2) Having to wait until one has passed an examination covering first-year mathematics before one can progress into second-year mathematics in a university course.

(3) Having to wait for four weeks before one's application for a passport will be processed.

These cases could all involve restrictions on an individual's life plans. But there are good reasons to have such waiting periods in place. Some aim at preventing harm to self or others; some aim to ensure competence is demonstrated; others are simple matters of administrative realities in the face of resource constraints. All affect our freedoms and could conceivably affect freedom of movement. But there are good justifications for such restrictions, regulations, or time-frame indications. While forcibly holding people against their will would require quite a lot of argument, if we characterize what is at issue as asking people to be a bit patient while they otherwise go about their business, the burden of proof is less onerous. In addition, if we emphasize that they have willingly entered such arrangements knowing that patience will be required, enforcing the agreement is entirely reasonable.

10.4.3 The Circumstances in Which Agreements are Forged

Blake might challenge that these people have been so willing to agree to these arrangements. Rather, he might suggest, they have been coerced into them and so they need not feel bound by the terms of the contract and should feel free to ignore them. Just as in the case of kidnapped hostages who have agreed not to report their captor to the police, the agreement becomes null and void because of the conditions under which it was made. Contracts to perform service or pay taxes are similarly made under duress.

While I understand the concern about excessive coercion undermining the validity of contracts, I do not see that the consideration applies convincingly here. No one is forcing students to pursue high-skill training—they willingly seek out such opportunities. There are thousands of others who would be pleased to take their places. Granted, students are being deprived of the opportunity to take expensive training on terms they might prefer, such as terms that do not require service or taxation payments on completion of studies. However, this is not an option to which anyone has a right or an option a state has a duty to make available.

It seems to me that the validity of these contracts is just as robust as contracts we regularly do consider quite defensible in developed countries, such as those that apply to a student who takes out a loan and agrees to pay back the sum borrowed under the terms and conditions specified. There are strong parallels here. Students are typically youngish. The ones who make use of these loans are often from low socio-economic groups, where they must borrow money in order to pursue the course of study. If they do not sign the loan agreements they will not be able to embark on tertiary-level training. Their options are therefore quite constrained by their lack of resources and the terms on which they can pursue education. If we think it acceptable to enforce student loan agreements in developed countries, as I suggest we do, then there is not much difference between such contracts and the sort developing countries may permissibly make use of when enrolling students in courses of study.

I would also resist Blake's characterization of my case concerning the permissibility of coercion as largely based on the fact that it would be socially useful. The person who will be taxed or must perform compulsory service has agreed to these arrangements, and I have argued that these are fair agreements and ones people can reasonably be expected to keep because of a conjunction of factors. To repeat, those factors include the conditions previously describing legitimacy, background conditions, accumulated responsibilities, reasonableness, and presence (when the latter is necessary to attend to deprivation).

10.4.4 Changing One's Life Plans

May we still hold people to their agreements when they no longer wish to work in the occupations for which they trained and have changed their life plans? In Blake's kidnapped local case, a Malawian trained in medicine discovers she dislikes medicine and would prefer to work in her father's restaurant. The idea is that if someone gives up her publicly funded occupation that assists with severe deprivation for another occupation, she will not be assisting with compatriots' needs. Someone who objects to my arguments might say: why think the case is any different when the state loses her not to restauranting but instead to another country? The objection is designed to show that there is an inconsistency in the arguments for compulsory service (and taxation), since we would not require service (or taxation) when people give up medicine for restauranting, but we would require contributions if they leave the country.

The first point to make in response to the challenge is that there would be no such inconsistency in my arguments. If people take up one of the scarce tertiary training positions they would be contractually obliged to fulfill their service terms before they could move in a new direction, be it restauranting in Malawi or practicing medicine in a foreign country.

Compare the medicine/restauranting example with someone who signs up to be in an orchestra for a season but wants to give that up to pursue surfing. The contractual agreement might include a commitment to stay for a certain period, such as completing the season's schedule. While we might concede this can be a bit inconvenient or disruptive for the person involved, it does not interfere with her life plans in a way that I would view as objectionable. People have to make commitments all the time, and others come to rely on these. People form legitimate expectations around the commitments we undertake and these expectations can have considerable weight. Moreover our taking on certain projects creates certain duties for us. Blake may wish he had the freedom to leave his current job on the day he wants to pursue other career options. But the University of Washington has responsibilities to its students such that it needs to execute plans to offer various courses, and it is reasonable for his employer to expect at least a certain period of notice be given, during which he may still be required to perform services and discharge professional obligations, even if he would prefer a different immediate path.

What about the fairness of taxation programs once someone wishes to, say, surf rather than be a doctor? I believe it is still reasonable to tax the surfer on his reduced income. Clearly the state will recoup less from the lower income stream than if he continued practicing medicine. But that is acceptable and anyhow seems to strike the right balance between letting him choose the course for his own life and asking him to make a contribution to support the state's legitimate and essential activities. Similarly for the case of the emigrant, it would be fair to keep taxing and recouping less. Again, this achieves a good balance.

Finally, we might note also that these changes of occupation are not standard cases. The vast majority of those who train in a particular field continue in the same field of initial training, even if we acknowledge that some people do change their minds about how they spend their working lives.

10.5 SOME REMARKS ON THE EMPIRICAL LITERATURE

I have indicated before that my argument is a conditional one: if there are important losses that result from high-skill emigration, what may poor developing countries do to solve their own problems? In response to this argument, some object (and Blake is a good example of this) that high-skill migration brings plenty of benefits, so there is no residual loss that we need worry about in many cases. In this section I comment on the empirical literature that attempts to show that many important benefits accrue from high-skill migration, and that these are often of such significance that there is no relevant loss with which we need to be concerned. Before I do so, two points are worth repeating. While we should identify types of losses that accompany high-skill migration so we can identify appropriate policy that can mitigate these categories of losses, we need not be committed to the view that the losses identified must always accompany high-skill migration. I should also remind the reader that I earlier (in Chapter 3) discussed some of the reasons to be cautious about the power of remittances to transform societies in the desired ways, so will not remark on the empirical literature on remittances again here.

10.5.1 Human-capital Formation

The prospect of migration can motivate citizens to undertake additional training and can therefore result in a phenomenon known as "brain gain." This effect can be especially noticeable in small countries like Cape Verde, Tonga, and Papua New Guinea.[7] However, the brain gain is not always beneficial to source countries, as enhanced training can be skewed toward usefulness in the targeted destination countries. Gibson and McKenzie find that it can lead to overinvestment in some fields (e.g., geriatric medicine) that have large payoffs overseas rather than in other fields that are more urgently needed locally (e.g., tropical medicine) but are not so attractive overseas.[8] When doctors who study geriatrics rather than tropical medicine remain, poor countries may not benefit much from the additional training, which is a form of brain waste.[9] So while there can be the noted stimulus for additional human-capital formation, we need to be careful about being overly optimistic about claims that the prospect of migration necessarily leads to beneficial brain gain in all cases.

Even when there is a notable brain gain, there is considerable variation in whether it is significant and sufficient to outweigh other factors. So, consider the migration of high-skill healthcare workers from sub-Saharan Africa. Does the prospect of emigration generate enough incentives to facilitate a net medical brain gain? Michael Clemens finds some evidence of this.[10] However, Frederic Docquier and Hillel Rapoport argue that "the effect of emigration becomes insignificant once controls such as GDP per capita, school enrollment, and ethnic conflicts are introduced and the number of emigrant physicians is instrumented using country size and linguistic links."[11] Alok Bhargava, Frederic Docquier, and Yasser Moullan find that while "migration prospects have a positive effect on medical training, the magnitude appears too small to generate a net brain gain in the medical sector."[12] Most worrisomely, even if there is this brain gain, it is not clear that it outweighs bad health outcomes in Africa from medical brain drain. Bhargava and Docquier find "that medical brain drain . . . is associated with a 20 percent increase in adult deaths from AIDS."[13] Also, as is widely documented, medical brain drain from Africa leads to "underprovision of healthcare staff in Africa and ultimately, to low health status and shorter life expectancy."[14] As this short foray into relevant literature suggests, even when human capital is enhanced by the prospect of migration, the net positive or negative effects are far from obvious.

10.5.2 Diaspora and Network Effects

Diaspora and network effects have long been recognized as important, though actual evidence about the exact channels seems to be more recent. One such channel involves increasing the source country's capacities to innovate or adopt technologies, and these enhanced capacities can have an effect on productivity and economic growth.[15] Migrants situated in host countries often facilitate the flow of knowledge and goods or in other ways reduce international transaction costs between home and host countries, which can lead to valuable trading and investment opportunities.[16] As Docquier and Rapoport note, "by reducing international transaction costs and facilitating the diffusion of knowledge and ideas, highly skilled diasporas settled in the developed countries encourage technology diffusion, stimulate trade and FDI [foreign direct investment] and contribute to improving domestic institutions."[17]

One highly studied example is migration from India, which has had positive effects on stimulating India's information technology (IT) sector. The role of the Indian diaspora has been powerful. Indians ran about 9 percent of Silicon Valley start-ups during 1995–1998 and they maintain strong business links with India.[18] There is regular beneficial exchange between Indian entrepreneurs resident in the United States and those in India. The Indian diaspora has been identified as the main cause of India's emergence into the international IT sector, providing "foreign investors with information on the Indian labor force, sparking demands for Indian IT specialists in countries without experience of Indian migrants (e.g., Germany and Japan) as well as international demand for IT services exported from India."[19] In these ways we can appreciate how through their presence in host countries, migrant workers can convey important information and also play an essential role in initiating business links.

Several studies show that there is a "positive relationship between the number of skilled migrants a country has in the United States and the level of foreign direct investment from the US economy to that country."[20] But, as Docquier and Rapoport urge, we should be cautious about generalizability here as these data sets contain only two countries with population rates below one million, "making it difficult to see whether this relationship holds in the smallest countries for which brain drain rates are highest. At the micro-level, . . . we find very low rates of high-skilled migrants being involved in trade facilitation or investment in business start-ups in their home countries: we estimate a small country like Tonga or Micronesia might gain at most $500–$2000 per high-skilled migrant from trade and foreign direct investment. This contribution is a positive one, but is unlikely to have large effects on development."[21] We might also wonder whether such small gains are sufficient to outweigh other negative effects associated with departure (such as fiscal losses).

More recently, researchers have examined diaspora and network effects on the quality of political and economic institutions, which is a rather significant development for my argument. Importantly, migrants residing in destination countries may engage in political or economic activities that may have consequences for institutional development in their home countries. And such migrants may increase awareness of and exposure to foreign political norms and values (such as democracy) that can have positive effects for source country institutions.[22] Again, caution should be exercised as there are only a small number of papers so far that explore this topic.[23] As even Docquier and Rapoport note, "the empirical assessment of these effects is still at an early stage."[24] Even among this sample we find a quite mixed result. For instance, Docquier and Marfouk find that in the study they undertook, brain drain may have had a "positive effect on political institutions but a negative effect on economic institutions at home."[25]

10.5.3 Temporary Migration and Return

Temporary high-skill emigration can be beneficial to the source country through mechanisms such as contributing to the diffusion of new technologies. Those who migrate often accumulate knowledge and financial capital while abroad. When they return they may bring back skills and assets that can increase productivity growth.[26] Returning migrants can also initiate or stimulate new projects and industries on their return.[27] Returnees from the diaspora became prominent advisors and played important roles in sector-wide reforms in India. Docquier and Rapoport note that organizations of Indian entrepreneurs in the diaspora have lobbied for "a better framework for entrepreneurship in India, and successfully lobbied the Indian government to change the regulatory framework for venture capital."[28] They note the potential for such lobbying organizations to achieve other political and institutional reforms.

While, in theory, returning migrants or members of the diaspora can promote reforms leading to more effective economic and political institutions, I am more skeptical about whether such links are always advantageous for the kind of institutional change that is beneficial for pro-poor development policy. Why think returning elites will necessarily want changes in home countries that benefit anyone other than local and international elites? These lobby groups may or may not be helpful for beneficial development, depending on their agendas, whether they lead to state or regulatory capture, whether they advance investors' interests at the expense of workers' interests, and so on. To put it mildly, the powerful who have influence with government do not always use that influence for purposes beneficial to the poor, vulnerable, or marginalized. Such lobbying might just as easily contribute to corruption of institutions rather than their improvement. To add some substance to my worry, it is not at all clear that all this influence in the case of India has made the slightest dent in the significant problem of widespread corruption in that country. Perhaps it has just exacerbated it.[29]

10.5.4 Taking Stock

It is important to note that the effects of brain drain will vary enormously across countries. Population size, skill levels in the source country, geographical features, levels of development, and language in home and host countries are all likely to be significant factors in determining whether high-skill migration is a net positive or negative for source countries. The consequences of medical brain drain from Africa seem to be vastly different from those of IT workers from India, for instance. So, the first point to note is that there is huge variation in effects and that makes generalizing difficult. While there are some winners from high-skill migration, there are many clear losers as well. For instance, small island states are the most affected by brain drain, typically quite negatively. By contrast, India has a very large population and a rapidly growing economy, and may therefore experience high-skill migration as a largely positive phenomenon. Large developing countries such as China, India, and Brazil are winners from high-skill migration, while small countries are generally losers.[30] Moreover, small countries lose more than large countries gain.[31]

However, there are some general patterns that might be worth noting here. First, as Docquier and Rapoport remark:

> High-skill migration is becoming a dominant pattern of international migration and a major aspect of globalization. *The fact that international migration from poor to rich countries is becoming more of the brain drain type is a serious source of concern in developing countries and for the development community.* Through the brain drain, it would seem, globalization is making human capital scarcer where it is already scarce and more abundant where it is already abundant, thereby contributing to increasing inequalities across countries, including among richer ones. (emphasis mine)[32]

Second, recent literature does indicate that high-skill emigration can generate some positive network externalities. Those developing countries that are largely winning are ones that have large populations and the abilities to capture the benefits of having a skilled, educated diaspora. Whether countries gain or lose is determined, to a large extent, by policies in the host and home country.[33]

Third, sheer numbers matter. In order to capture some of the positive externalities from diaspora effects you may need a large (or at least a critical mass of) skilled workers to settle in certain locations. So what is possible for Indian expatriates in the diaspora may not be readily achievable for smaller countries not able to reach the same threshold levels of visibility to gain the confidence of foreign investors. Small countries with small populations may have fewer skilled workers to begin with. Plus, if they do not settle in geographically concentrated ways, they may not be able to capture these benefits. What is achievable for some countries may be completely unfeasible for others. As noted, population size matters, as does the size of the pool of skilled workers. India and the Philippines have huge numbers of skilled workers to draw from and if some work abroad it may not matter much to the remaining population, unlike other countries where the skilled worker bases are smaller. Again, what might be the case for India may not be the case for different countries with different skill levels, population size, and other demographic features.

Fourth, there is much we do not know. In particular, further research on the connections between migration and economic development would be welcome.[34] We need to understand better the externalities that a scientist, engineer, or entrepreneur confers on the host and home countries. Furthermore, because of data constraints, "many of the macro studies surveyed do not identify the causal effects of high-skill emigration on development in a fully convincing way. As a result, the sign and magnitude of these effects remains a source of controversy among economists."[35] We clearly need more research on a range of issues, including the actual effects of policies aimed at reducing or capitalizing on high-skilled immigration.

I make one final cautionary point before closing this section. Research trends can follow fashions. Early waves of research on brain drain (especially in the 1970s) indicated a bleak picture. When one trend seems to be dominant, this often stimulates theorists to look for other data. Current research may especially be trying to find contrary data or just to show that some of the earlier research was not sufficiently nuanced. And researchers working on this topic in the future will, in part, respond to earlier research. We should be cautious about resting too much weight on what any one current trend might suggest is the new received wisdom. At any rate, I want to underscore a point made in the previous paragraph, namely that our current state of knowledge suggests there are some positive, some negative, and some quite mixed results. Importantly, there is also much that we have yet to learn about the effects of high-skill migration. There are very few "all things considered" claims that we can plausibly make about what the empirical literature currently reveals concerning the effects of high-skill migration that apply to all countries.[36]

10.6 THE BRAIN DRAIN AS MORAL TRAGEDY

Blake suggests that the brain drain represents a moral tragedy because our world is unjust; however, we cannot move away from it in ways that are both effective and just. Blake believes there are a few strategies that developing states can pursue, consistent with the demands of liberal morality in response to the brain drain. For instance, they may try to improve working conditions in countries of origin; they may permissibly introduce conditional repayment schemes for education under certain conditions; and they may impose schemes that tax worldwide income on citizens who do not renounce their citizenship, when this would not be counterproductive. He gives very limited support to the possibility that developing countries may sometimes, under heavily qualified conditions, also make educational provision contingent on signing a contract; however, in practice, very few states will be eligible to avail themselves of this strategy, or indeed the option concerning conditional repayment schemes. I briefly comment on Blake's views on each strategy.

In many poor developing countries there is genuine political will to work toward better working conditions, but lack of resources severely constrains what they can feasibly achieve in the near term. So, I think this is probably not going to advance the effort to eliminate the brain drain much. I agree with Blake's assessment that this may be somewhat akin to blaming the victim. However it is not worthless as a statement of advice: incremental changes can sometimes be made at low cost and the cumulative effect might, over time, considerably reduce push factors for migrants.

Blake also argues that taxing citizens who do not renounce citizenship may be permissible, but urges that we should be cautious about using it in case it has perverse effects. I agree with this cautionary qualification.

Another option he endorses is that developing countries might introduce conditional loans, which specify a
period of service as a condition of receiving an education
loan for, say, a nursing degree, as Ghana currently does. He
believes these conditional loans are permissible under the
right conditions. Similarly, while Blake agrees that some
contracts to serve in exchange for educational attainment
are permissible, he again cautions against the possibly
coercive circumstances under which they are signed. Blake
suggests that the circumstances surrounding students
signing contracts can be reasons for invalidating contracts.
He does not say directly that this should apply in my case
of "responsible, but poor" countries, but he does heavily
qualify the range of states that are able to avail themselves
of this option.

So let us return briefly to the issue of circumstances
and how they matter. We can bargain away our rights, and
under the right circumstances, these agreements are morally binding. The right circumstances obviously exclude
cases such as that of striking bargains while being held
hostage. And when someone's rights are not adequately
protected, this situation is comparable to that of being held
captive, in Blake's view. Citizens would be agreeing from
within a society that is not adequately rights-protecting to
remain in such an environment. But how can this be a valid
contract? It is like holding hostages to any agreements they
strike with their captors, and we clearly would not do that.
So, in practice, not every state that might want to make use
of contracts for conditional repayments, compulsory service, or any other conditions as constraints on educational
provision is legitimately able to do so. A minimal level of
state adequacy is required before we have a valid contract

that could be enforceable. And a state that permits or causes widespread human rights abuses does not meet that adequacy threshold. So some of the states that might most like to avail themselves of such strategies will not be able to do so. Like Blake, I agree that it looks like countries such as Ghana have a reasonable chance of reaching the adequacy threshold, whereas others such as the Central African Republic do not. I would also add that other reasonable contenders might include the Philippines, Mexico, India, Peru, and Brazil, though we would need to engage in extensive analysis concerning rights protections in those countries before we could make more definite claims. The list of states that are not currently in contention would be long and would include Zimbabwe, North Korea, Iran, Chad, the Sudan, and Uganda.

Now it is important to note that not just any signed contract matters. Neither Blake nor I hold this position, and there are good reasons for this. If some action the state would take is completely unjust, how could someone's signing a contract remove all the injustice or the worrisome aspects? The worry would transform into one that people are being coerced into signing unjust contracts. If slavery is deeply unjust, it is not clear how signing a contract to be enslaved can be just. Indeed, it is often thought that contracts to bind oneself into slavery have no validity. So, signing a contract does not make morally worrisome aspects of the deal disappear; rather, it infects the contract rather than relieving it of moral taint. Signing a contract cannot bestow this kind of magic in making morally troubling aspects disappear; the signed contract cannot have special standing when the terms are blatantly unfair.

I take it to be an important project that one must offer significant arguments as to why asking people to sign contracts to bind themselves into compulsory service would be fair ones to sign. In fact, much of what I do in Part I is offer arguments as to why compulsory service contracts would be such. We can too easily get students to sign all sorts of contracts, especially if we have a monopoly on the goods they want (tertiary education) or on regulating the terms by which those goods can be offered in our state (as state agents do). But if this is not just to be a brute exercise of state power and is part of the give and take of governments justifying their actions to citizens in attempts to be accountable in the use of that power, governments must offer compelling arguments for any contracts they can defensibly ask students to sign. This is what I take myself to have done in Part I. The most important piece in those arguments is my demonstration that expecting students to sign such contracts would be fair and reasonable. The status of signed contract matters. But what matters more is the case for why the terms offered are fair.

Blake expresses the view that the brain drain is not a problem that can be solved apart from working on global injustice generally. Indeed, he states that "dealing with the brain drain without dealing with these more central forms of inequality is likely to prove futile" (p. 224). While I agree that we do need to have firmly in view treating the root causes when we consider good solutions to the problems that brain drain creates, sometimes this option is not available. In some cases we cannot first fix global injustice and then prioritize fixing problems created by brain drain. Part of the solution to global injustice is remedying the negative effects created by brain drain. Tackling global injustice involves ensuring basic goods and services are actually supplied, which entails that those who can deliver them be encouraged, nudged, or coerced into doing so. And developing countries need to explore how to solve their own problems. This includes considering the ways to retain a critical mass of skilled citizens who are likely to be important assets in allowing developing countries to transition to more just societies. In short, dealing with the brain drain is *part of the solution* to dealing with the more central forms of inequality that underlie this problem.

So, we might wonder, is Blake correct about the brain drain representing a moral tragedy of the kind he describes? While we both believe there is much scope for remedying the brain drain by addressing the poor conditions that give rise to the phenomenon, I see programs aimed at combatting the burdens associated with brain drain (such as compulsory service or taxation arrangements) as a helpful set of remedies that can aid the transition to a more just state of affairs rather than as morally forbidden measures. Even if the brain drain represents a sort of moral tragedy, we are faced with the issue of what is a permissible transitional strategy while injustice is still pervasive. The courses of action for which I argue might be the best we can do in pursuing transitional justice, as we try to progress toward a more just state of affairs in less than ideal circumstances.

I should add that I think there is plenty more that developing countries may be permitted to do in their quest to retain more of their skilled citizens and mitigate the worst effects of the brain drain. For instance, there is a case also for changing tertiary-level training curricula to make citizens less marketable and more useful in countries of origin. Like Nir Eyal and Samia Hurst, I also believe that locally relevant medical training programs are entirely justified, such that the curriculum is focused on treating locally endemic diseases using cost-effective, low-technology solutions, rather than diagnostic and treatment methods which might be more reliable but are completely unsuitable outside of developed-world contexts where reliable power and clean water supplies cannot be taken for granted.[37] This might make medical graduates less marketable and attractive to foreign recruiters, but would make them more useful in their social settings. Educational reforms could also include training more health practitioners to do routine jobs, such as administering vaccinations or providing treatments for prevalent diseases, which would not involve lengthy and costly training programs.

10.7 PERMISSIBLE POLICIES: SOME CONVERGENCE

In this final section I discuss the extent to which Blake and I agree on some policy options that can permissibly be implemented here and now, and if so, whether this convergence is problematic.

Blake and I agree that developed countries should pursue a number of strategies including appropriately investing in creating sufficient human resources for necessary jobs and revising ethical recruitment guidelines. Blake believes that revising ethical recruitment practices is one of the most promising strategies available to those concerned about brain drain. I am less optimistic, given that revisions have so far yielded few notable gains.[38] By contrast, I wholeheartedly agree with Blake that we must attend better to the circumstances that give rise to the problems in the first place and play a crucial role in reducing global injustice on a wide scale. I do not share Blake's pessimism about not having much knowledge about how to go to work on helping impoverished societies transition toward prosperity. We may not have perfect clarity about recipes for success, but we know enough that we have no excuse based on alleged ignorance to refrain from making a concerted effort with respect to those institutions, practices, and activities we know play an important role in improving people's lives.

While Blake and I agree largely on all the actions developed countries can and should be taking, this is only one area where efforts could and should be made. On the matter of what developing countries may do, Blake believes the right to freedom of movement deserves a kind of privileged status in our moral universe, and, as liberals, we tread on thin ice when we restrict it. The right to keep one's citizens from exiting is a right that would lead to bad results if widely endorsed as permissible; restricting the right would also send bad signals to malign states that the right to exit is not all that important. For these and other reasons, it is a very bad idea to restrict movement across borders. From my perspective, liberal practice already widely accepts states' rights to restrict movement across borders. Consider how the state may restrict citizens' departure when they have not paid all their speeding fines or when they are suspected of being threats to public safety. We already have a fairly well entrenched practice of interfering with freedom of movement at borders in the name of protecting citizens from risks of harm—witness the elaborate apparatus already in place to restrict movement and subject people to scrutiny in the name of protecting citizens from terrorist threats and other alleged risks to safety and public order. This apparatus can constitute an enormous violation of our freedom and interference with our life plans, when we consider how we can be detained or our property can be confiscated for however long it takes for authorities to determine whether we do in fact pose any risks to others. Given there is already precedent for such restrictions within liberal practices, my inquiry into whether less invasive restrictions can be justified (from within the perspective of liberal theory and practice) does not seem to be so peculiar.

Despite these fundamental differences concerning the way we view the role of freedom of movement within liberal theory and practice, Blake and I agree on some strategies developing countries could deploy. These include (1)– (6) below.

(1) Some contracts to serve are permissible. We might well differ over how often this strategy may permissibly be used in practice, but in theory we both agree that only adequately rights-protecting states can deploy this strategy.

(2) Some forms of taxing non-renouncing citizens may be permissible (so long as they do not produce perverse results).[39]

(3) Conditional repayment programs for education are permissible, whereby loans are forgiven (in whole or in part) when skilled workers remain in the country.

(4) Some domestic reorganization may be permissible, such as reforms to educational curricula that

make citizens more useful to countries of origin and less attractive to others.

(5) Preventing exit under emergencies may be permissible.

I make some brief comments on each next.

Blake argues that developing societies may deploy strategies such as (1), (2), and (3), but his endorsement especially of (1) and (3) is heavily qualified by concern with the right circumstances. As noted, I agree that people who make bargains in societies that are insufficiently rights-protecting are not in the right circumstances to make valid contracts that are morally binding, because they are making agreements against a backdrop of a lack of freedom. So, I agree with Blake that in cases of duress, such as being held hostage, those who make agreements should not feel morally bound by those agreements. But I disagree with Blake that there is sufficient duress in the case of "responsible, but poor" countries that those who make agreements should be morally released from them. My argument is that only legitimate states may permissibly deploy this strategy of compulsory service for educational provision and to be such they must have reached a threshold of making good-faith efforts to protect rights even if they have not yet entirely succeeded. I also agree with Blake that in practice, there will be states who might like to make use of the strategy but are not permitted to do so, because they fall too far short of the rights-protecting threshold. There is clearly a minimal level of state adequacy. In particular, I agree with Blake that a state that permits or causes wide-scale human rights abuses falls too far short of the adequacy requirement. And like Blake, I can tentatively endorse the view that Ghana may well meet the legitimacy requirements while the Central African Republic does not. Like Blake, I believe these judgments require some further analysis and specifics of rights protection in these two societies.

There is a worry here that Blake has not mentioned, but I think could be about this strategy. Only sufficiently rights-protecting states may enforce valid contracts. But if they are sufficiently rights-protecting, perhaps they do not need to extract such bargains to provide the core goods protected by rights. So the strategy can only be deployed when it is, in effect, not needed. Some of those most in need of the strategy will not be able to use it. While I see the worry, I would emphasize that its force is somewhat mitigated by some of the qualifications I introduce to my argument. For instance, I believe those that are making good-faith efforts to protect rights (and succeeding to some extent, though still falling short of what is needed) may legitimately be able to use the strategy depending on certain threshold considerations, what they are actually doing to protect rights, an account of which rights they fall short of protecting and in what ways, and so forth.

Like Blake, I believe there is more that developing countries can do to make practicing medicine at home more attractive and the options to practice abroad less available. Clearly, in so far as it is in the power of countries of origin to improve conditions directly and indirectly related to living and working at home, they should take them. But often this is more of a resourcing issue than a lack of will and care on the part of governments.

I also agree with Blake that it can be permissible for developing countries to reshape their educational curricula to have them focus more on training to solve widespread local problems, using local resources appropriate to circumstances, with a keen eye on resourcing and constraints in those conditions. If the state is under no obligation to provide tertiary-level training to any particular individual, it is not under an obligation to provide training that will be maximally attractive to foreigners and is well within its rights to offer training that will be of most use in domestic contexts.

Both Blake and I agree that emergency circumstances may justify more unusual courses of action, though we may well differ over what constitutes an emergency. For Blake, there are four conditions that must obtain before this emergency-based justification could succeed. First, the emergency needs to be sufficiently grave to justify the wrong proposed; second, the rights violation envisaged should be likely to lead to a significantly better rights protection situation within a reasonable time period; third, there should be no other pathway available toward the justice we seek; and fourth, we would need to later compensate those for the evils we have imposed on them. Blake believes the conditions to be rather demanding and is unsure any of the tests can be met. I do not share Blake's pessimism or his sense that the last two criteria are strictly necessary for us to invoke emergency considerations to restrict movement, but since neither Blake nor I use emergency considerations to make our central arguments I leave these disagreement to one side.[40]

To conclude, there are important policies that we can both agree are permissible in addressing issues associated with brain drain. Even when we agree on which are permissible, we disagree perhaps on how often these can be used in our actual world, and we have very different reasons for

our thinking this is so. The fact that we reach similar conclusions about which policies are permissible from such
different perspectives gives us strong reasons to think the
policies we do agree on can be cogently defended. So one
fairly optimistic result of this work, then, is that certain
courses of action have been shown to be defensible when
the justifying conditions we offer are sufficiently well met.
Of course, we still disagree in many important ways about
the nature of our freedoms, particularly freedom of movement. There are, apparently, some importantly different
ways to view these from within a liberal framework. I hope
the debates that we have begun in this book will stimulate
readers to continue to explore the nature of the freedoms
and rights we should have in liberal societies, especially in
those that are quite far away from being perfectly just.

NOTES

1. Examples include Norway, Denmark, Switzerland, Finland,
   and Greece.
2. Such as p. 112.
3. In fact, when one reflects on the issue, there are some deep
   contradictions in our views that everyone has a right to certain goods and services, but that no one can be obligated
   to provide them. For an excellent analysis of the issues, see
   Lucas Stanczyk, "Productive Justice," *Philosophy and Public
   Affairs* 40 (2012): 144–164.
4. That measure will serve as a concise proxy for the relevant
   issues, though legitimacy includes also making good-faith
   efforts to provide sufficient public goods, operating an
   impartial system of justice, collecting and spending public
   resources judiciously, and so on.

5. These considerations also highlight the vast differences between leaving a religion and leaving a state under the conditions characterizing the case of "responsible, but poor." The analogy Blake attempts to draw with apostasy can be easily blocked by highlighting the different circumstances, associations, and harms involved.

6. Again, these are vast differences with why "managing apostasy" and "managing migration" are not at all similar. I should emphasize also that what does important work here is the circumstances and there being fair and reasonable terms attached to contracts, not just the status of signed contract. We discuss these issues in more detail later in this chapter.

7. John Gibson and David McKenzie, "Eight Questions about Brain Drain," *Journal of Economic Perspectives* 25 (2011): 107–128, at 122.

8. Gibson and McKenzie, "Eight Questions about Brain Drain."

9. Carrado DiMaria and Piotr Strszowski, "Migration, Human Capital Accumuluation and Economic Development," *Journal of Development Economics* 90 (2009): 306–313.

10. Michael Clemens, "Do Visas Kill? Health Effects of African Health Professional Emigration," *Center for Global Development Working Paper 114*, (Washington, DC: Center for Global Development, 2007).

11. Frederic Docquier and Hillel Rapoport, "Globalization, Brain Drain, and Development," *Journal of Economic Literature* 50 (2012): 681–730, at 705.

12. Alok Bhargava, Frederic Docquier, and Yasser Moullan, "Modeling the Effects of Physician Emigration on Human Development," *Economics and Human Biology* 9 (2011): 172–183.

13. Docquier and Rapoport, "Globalization, Brain Drain, and Development," 714. Alok Bhargava and Frederic Docquier, "HIV Pandemic, Medical Brain Drain, and Economic Development in Sub-Saharan Africa," *World Bank Economic Review* 22 (2008): 345–366.

14. Peter E. Bundred and Cheryl Levitt, "Medical Migration: Who are the Real Losers?" *Lancet* 356 (2000): 245–246. See

also Edward Mills, William A. Schaba, Jimmy Volmink, et al., "Should Active Recruitment of Health Workers from Sub-Saharan Africa be Viewed as a Crime?," *Lancet* 371 (2008): 685–688.

15. Docquier and Rapoport, "Globalization, Brain Drain, and Development," 707–708.
16. Docquier and Rapoport, "Globalization, Brain Drain, and Development," 707.
17. Docquier and Rapoport, "Globalization, Brain Drain, and Development," p. 709. Docquier and Rapoport's observations about contributions to improving domestic institutions are interesting, but there are at least two cautionary points that deserve mention about these results. In order to reap these rewards, the numbers of highly skilled emigrants who leave and whether they settle in geographically concentrated ways are relevant. And it is not at all clear that whatever positive effects on institutions accrue necessarily outweigh drawbacks that also result from migration. So whether or not the net effect of migration is positive will vary a great deal depending on a range of other factors.
18. AnnaLee Saxenian, *Silicon Valley's New Immigrant Entrepreneurs* (San Francisco: Public Policy Institute of California, 1999); AnnaLee Saxenian, *Local and Global Networks of Immigrant Professionals in Silicon Valley* (San Francisco: Public Policy Institute of California, 2002).
19. Docquier and Rapoport, "Globalization, Brain Drain, and Development," 717.
20. Maurice Kugler and Hillel Rapoport, "International Labor and Capital Flows: Complements or Substitutes?" *Economics Letters* 94 (2007): 155–162; and Beata S. Javorcik, Çağlar Özden, Mariana Spatareanu, and Cristina Neagu, "Migrant Networks and Foreign Direct Investment," *Journal of Development Economics* 94 (2011): 231–241.
21. Gibson and McKenzie, "Eight Questions about Brain Drain," 122.
22. Docquier and Rapoport, "Globalization, Brain Drain, and Development," 711.

23. Docquier and Rapoport, "Globalization, Brain Drain, and Development," 711. See also Aart Kraay, Massimo Mastruzzi, and Daniel Kaufmann, "Governance Matters IV: Governance Indicators for 1996–2004," *World Bank Policy Research Working Paper 3630* (Washington, DC: World Bank, 2005); and Frederic Docquier and Abdeslam Marfouk, "International Migration by Education Attainment, 1990–2000," in Çağlar Özden and Maurice Schiff (eds.), *International Migration, Remittances and the Brain Drain* (Washington, DC: World Bank, 2006), 151–199.

24. Docquier and Rapoport, "Globalization, Brain Drain, and Development," 711.

25. Docquier and Rapoport, "Globalization, Brain Drain, and Development," 711.

26. Docquier and Rapoport, "Globalization, Brain Drain, and Development," 705; Manon Domingues Dos Santos and Fabien Postel-Vinay, "Migration as a Source of Growth: The Perspective of a Developing Country," *Journal of Population Economics* 16 (2003): 161–175; also Christian Dustmann, Itzhak Fadlon, and Yoram Weiss, "Return Migration, Human Capital Accumulation and the Brain Drain," *Journal of Development Economics* 95 (2011): 58–67; and Karin Mayr and Giovanni Peri, "Brain Drain and Brain Return: Theory and Application to Eastern-Western Europe," *B.E. Journal of Economic Analysis and Policy* 9 (2009).

27. Examples of this would include Hsinchu Science Park in Taipei or the information technology sector in India. See, for instance, Docquier and Rapoport, "Globalization, Brain Drain, and Development," 707.

28. Docquier and Rapoport, "Globalization, Brain Drain, and Development," 718.

29. It is probably worth pointing out that although there is the potential benefit of skill sharing and this improving health-care knowledge and treatment (for instance), there is also the reality that the vast majority of migrants never return. On balance then, healthcare worker migration constitutes a net loss for poor rural populations. See, for instance, Nir

Eyal and Samia Hurst, "Physician Brain Drain: Can Nothing Be Done?" *Public Health Ethics* 1 (2008): 180–192; Fitzhugh Mullan, "The Metrics of the Physician Brain Drain," *New England Journal of Medicine* 353 (2005):1810–1818; also Joseph N. Ana, "Africa's Medical Brain Drain: Brain Gain and Brain Circulation Result when Drain is Reversed," *British Medical Association* 331 (2005): 780–781.

30. Michel Beine, Frederic Docquier, and Hillel Rapoport, "Brain Drain and Human Capital Formation in Developing Countries: Winners and Losers," *The Economic Journal* 118 (2008): 631–652.

31. Beine, Docquier, and Rapoport, "Brain Drain and Human Capital Formation in Developing Countries."

32. Docquier and Rapoport, "Globalization, Brain Drain, and Development," 725.

33. Docquier and Rapoport, "Globalization, Brain Drain, and Development," 725.

34. "Data limitations continue to be a huge challenge to work in this area." Gibson and McKenzie, "Eight Questions about Brain Drain," 125.

35. Docquier and Rapoport, "Globalization, Brain Drain, and Development," 725.

36. There seems to be wide variation in reports concerning people's motivation to leave states experiencing problems of brain drain. Some highlight more push than pull factors; others the reverse. Consider as one such sample the following studies. Anna Maria Mayda shows that push factors have a relatively small impact on migration compared to that of pull factors and distance (in "International Migration: A Panel Data Analysis of the Determinants of Bilateral Flows," *Journal of Population Economics* 23 [2010]: 1249–1274.) Magda Awases, Akpa R. Gbary, Jennifer Nyoni, and Rufaro Chatora found that in the six countries surveyed in Africa, 50 percent declared that they were thinking of emigrating and the reasons cited were better access to wages, working conditions, and lifestyles, while also wanting to avoid risks aligned with caring for HIV/AIDS patients. (*Migration of Health Professionals in Africa: A Synthesis Report*

[Brazzaville: World Health Organization, 2004], pp. 38–47). John Gibson and David McKenzie found that emigration was largely driven by career concerns, family and lifestyle considerations, rather than income ("Eight Questions about Brain Drain," 117). Michael Clemens has a similar finding at least in the case of health workers migrating from Africa ("Skill Flow: A Fundamental Reconsideration of Skilled-Worker Mobility and Development," *Center for Global Development Working Paper 180* [Washington, DC: Center for Global Development, 2009]). Almon Shumba and Douglas Mawere find that push factors (e.g., low remuneration, declining currency regimes, low job satisfaction and collapse of funding) and pull factors (e.g., attractive salaries and research and study opportunities) caused brain drain in Zimbabwe ("The Causes and Impact of Brain Drain in Institutions of Higher Learning in Zimbabwe," *International Migration* 50 [2012]: 107–123).

Like several other issues in this book that require empirical treatment, we cannot decisively conclude what the case is for all countries and all sectors at all times. No doubt the story is complex, multi-faceted, and varies greatly among states. While Blake makes the claim that most emigration occurs to avoid violence, I do not believe we are in a position to know this, given this very brief survey of different views.

37. Eyal and Hurst, "Physician Brain Drain: Can Nothing Be Done?"

38. For more discussion, see Gillian Brock, "Health in Developing Countries and Our Global Responsibilities," in Angus Dawson (ed.), *The Philosophy of Public Health* (Farnham: Ashgate, 2009), 73–83.

39. Worldwide taxation programs may have attendant perverse consequences if not carefully crafted in that they might give high-skilled persons sufficient reason to renounce their citizenships, which could have bad consequences for countries of origin, shutting off potential useful avenues by which pro-poor development can result, such as circular migration.

40. Emergency circumstances can justify more unusual courses of action. We both agree with this view. We could explore whether the state of unmet need and institutional development are currently so grave that they constitute an emergency situation. I believe a plausible case could be marshaled for this line of argument when one considers some of the figures concerning health, healthcare, educational attainment, disease burden, unsanitary and unsafe living conditions, and the like. Arguably, the lack of provision for certain basic needs does in some cases amount to a serious threat to those needs, such as where the lack of personnel available to provide healthcare does constitute a serious threat to the health of those living in particular developing countries. And similarly, a case could be marshaled that lack of provision for education, clean water, and other basic needs is so dire that the situation constitutes an emergency, and does rise to the level of pressing public concern. Blake concedes that the situation of public health is a grave one and, in that case, it is plausible that the situation reaches the threshold for being dire. Rather, it is the other three criteria he offers that he believes cannot be met. In response we might challenge some of the criteria Blake uses. They do not all seem necessary or important to include in an account of under what conditions considerations of emergency might justify requiring service. In my arguments here I leave to one side the emergency defense as I believe we can make the central case needed without resorting to this line of argument.

11

Blake Responds to Brock

NEAR THE END OF TERRY Pratchett's *The Fifth Elephant*, Commander Vimes discusses the issue of the brain drain with the King of the Dwarves:

> "It seems all our best go to Ankh-Morpork, where they live in squalor. You leave us dry."
>
> Vimes was at a loss. It was clear that the little figure now sitting at the long table was a lot brighter than he was, although right now he felt as dim as a penny candle in any case. It was also clear that the King hadn't slept for quite some time. He decided to go for honesty.
>
> "Can't really answer that, sir," he said, adopting a variant on his talking-to-Vetinari approach. "But . . ."
>
> "Yes?"
>
> "I'd wonder . . . you know, if I was a king . . . I'd wonder why people were happier living in squalor in Ankh-Morpork than staying back home . . . sir."[1]

Vimes's political sense is, perhaps, lacking, but his moral sense is not. In dealing with the issue of the brain drain, the focus must be kept squarely on the issue of human (or, in this case, dwarf) freedom. Whatever can be done to keep the "best" of a given population in its home jurisdiction must be compatible with the rights of people to seek their own happiness, to form new relationships, and to decide for themselves where they will do both. If people are not happy with the society where they are, they have a right to leave, and this right can only be overcome by something with a character that demonstrates respect for human agency: by a free and fair contract, perhaps, or by an emergency of the sort that allows for conscription. This way of looking at humans (or dwarves) makes the world a fundamentally *messy* place: we cannot move people around, or keep them in place, simply because it would be *useful*, even when what it is that they are being used for is the creation of morally required institutions. The world is, indeed, a *tragic* place: we find that we cannot, consistent with human rights, make the moves that might lead to more people's having their human rights protected. The nature of morality is such that we are precluded from moving directly to where we would most want, morally speaking, to be.

I have defended this vision in what has gone before, and will be comparatively brief in what follows. This seems only right; those who defend the status quo have an easier job than those who critique it, and I take it that the defense of a "liberal orthodoxy" might therefore require less space than an argument against that orthodoxy. I want therefore only to emphasize that, despite Brock's very capable defense of an alternative vision, I hold a vision of the right to exit that allows us to do less good for the world than we might. I want to highlight three differences between Brock's vision and my own, since I believe these are keys to understanding how Brock and I understand the morality of the brain drain.

First, I believe that we cannot always be coerced into doing what is most right for us to do. Look, for example, at Brock's analysis of my employment with the University of Washington. She asserts that I might want to have the freedom to leave at a moment's notice, but that I do not have such a right; I have, instead, an obligation to the administration and students to remain where I am, doing the job I agreed to do. I might agree with Brock as a matter of moral duties; I cannot agree with her that these duties could ever be made a matter of rightful *enforcement*. If I were to discover that my own happiness requires me to become a surfer—an unlikely eventuality, but logically possible—then I believe I have a moral right to be free from legal interference with my pursuit of that vocation. I would be, morally speaking, a bit of a cad in leaving the University in the middle of the quarter; but I cannot think that it would ever be rightful for the University to coercively prevent me from leaving, or to demand that the state of Washington punish my attempt to depart. Indeed, since the terms of my employment with the University do not include any specific terms to the contrary, I believe I would be unlikely to even have to pay damages to the University or its students were I to stop teaching.[2] Certainly, it would be hard to imagine that the University could ever rightly insist upon specific performance in my fulfillment of my duties; the thought that I could be made, upon threat of imprisonment, to deliver lectures on ethics to undergrads is a bit fanciful. This image, though, is implicitly what is at stake in the debate surrounding the brain drain. To "condition," "manage," or "delay" exit is, implicitly, to threaten with legal punishment those who seek to depart ahead of schedule; it is to use legal coercion to prevent someone from going where they want to go. It is to say that the state has the right to threaten people with prison if they want to leave. Contrary to Brock's vision, I think we do have the right to be free from this sort of coercion. The

University of Washington does not have the right to coercively prevent me from being a cad.[3] Neither, I believe, does any state have the right to prevent people from leaving, even if they would be most useful to the world by staying in their states of origin. Thus, Brock and I differ quite deeply in our reaction to cases such as the prevented local. Brock believes that the only thing wrong with the case, as I have described it, is that the prevented emigrant has not been given enough advance warning before being subjected to state coercion. I think the wrong done to the emigrant is more profound; we have no right to prevent her emigration, any more than we would have to prevent her apostasy, and no amount of advance warning would make this wrongful act right. If I let you know ahead of time that I plan to violate your rights, I am—perhaps—a considerate villain. We should not, however, think that the act proposed is therefore *justified*. If I have no right to prevent your exit, as I think I do not, then I do not acquire this right simply because I inform you of my plans.

Second, we do not always have an obligation to meet the expectations of others. If you give me a car, in the expectation that I will shuttle you to work every day, then I am perhaps a cad if I decide to go to the beach with that car instead. But the mere fact that you *expected* to benefit from your gift is not enough to create enforceable obligations on my part. In order for your claim on my actions to be rightful, it has to issue from a fair and free contract, one that specifies exactly what is to be done. To use the terms of contract law: we are not bound merely by expectations in the minds of others; we are bound, instead, when we have entered into mutual *agreement* with those others to regard ourselves as bound.[4] The mere existence of expectations is not enough to create obligations that can be rightfully enforced. A society that builds an institution of learning in the expectation that those who graduate will use their learning in some particular way does *not* thereby create binding obligations on the part of those educated. For that binding to take place, there must be something more; something much more like an explicit acceptance, on the part of the one being educated, of that burden. The one issuing the contract, moreover, must be in a position to create such a contractual obligation. I do not think these two tests are likely to be easily met, in the concrete cases of the brain drain we have been discussing. The state must be explicit that education is provided only upon acceptance of an obligation of repayment, and it must be sufficiently robust as a state to make the one who enters into the contract able to do so fairly and freely. These tests, again, may prove difficult to meet, but more importantly, they differentiate the potentially enforceable contractual obligation from the mere knowledge that others expect performance. The freedom to determine the course of one's life from the inside is sufficiently important to make the latter an insufficient ground for legal enforcement. The one who walks away from known expectations is perhaps a jerk but, once again, not rightly subject to legal punishment.

Finally, the suspension of a right is not minimized simply because of its temporary or brief nature. The Supreme Court, in *Robinson v. California*, emphasized that the brief nature of incarceration for the status of being an addict was not enough to make that incarceration rightful; even a day's incarceration was impermissible, since there were no rightful grounds for the use of this sort of coercion in light of this sort of "crime."[5] So it is with the right to exit. We cannot think that a violation of human rights is legitimated simply because it is brief. We cannot, similarly, impose a temporary suspension of the right to leave a religious community and justify it by saying that we are "managing" or "administering" the right to free exercise of religion; saying "wait a bit" is only rightful if the purposes for the coercive delay are rightful. Imagine, here, that my church insists that I continue to attend services for a year or two, prior to being allowed to leave; they are only trying to "manage" apostasy, after all, and my absence would make that church less able to serve the important spiritual needs of other parishioners. They have no right to do this, even if they are right about the negative effects of my absence. A brief delay is not justified with reference to brevity, when it is the delay itself that is wrongful. Being made to wait until age sixteen to drive reflects a valid limitation on the rights of children and their comparative immaturity; being made to wait until one's passport is processed reflects the necessary limitations on the capacities of bureaucracy. Being told that one may not cease religious practice for some similar period is akin to neither. If the religious community in question were to have the right to coercively prevent exit, it would be in possession of a power it is not rightly able to administer—no matter how brief its use of that power. So, too, with emigration. If a person is told that they cannot leave until some eventuality occurs—until, perhaps, they have repaid their supposed debt to society, or until they have worked in a disfavored location for sufficient time—we have to ask whether or not that right to coerce is rightly pressed against this person. That person, after all, would be subject to criminal enforcement if they tried to leave prior to that eventuality; they would be put in prison, perhaps, or subject to fines. What right, though, does the state have to do any of that? If what I have said before is true, the liberal state does not have the right to deploy this sort of coercive power; it does not have the right to prevent exit, since this sort of power could never be justified to the exiting individual considered *as* an individual. The state must, for its coercion to be rightful, justify its powers with reference to the interests and rights of the one being coerced, as Rawls emphasized. Here, no such justification can be made, and the state that seeks to deploy jails and monetary penalties for "early departures" cannot justify its right to do so. The fact that the punishment is in place only for a limited time does not negate the fact that it is wrongful punishment; a temporary violation of human rights is a violation nonetheless.

All of this, of course, is only to reiterate the view of liberalism I have been defending against Brock. I would close with two brief notes: one in favor of a moderate and tempered conservatism, and one noting the range of agreement that remains even in light of our profound disagreement.

I am not, I should say, a conservative, at least as the modern world understands the concept. (Indeed, in the United States it is now hard to understand exactly what that concept entails.[6]) I do think, though, that the following moderate conservative proposition might hold true: those who propose to violate or suspend basic human rights must have extraordinary evidence before they do so. The human rights we have articulated, on this vision, are hard-won and worth conserving, and we should have extraordinary evidence before they are suspended.

I believe that the right to leave, as described in the UDHR, is a core human right, and should continue to be treated as such. It may be true, in the end, that Brock has given us good reason to think that the right should not deserve this treatment. But I believe that there is a special burden upon her to provide us with these reasons. There are two aspects to this burden: she owes us particular moral justifications that are of sufficient power to demonstrate that the right is not as important as we think, and she owes us a strong empirical story to explain why the suspension of the norm will lead to good results. As should be obvious at this point, I do not believe that either of these has been adequately provided. I believe her moral analysis, while powerful, is inadequate, and I am entirely unsure that the empirical effects of the suspension of the right to exit will be beneficial. What I emphasize here, though, is that we should in general await convincing cases for both before we decide to start adjusting basic norms of human rights. Where the arguments and evidence are in equipoise—let alone where they both lead to a defense of the human right, as I believe is the case—we should generally favor the protection of the human rights we now enjoy. This much, I think, is at the heart of the moderate conservative idea I would defend: that we have reason to be extremely careful before we begin making fundamental alterations to those institutions and norms that protect us. The idea is not a prohibition on novelty; it is not reactionary; it is not a blanket defense of the status quo. It is, however, a standing demand that deviations from the rights provided by that status quo require extraordinary justification—justification, again, that I do not believe can be provided.

With that said, I believe that there is reason to look at the significant degree of overlap between Brock and myself as far as permissible means by which the brain drain might be addressed. We disagree about the coercive prevention of exit; we agree, however, that both developing and developed states might work to make the world within which employment decisions are made a less thoroughly unjust one. I will not rehearse these agreed-upon points here; I will restrict myself to saying, as I have before, that for me these are the limits of the rightful responses to the brain drain, and that they are likely to be ultimately partial responses to these issues. The world in which we live is, as has so often been said, a deeply unjust one. I believe that this world has a deeply tragic aspect as well. We can, and should, work against the worst excesses of the brain drain; we cannot expect, however, that we will ever rightly possess the tools required to eliminate the problem. The world in which we live will, as it so often does, make the problem one we cannot rightly eliminate with the tools at our disposal. The response to this should not be quietism or desperation; it should instead be a renewed commitment to those permissible tools that could eventually make the problem less serious, even if those tools cannot make the problem go away. In the end, I will be happy if the exchange between Brock and myself counts as one of these imperfect tools.

NOTES

1. Terry Pratchett, *The Fifth Elephant* (New York: Harper Collins, 2004).
2. And, of course, my contract with the University of Washington would have to be both free and fair—attributes I think would

be more likely to apply here than they would in contracts made with (many) developing societies.

3. Indeed, there is some evidence that universities systematically benefit from a sense of professionalism that undermines the ability of contingent faculty to find better-paid jobs. See L. V. Anderson, "Why It's Hard for Contingent Faculty to Find Different Work," *Slate*, November 19, 2013, available at http://www.slate.com/blogs/browbeat/2013/11/19/ adjunct_professor_job_mobility_why_it_s_hard_for_contingent_faculty_to_find.html.

4. See Restatement (Second) of Contracts, § 24.

5. Robinson *v.* California, 370 US 660 (1962).

6. The word *conservatism* in the United States now seems to refer to a mishmash of distinct, and not always compatible, ideas. See Sam Tanenhaus, *The Death of Conservatism* (New York: Random House, 2009).

INDEX